DECLASSIFIED

DECLASSIFIED

50 Top-Secret Documents
That Changed History

Thomas B. Allen

Foreword by Peter Earnest,

Executive Director, International Spy Museum

NATIONAL GEOGRAPHIC
WASHINGTON, D.C.

ISBN: 978-1-4262-0222-3

Library of Congress Cataloging-in-Publication Data
available upon request.

Founded in 1888, the National Geographic Society is one of the largest nonprofit scientific and educational organizations in the world. It reaches more than 285 million
people worldwide each month through its official journal, NATIONAL GEOGRAPHIC, and
its four other magazines; the National Geographic Channel; television documentaries;
radio programs; films; books; videos and DVDs; maps; and interactive media. National
Geographic has funded more than 8,000 scientific research projects and supports an
education program combating geographic illiteracy.

For more information, please call 1-800-NGS LINE (647-5463)
or write to the following address:

National Geographic Society
1145 17th Street N.W.
Washington, D.C. 20036-4688 U.S.A.

Visit us online at www.nationalgeographic.com/books

Interior Design: Sanaa Akkach
Design Assistant: Al Morrow

Printed in the United States of America

CONTENTS

INTRODUCTION

If These Documents Could Talk

THERE IS A SPECIAL EXCITEMENT IN DISCOVERING HIDDEN WORLDS, whether revealed on a hazardous trek through dense jungles or discovered after scholarly research into dusty archives. The archaeologist coming unexpectedly upon ancient ruins changes forever our view of the world, or rather, shows that world to us through new eyes. So, too, the lone scholar culling through dimly lit stacks and sealed archives has a similar experience, uncovering hidden words that have been buried under layers of fragmentary information, falsehoods, and in some cases outright deception.

Documents and records in themselves, of course, are but words on paper, but they serve as windows into the principal actors, policies, and machinations that have played a role in revolutions, wars, assassinations, and other momentous events that changed the course of history.

One of the International Spy Museum's prized artifacts is a letter from General George Washington to one Nathanial Sackett with instructions for him to form an espionage network in British-occupied New York City. Always fascinating to visitors, the letter bears silent testimony to Washington's keen interest in timely and accurate intelligence from firsthand sources.

That and his employment of classic espionage tradecraft and covert deception led later generations of intelligence officers to consider him the Father of American Intelligence.

Serving in the Clandestine Service of the Central Intelligence Agency for 36 years, I dealt firsthand with highly classified and sensitive files and records. On one occasion, I signed the approval for the first collection of declassified records of the Office of Strategic Services (OSS), the CIA's predecessor, to be transferred to the National Archives and Records Administration for eventual release to the public. These were secrets of wartime covert operations that had been under seal for over 40 years.

Later in the CIA, I was responsible for a roomful of records bearing on the assassination of President John F. Kennedy. Agency sources all over the world had been tasked for any information in any way relating to that traumatic event. These records too would eventually be brought to light. On each occasion, I sensed that blanks in the historical record would finally be filled.

In 1994 Benjamin Weiser, then a reporter with the *Washington Post*, sent Director of Central Intelligence Robert Gates a request for special permission for me to research the top secret records of the CIA's most secret and productive source in Poland during critical years of the Cold War, 1972-1981. The source was Col. Ryszard Kuklinski who served on the Polish General Staff and who secretly volunteered to act as a source for American intelligence. That research served as the narrative basis for Weiser's book, *A Secret Life: The Polish Officer, His Covert Mission, and the Price He Paid to Save His Country*.

Kuklinski provided his agency handlers with over 40,000 top secret documents on the Soviet-run Warsaw Pact and early warnings of Polish government plans to impose martial law and to facilitate Soviet military entry into Poland. Kuklinski's timely intelligence led the Carter administration to warn the Soviets against invading Poland—a major setback for the USSR at the height of the Cold War.

In *Declassified*, Tom Allen, a respected writer of American history, describes 50 documents and records that were either "classified" or whose origins were shrouded in mystery and deceit. They range widely: Spain's top secret plans to launch a naval armada against England obtained by Sir Francis Walsingham, spymaster to Elizabeth I; the captured encrypted message of Dr. Benjamin Church, a prominent American revolutionary, which exposed him as a spy for the British; Maj. Gen. Benedict Arnold's secret message to the British offering to sell American secrets and change sides; and, finally, the secret letter FBI turncoat Special Agent Robert Hanssen sent to Soviet Intelligence offering to spy for them—which he successfully did for almost 20 years!

But more than simply listing and describing these fascinating documents, Allen gives us a context, a picture of the world and times in which they were created and in which they were to play a pivotal role. He takes us behind the scenes and enables us to see and understand those times more clearly.

As you read these documents—some declassified by governments, others that have come to light via more circuitous routes—recall and reflect on the headline-making events they affected. Consider the dark secrets they concealed until the passage of time brought them to light. Would history's course have run differently had their secrets been uncovered earlier? And what secrets still lie buried that could alter the course of our own times?

–Peter Earnest, Director, International Spy Museum

ONE

Secrets of War

WAR IS OLDER THAN HISTORY. BATTLE AXES OF POLISHED STONE EMERGED IN LATE Neolithic culture, and the arms of war have appeared in every society since, escalating from cavemen's weapons of personal destruction to nations' weapons of mass destruction. Savage fights evolved into nation-versus-nation wars. Concealed within every war is a secret war whose actions may never be chronicled. Because of the lack of documents, historians who write about battlefield wars often ignore the secret wars. In times of peace, secrets still hide, resisting history's attempts to ferret them out. But eventually, sometimes decades after the end of war, documents do emerge, disclosing the hidden roots of celebrated victories and defeats.

Spying, the secret servant of war, is there when the war is being planned, when the war is being fought, and even when the war ends and peace negotiations are beginning. This has been true for a long time. According to the Bible, when powerful Philistine lords were planning war against the Israelites, they recruited beautiful and seductive Delilah and told her to spy on Samson, an Israelite hero: "Coax him, and find out what makes his strength so great, and how we may overpower him . . . and we will give you each eleven hundred pieces of silver." Elsewhere in the Bible, Moses picks a man from each of the

12 tribes and sends them on a mission into the Promised Land of Canaan. He gives them explicit orders to see whether the Canaanites are "strong or weak, few or many" and whether they live "in tents, or in strong holds."

In another ancient theater of war, the Chinese empire of the sixth century B.C., no less than five kinds of spies were working for the emperor. "Local agents" spied on their own people. Enemy officials who provided intelligence to the emperor were known as "inward spies." Enemy spies working for the emperor were called "converted spies" (today, they're called "double agents"). "Surviving spies" managed to bring back intelligence after burrowing deeply into the enemy's hoard of secrets (today, "moles"). Finally, there were the "doomed spies," agents who were deliberately exposed by the emperor's own spies so that enemy counterintelligence operatives would be deceived into believing that they had caught real spies.

Our knowledge about those varied spies comes from Sun Tzu, a Chinese military strategist who wrote *The Art of War* in the sixth century B.C. To Sun Tzu, the most vital weapon of war was intelligence. "If you know the enemy and know yourself, you need not fear a hundred battles," he wrote. "If you know yourself and not the enemy, for every victory you will suffer a defeat. If you know neither yourself nor the enemy, you are a fool and will meet defeat in every battle."

Sir Francis Walsingham, the brilliant spymaster who worked his wonders for Queen Elizabeth I from 1573 to 1590, did not have the benefit of Sun Tzu's advice. *The Art of War* remained unknown outside the East until the late 18th century, after it had been translated by Jean Joseph Marie Amiot, a French Jesuit missionary in China. But Walsingham would understand one of Sun Tzu's basic beliefs: "A hundred ounces of silver spent for information may save ten thousand spent on war." Walsingham said it more succinctly: "Knowledge is never too dear."

Secrets, especially secrets of war, are priceless—and expensive. Spying is often costly, and that cost has usually been one of the major secrets in the secret world of espionage. The espionage-is-expensive warning has been repeated down the centuries by spymasters, especially in times of war. Spymasters, unlike most other government officials, do not have to publicly reveal just how expensive their dark arts happen to be.

The amount of money the United States spends each year on intelligence has long been a secret. But the U.S. Government revealed in October 1997 that the total annual budget for the 16 agencies that make up the U.S. intelligence community was $26.6 billion. And with the Iraq War came demands for more spying. The budget for fiscal year 2007 was revealed to be $43.5 billion.

The letter from Anthony Standen to Sir Francis Walsingham,
imparting information on the plans for the Spanish Armada.

Spying on the Armada

[
CREATED: MARCH 1586
SUBJECT: FORMATION
OF THE SPANISH ARMADA
]

1 | For the dual mission of protecting Queen Elizabeth I and her realm, Sir Francis Walsingham formed a network of "intelligencers," as he called his agents, in merchant communities and even in royal courts throughout Europe. His official title was "principal secretary" to the queen. Unofficially, he was her spymaster. After Spain and England began an undeclared war in 1585, Walsingham focused his spying on Spain. In 1587, Walsingham believed from reports he received that King Philip II of Spain was planning to invade England. Walsingham told one of his best agents, Anthony Standen, to show "diligence in intelligence" about Spain. Standen, an English Catholic in exile at a time when Catholics were considered potential traitors in England, used his religion to penetrate the inner circle of Catholic Spain.

Philip II had an efficient spy service, which worked closely with the Vatican's far-flung network, and he was well aware that he was constantly being spied upon by agents working for several governments. He firmly ordered his ambassador in Paris to handle "secret matters . . . by word of mouth, without writing them down." But Standen was not deterred.

Standen's secret communications included a letter sent to Walsingham, using one of the spymaster's servants as a cutout.

(A cutout enables a spymaster to contact an agent without meeting directly with the agent.) Standen, using the cover name Pompeo Pellegrini, enciphers some words in this report (shown on page 16), which says that he has learned from an ambassador that four galleys, additions to the planned Armada, have been sent to Spain from Genoa.

Standen also recruited a spy—still unidentified—who in March 1586 copied an admiral's detailed plan for the Armada, listing the ships, material, and men needed for the invasion. The spy who produced this invaluable document probably was a valet in the admiral's house; the valet's brother worked for Standen. The spy carried the copied document to Madrid, where he gave it to an ambassador who sent it on to Florence, Italy, where Standen picked it up and sent it on to Walsingham in London, in a classic example of espionage networking.

Analysis of the admiral's plan showed that it would be some time before the Armada ships could be assembled and properly manned. Elizabeth had more time than she had expected to prepare for invasion.

Spain's counterintelligence was also at work. In January 1588, Spain's highly placed spy, Sir Edward Stafford, the British ambassador in Paris sent a dispatch to Elizabeth saying that the Spanish Armada had been disbanded. But Elizabeth, primarily through Walsingham's network, was getting a constant stream of intelligence showing that Spain was still planning to launch a mighty fleet. An intercepted letter from an Italian merchant revealed that troops were being mustered for an invasion; enclosed with the letter was a copy of a papal promise of an indulgence for anyone who aided in the "crusade" against Protestant England. Diplomats' dispatches, often unencrypted, traveled by couriers, who could be bribed or threatened. From such intercepted dispatches Elizabeth's wily advisers could piece together what became known as Philip's Grand Strategy: the conquest of England.

In July 1588, the Armada—a fleet of more than 130 ships— sailed into the English Channel and waited off Calais for the troop barges that would be escorted to the invasion beaches. On the night of July 28, an English fleet set adrift eight "Hell Burners," old ships loaded with tar, firewood, and gunpowder. In a fiery panic, Spanish ships cut their anchor cables and headed to sea, breaking up their tight, crescent-shaped defensive array. Next day, the English fleet struck, sinking three ships and running four others aground.

A sudden change of wind blew the Armada beyond the range of English guns. Then the wind whipped into a gale, dashing some ships against rocky shores and driving the fleet northward. Storms kept battering the dwindling fleet as the ships fought the winds up the eastern coast of England, then around Scotland and down Ireland's western coast. Only about half of the ships that had sailed off found their way back to Spain.

Spies, guns, and storms had defeated the Armada. Anthony Standen returned to England from exile in 1593. By then, Walsingham was dead. Enmeshed in religious and royal intrigue, Standen no longer had a patron. He was imprisoned in the Tower of London for ten months and drifted out of spy history.

Impact on History: Standen's spying and Walsingham's skillful handling of intelligence gave Elizabeth and her strategists invaluable knowledge, enabling Britain to thwart Spain's invasion plans. The defeat of the Armada ended the anti-Protestant crusade of King Philip II of Spain and weakened the political power of the pope. Victory over the Armada launched a British navy that would eventually rule the waves.

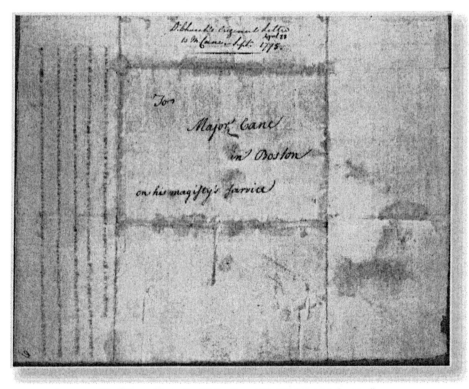

The letter, addressed to Major Cane "On His Magisty's Sarvice," that eventually revealed to General George Washington that a trusted patriot—Dr. Benjamin Church—was acting as a spy for the British.

Washington Finds a Spy

CREATED: JULY 1775
SUBJECT: REVOLUTIONARY WAR—
THE EXPOSURE OF A RESPECTED
PATRIOT AS A BRITISH SPY

2 | One day in July 1775, a young woman called on her former boyfriend, a baker in Newport, Rhode Island. To his surprise, she handed him a letter and asked him to deliver it to the captain of His Majesty's ship *Rose*. The Royal Navy frigate, on patrol off Newport, was part of the British land and sea force deployed to put down the American Revolution. Only three months before, the revolution had become a shooting war when American militiamen and British redcoats had clashed at Lexington and Concord.

The baker put the letter away and forgot about it. In September he received a letter from the woman, who sharply reminded him that he had not kept his promise. The baker, now finally suspicious, took the letter to a Patriot official, who saw to it that the baker was escorted to Cambridge, Massachusetts, where Gen. George Washington, newly commissioned commander in chief of the Continental Army, was shown the letter, which was obviously a message in cipher. (In a cipher, each letter is replaced with another letter. In a code, each word or phrase is replaced with another character or set of characters taken from a codebook.)

Washington gave the letter to the Reverend Samuel West, an amateur cryptanalyst who was familiar with encryption techniques that had been used for a long time by merchants who did not trust the colonial mail service. Washington also asked that a separate decryption be done by Elbridge Gerry, a member of the Massachusetts Provincial Congress and the Committee of Safety. (He would become the fifth vice president of the United States.) Working with Gerry was Colonel Elisha Porter of the Massachusetts militia. The two attempts at decryption produced identical translations of the message, which was addressed "To Major Cane in Boston, On His Magisty's Sarvice."[cq] Cane was on the staff of Gen. Thomas Gage, who had been dispatched to Boston from England with orders to tame the rebellious colony. Gage had started developing a spy network. The 861-word message revealed the work of an American spy providing the British with military information.

"I hope this will reach you; three attempts have I made without success," the letter begins. The agent tells of his visit to Philadelphia, where "I mingled freely & frequently with the members of the Continental Congress." Besides giving a standard agent report on the number and location of cannons and soldiers, he provides some political observations: The Congressmen "were united, determined in opposition, and appeared assured of success" and "A view to independence gr[ows] more & more general." Revealing his fear of being caught, he concludes: "Make use of every precaution or I perish."

The letter also revealed the following intelligence:

Provisions are very plenty. Cloaths are manufacturing in almost every town for the soldiers. Twenty tons of powder lately arrived at Philadelphia, Connecticut & Providence. Upwards of 20 tons are now in camp. Salt petre is made in every colony. Powder mills are erected and constantly employed in Philadelphia & New York. Volunteers of the first fortunes are daily flocking to camp. 1000 rifle-men (in 2 or 3 days recruits) are now levying to augment the army to 22 thousand men. 10 thousand militia are appointed in this government to appear on the first summons.

A page from the encrypted message from Benjamin Church to Major Cane, detailing the state and extent of colonial troops and resources.

The woman who had given the baker the letter was found in Boston and brought before Washington. "I immediately secured the woman," Washington later wrote. He began questioning her and "for a long time she was proof against every threat and persuasion to discover the author." Then, suddenly, she broke and gave up the name of the man who wrote the letter—her secret lover, Dr. Benjamin Church.

Washington was astounded and disheartened. During Boston's long journey to revolution, Dr. Benjamin Church had been a respected patriot. He served with John Adams and other revolutionaries on the underground Committee of Correspondence, and when the shooting war began, he treated the wounded of the Battle of Bunker Hill. Washington had made Church director of the army's first hospital. Because of his knowledge of Massachusetts defenses, he had gone to Philadelphia to discuss the war against the British with members of the Continental Congress.

The message hid its contents in what cryptographers call a monoalphabetic substitution cipher. A character in Edgar Allan Poe's *The Gold Bug* notes another aspect of this kind of cipher: "You observe there are no divisions between the words."

Washington's code breakers probably began by noting the most frequently occurring letter in the message and then assuming that it stood for *e*, the most commonly used letter in the alphabet. If the presumed letter for *e* was, say, *l*, then they might have started looking for *l* in a combination called a trigram, such as *rkl*. Perhaps *rkl* was *the*. If so, a big break would come with the discovery of the digram *kl*, which would be *he*. Through a similar process, the codebreakers could track down letter combinations for common trigrams, such *as, and, ion, ent*, or digrams, such as *an, as, in, on, is, ed*, and *ou*. As in a crossword puzzle, each small discovery would lead to another and then another.

When Washington learned that Church was a spy, he ordered officers to search Church's home and bring him every piece of possibly incriminating paper. They found nothing, leading to suspicions that another British spy had got there before them.

Hanging was the usual fate of spies, but Congress had not passed any laws about treason or espionage. So Washington decided that he, as commander in chief, had the power to call a court martial. As the head of the court martial, Washington listened to Church insist that he was innocent. But Washington found him guilty of "holding criminal correspondence with the enemy." Congress ordered Church put in a Connecticut prison. Later, claiming illness, he got himself transferred to Massachusetts. Finally, around 1778, he was allowed to sail to the West Indies. His ship was lost at sea.

Impact on History: The shocking discovery of Church's treachery began Washington's on-the-job training as a spymaster. Throughout the war, he personally handled many agents and, under the code name Agent 711, organized a highly effective spy network, some of whose members are still unknown. Washington played his spymaster role so well that Maj. George Beckwith, the head of British intelligence operations in the Colonies, later wrote: "Washington did not really outfight the British, he simply outspied us."

Encrypted letter from Benedict Arnold to John André,
offering in "book code" to hand over West Point to the British.

Benedict Arnold Becomes a Spy

CREATED: JULY 1780
SUBJECT: REVOLUTIONARY
WAR—BENEDICT ARNOLD'S
OFFER TO SELL WEST POINT

3 | As soon as word of fighting in Lexington and Concord reached Connecticut in April 1775, Capt. Benedict Arnold mustered his men of the New Haven militia and told them they were heading to Boston to aid the embattled patriots. When he demanded the keys to the town's powder magazine, a selectman refused. An enraged Arnold shouted, "None but Almighty God shall prevent my marching!" The frightened selectman handed Arnold the keys and he marched off to war. By July 1780, when he wrote the letter shown on the facing page, he was a major general and a hero who had been wounded in battles in Canada and New York. He had served with his friend George Washington at Valley Forge, where he, along with all other officers, signed an oath of allegiance that denounced King George III.

Washington led his men out of Valley Forge in the spring of 1778, pursuing the British troops who had just evacuated Philadelphia. Arnold, hobbling from his wounds, was left behind as the military governor of the city until Congress returned and civil rule was reestablished. Soon after arriving in Philadelphia, Arnold found a man who served as a cutout between British intelligence officers and agents in British employ. The cutout, a Philadelphia merchant, worked for Maj. John André, a British spymaster for the commander in chief of British forces in North America, Gen.

Sir Henry Clinton. Clinton's headquarters were in New York City. Arnold began an encrypted correspondence with André.

Historians still speculate on Arnold's motive for treason. Modern American counterintelligence officers coined "MICE," a simple acronym for the four common motives they believe inspire traitors: money, ideology, coercion, and ego. Arnold was not coerced, and, though he was bitter about not being given enough recognition, his motivation was money, which he demanded for his services. He also dubiously claimed inspiration by ideology, saying that even though he had fought valiantly for the Revolution, he had doubts about the wisdom of breaking away from Britain.

During the British occupation of Philadelphia, André was a dashing young officer. He attended numerous parties and balls hosted by pro-British Americans, self-proclaimed "Loyalists" despised as "Tories" by Patriots. One of André's most ardent admirers in Philadelphia was a beautiful teenager named Peggy Shippen. When Arnold arrived as military governor, he fell in love with Peggy. In April 1779, when he was 37 years old and she was 18, he married her. His offer to spy for the British seems to have been inspired by his obsessive dissatisfaction over his army career and his desperate need to maintain Peggy's lavish lifestyle. After learning that Arnold was offering to spy for the British, André wrote a seemingly innocent note to Peggy, sending it through the unofficial postal system that existed between American-occupied Philadelphia and British-occupied New York.

Peggy, in an equally innocent-looking letter, assured André that Arnold was ready to go to work. Through the cutout, André taught Arnold how to use a "book code," a tough code to break. As André explained the code, "Three Numbers make a Word." The first number is the page of the book, the second is the line on that page, and the third is the word on that line, counting from the left. 293.9.7, for example, directs André to the seventh word on the ninth line of page 293 of the book that the spy and spymaster were using (William Blackstone's *Commentaries on the Laws of England*).

Not every word was put into numbers. To keep the spy letters looking like conventional merchant letters, André told Arnold not to put every word in code. So in the decoded version of the opening lines of the message, the very first word, *I*, is not encoded. Nor is *to*. And the following combination C t B. could be a part of a name—a convention used in merchants' coded letters. In this letter, the first number combination, 293.9.7, sends André to page 293, line 9. He sees that the seventh word in that line is *wrote*.

As André decrypted the message, he would have mentally filled in the missing letters, as indicated in the brackets:

I wrote to C[ap]t B[eckwith] on the 7th June, that a F[rench] fleet and army were expected to act in conjunction with A[merican] army. At the same time I gave Mr. S[tansbury] a manifesto intended to be published in C[anad]a, and have from time to time communicated to him such intelligence as I thought interesting, which he assures me he has transmitted to you.

Captain Beckwith was an intelligence officer attached to Clinton's forces. London-born Joseph Stansbury, an avowed Tory, had aided the British occupiers in Philadelphia. When the British withdrew, thousands of Tories fled the city, joining the British in New York City. But Stansbury remained as what today would be called a "stay-behind agent." Acting as a cutout, he could easily slip into New York to report to André.

In the message, Arnold discloses important information about French involvement in the war. He had learned directly from Washington that French troops and ships were on their way to aid the American cause. The "manifesto" refers to a bit of deception masterminded by Washington: He would release a fake proclamation that said a combined French and American force was about to attack Canada, forcing the British to divert troops. Washington had even given Arnold the proclamation and told him to print and distribute 500 copies.

*Benedict Arnold, notorious traitor to George Washington
and the Continental Army.*

In Arnold's next letter (shown on page 26), he says he is about to become commander of West Point, the fortress that commands the Hudson River. He offers to hand West Point over to the British for £20,000, which would be equal to well over $1 million today. And he asks for a face-to-face meeting with André.

The first attempt at a meeting failed. At the next one, on September 23, Arnold handed André sketches of West Point defenses, which André put inside his boots. He headed south, through American lines, toward safety in British-held territory. But three suspicious American militiamen stopped André, searched him, and found the sketches. Under questioning by Washington's top intelligence officer, André insisted that he was a British officer, not a spy.

Arnold learned of André's capture and managed to escape to a British warship, which carried him to New York. There, he took command of a Tory regiment called the American Legion. André, found guilty of spying by a military court martial, was hanged. As the war was ending, Arnold, Peggy, and their three children sailed to England. Arnold, who never was accepted into British military society, died in England in 1801, Peggy in 1804.

Impact on History: Arnold handed André documents that would have provided the British with the intelligence needed to take West Point. Conquest of that vital fort would have given the British control of the Hudson, cutting off the northeastern colonies from those in the south. Washington would then have had to fight a two-front war, though he almost certainly would have been doomed by a lack of manpower and resources. France would have seen this situation as a sign of an inevitable British victory, and no longer would have planned to aid the Americans.

Draft of a report written by Confederate spy Rose Greenhow, providing information on Union Army troops. She tried to destroy this and many of her other letters before they were seized, but detectives pieced them back together.

The Lady Is a Spy

CREATED: AUGUST 1861
SUBJECT: CIVIL WAR—
ROSE GREENHOW'S CAREER
AS A CONFEDERATE SPY

4 | Within a month after the election of Abraham Lincoln in November 1860, the breakup of the Union began. In Washington, Southern Senators and House members were resigning and heading for their seceding states. On January 21, 1861, Senator Jefferson Davis of Mississippi, who would become the president of the Confederacy, said farewell to the Senate. In the Senate gallery, Mrs. Rose O'Neale Greenhow, a beautiful and popular Washington hostess, was seen to weep. Her sentiments were well known, as were those of the U.S. Army and Navy officers in Washington who were quietly resigning their commissions and returning to their native South, ready to fight in a civil war.

U.S. Army Capt. Thomas Jordan, a Virginian and a West Point graduate, became a Confederate spy while on the staff of Lieut. Gen. Winfield Scott, commander in chief of the U.S. Army. Jordan soon left to serve in the Confederate Army. But he had set up a spy network in the capital, and one of his best agents was Rose Greenhow.

The vivacious 44-year-old widow had friends in high places, including a lover who was a leading northern Senator. She passionately began her new career, obtaining intelligence from her wide circle of influential Washingtonians and sending reports to Jordan in a simple, 26-symbol cipher. Some of her reports, she later wrote in a memoir, included verbatim transcripts of Cabinet meetings.

One of her reports helped the Confederate Army win the first major battle of the war at Bull Run Creek on the road to Manassas, Virginia, on July 21, 1861. Many historians attributed the victory to Union errors that led to a rout. But Confederate Gen. P.G.T. Beauregard and President Davis both thanked Rose Greenhow for her information, which alerted the Confederates to the Union Army's decision to advance toward Manassas.

While marching on Manassas, Union troops overran a Confederate outpost, where soldiers found papers and maps that incriminated Greenhow. Allan Pinkerton, nationally famous as director of a private detective agency, put her Washington mansion under surveillance and kept track of her visitors, many of them suspected spies. Pinkerton had been appointed military intelligence officer for Maj. Gen. George B. McClellan, who had taken command of the Union Army's Division of the Potomac after the Bull's Run rout.

Pinkerton and his detectives, in a search of Greenhow's mansion, found, among other incriminating documents, a seven-page War Department plan about the structure of an expanded U.S. Army. She attempted to destroy documents by burning them, tearing them up, or cutting them into pieces. But the detectives seized the pieces and the singed papers, including the one on page 32—a draft of a report she prepared in August 1861, after the Bull's Run battle when, fearing a Confederate invasion, the capital was building defenses. "During the present week," the draft begins, "the movement of troops & ordnance and munitions, has been active . . ." (The white spaces indicate missing pieces from the torn-up draft.)

The seized papers showed that she made a grave mistake for a spy: She kept drafts and copies of her reports after she sent them. She also saved her notes about enciphering her reports, making decryption easy. On the facing page is one of those cipher notes.

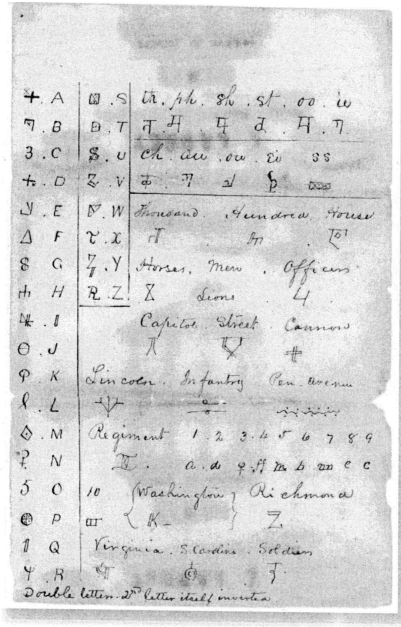

One of Rose Greenhow's greatest errors as a spy—a preserved note
on the methods she used to encipher her reports.

Rose Greenhow, celebrated spy for the Confederacy and one of the first women during the Civil War on either side to play a vital part in espionage.

Greenhow was arrested on August 23, 1861, and charged with "being a spy in the interest of the rebels and furnishing the insurgent generals with important information relative to the movements of the Union forces." For five months, she and several female friends were kept under house arrest. Because she kept trying to smuggle out messages, she was put in the Old Capitol Prison (now the site of the United States Supreme Court Building). In June 1862 she was released and sent through Federal and Confederate lines to Richmond.

Hailed as a heroine but exposed as a spy, she was given a new mission: touring Britain and France to spread Confederate propaganda in speeches and writings. Her memoirs became a best seller in Britain. After a year overseas, she sailed for home aboard a British blockade-runner that ran aground off Wilmington, North Carolina. She was put in a lifeboat, which capsized. Legend says she drowned because she was dragged down by the weight of the gold she carried. According to one version, the gold came from book royalties; in another, she carried gold destined for the

Confederacy's Secret Service. She was buried with full military honors in the Oakdale Cemetery in Wilmington. A marble cross marks her grave and bears an epitaph: "Mrs. Rose O'N. Greenhow, a bearer of dispatchs [sic] to the Confederate Government."

Impact on History: Rose Greenhow's intelligence helped the Confederacy win the first battle of the war. Had the North's strategy not been known in advance, victory for the Union Army—given its strength—was possible. At that early point, with the North ready to march on to Richmond, a negotiated end of the short-lived Civil War would have been possible. In negotiations, President Lincoln, whose war aim was preservation of the Union, may not have been inclined to demand an end to slavery.

Executive Office

Department of State,

Richmond, *Apl 25*, 186*4*

TO THE SECRETARY OF THE TREASURY,

Sir:

Please cause a WARRANT for the sum of One Million *XX* dollars

payable out of the Appropriation for "Secret Service" Act of 15 Feb 1864

to be issued in favor of Hon. J. P. Benjamin Secretary of State

Payable in foreign Countries

£ 206,185. 11. 4

Exchange on England requested

Jefferson Davis
President C.S.A.

~~Secretary of State.~~

Appropriation for "Secret Service" $1,000,000

The "warrant" signed by Jefferson Davis allotting $1 million to covert missions
and operations out of Canada during the Civil War.

A Golden Export to Canada

CREATED: APRIL 1864
SUBJECT: CIVIL WAR—$1
MILLION ALLOTTED TO COVERT
CONFEDERATE MISSIONS

5 | In the early months of the Civil War, the Confederates had a highly effective espionage ring in Washington. Besides Rose Greenhow, there was, for instance, a man—working as a Confederate spy—employed in the quartermaster office of the U.S. War Department. Much of the agents' intelligence traveled from Washington to Richmond on what the Confederates called "The Secret Line," a network of men and women who used boats and wiles to get documents across the Potomac River from Washington or Maryland to Virginia and then on to spymasters in Richmond.

As the war raged on, the Confederacy expanded its espionage activities, forming the Secret Service Bureau, a clandestine unit within the Confederacy's Signal Corps. The bureau ran spy networks and covert missions out of Richmond, Canada, Great Britain, and Continental Europe. To finance the secret Canadian operations, Jefferson Davis, president of the Confederate States of America, signed this "warrant" (opposite page) requesting $1 million from the Secretary of the Treasury, payable for "Secret Service."

Thompson, which appears at the upper left of the warrant, refers to Jacob Thompson, who would take the money, in gold, to Canada. A Washington insider, Thompson had served in

Congress and had been Secretary of the Interior under President James Buchanan. He had no experience in espionage—or in sabotage, which was to be one of his missions.

In February 1864, the Confederate Congress had secretly passed a bill authorizing sabotage against "the enemy's property, by land or sea." Thompson's $1 million came from the $5 million Secret Service fund granted by the Confederate Congress. The bill also allowed saboteurs to get rewards based on how much damage they caused.

Thompson's star operative was Confederate Army Capt. Charles H. Cole, a veteran of battle who had been assigned to Secret Service missions operating out of Canada. Cole slipped into the United States and, assuming the identity of a Philadelphia banker, became an actor in a complex plot.

Near the U.S.-Canadian border were two large camps for Confederate prisoners of war. One was on Johnson's Island, off Sandusky, Ohio, on Lake Erie, and the other was at Fort Douglas in Chicago. The Canadian plotters planned to take over Lake Erie passenger ships and then use them to seize the USS *Michigan*, a warship that patrolled the lake for the Union. After seizing the *Michigan*, the conspirators would then attack the camp at Johnson's Island and free thousands of prisoners. Joined with prisoners freed at Fort Douglas in another operation, the ex-POWs, along with anti-Lincoln militants, would assume control of the region and force the Union to end the war.

Cole, who had been given about $4,000 in gold for his mission, was supposed to charm the officers on the *Michigan*, get them to be less vigilant (perhaps by slipping drugs into their drinks), and signal when the ship was ready for boarding. The signal was to go to John Yates Beall, leader of a guerrilla band of about 20 men. They had seized a small passenger steamer that sailed between Detroit and Sandusky.

Beall waited in vain for the signal, unaware that the seemingly charmed or drugged *Michigan* officers had been tipped off about Cole by a Confederate prisoner aware of the plot. Beall, rightfully assuming that Cole had failed, sped to the Canadian shore, abandoned the ship, and set it afire.

Toward the end of the war, the $1 million in gold financed several other bizarre operations. About 20 men crossed the border to raid St. Albans, Vermont. They robbed three banks of about $200,000 and, trying to burn down the town, managed only to set fire to a woodshed.

A much larger incendiary plan was hatched for New York City in November 1864. Eight agents entered the city and obtained from a sympathetic chemist bottles containing a mixture of phosphorous and carbon disulfide that would burst into flame when exposed to air. The agents left open bottles in hotel rooms and a theater and broke a bottle on a stairway in P.T. Barnum's American Museum. The fires were quickly put out, New York did not burn down, and no one panicked.

In December 1864, John Beall tried to derail Union trains near Buffalo. Union counterintelligence agents trailed him to a station where he waited for a train to Canada. He was tried and convicted as a spy and a guerrilla and was hanged. Union agents next caught Robert Cobb Kennedy, one of the New York arsonists. In his confession he admitted trying to set the museum on fire, adding "but that was only a joke." He also was hanged.

Shortly after the war ended, Canadian authorities arrested another Confederate terrorist: Luke Pryor Blackburn, a Kentucky doctor. He was charged with conspiracy to murder in a foreign country. While in Bermuda caring for victims of a yellow fever epidemic, Blackburn had secretly collected victims' sweat-soaked clothing and blankets and shipped them to Canada. Believing that yellow fever could be transmitted by the victims' clothing, he hoped to start an epidemic in Northern cities. President Lincoln was to be presented with a gift of dress shirts packed with rags of fever victims' clothing. Blackburn was acquitted for lack of evidence. He returned to his native Kentucky, where he resumed his medical practice and was elected governor in 1879.

Although the Confederates' $1 million operation in Canada had little effect on the war, a plot discussed in Canada had profound consequences. Shortly before the Vermont raid, John Wilkes Booth arrived in Montreal and checked into a hotel that served as a Confederate headquarters. Rumors there swirled about plans by Booth and others to kidnap President Lincoln and hold him until he freed all Confederate prisoners of war; presumably they would fight again and help win the war. While in Montreal, Booth went to a bank and traded $300 in gold coins—presumably Confederate gold—in a currency transaction. (He later left for New York, where, coincidentally, he was on the stage of a theater when the Confederate arsonists struck.)

The kidnapping was to take place in March 1865. But a change in Lincoln's schedule thwarted Booth and his associates. After Gen. Robert E. Lee's surrender on April 9, 1865,

THE ASSASSINATION OF PRESIDENT LINCOLN.
AT FORD'S THEATRE WASHINGTON, D.C. APRIL 14TH 1865

Booth's assassination of Abraham Lincoln in Ford's Theater in Washington, D.C. After the South surrendered, there was little for Booth to gain through a mere kidnapping.

there was no need for a kidnapping; the war was over. But five days later, Booth, on his own, changed the plan from abduction to assassination, with the aid of others in the original plot. Booth entered Ford's Theater in Washington on the evening of April 14, opened the door of the presidential box, shot Lincoln in the back of the head, leaped to the stage, shouted "*Sic Semper Tyrannus*"—"Thus always to tyrants"—and escaped. Lincoln died the next morning. On April 26, Booth was killed while resisting capture, and the full story of the original plot died with him.

Impact on History: By a setting up a base for covert action and pouring money into neutral Canada, the Confederate Secret Service created a clandestine network that allowed like-minded conspirators to plot freely against the Union. This eventually led to the plan to first abduct and then kill Lincoln.

From Secretary of Navy.
To COM'DR-IN-CHIEF

Date February 26, 1898.

Subject Assemble Squadron
at Hongkong.
Prepare for war.

Received Hongkong Feb. 26,
8:30 p.m.

Secret and confidential.

Order the Squadron except Monocacy

to Hongkong.

Keep full of coal.

In the event of declaration of war

Spain, it will be your duty to see

that the Spanish squadron does not

leave Asiatic coast and then offensiv
e

operations in Philippine Islands.

Keep the Olympia until further

orders.

(Signed Roosevelt).

Theodore Roosevelt's cable as received by Adm. George Dewey,
ordering him to prepare for war against Spain.

T.R. Remembers the *Maine*

CREATED: FEBRUARY 1898
SUBJECT: SPANISH-AMERICAN
WAR—ROOSEVELT'S DECISION
TO PREPARE FOR WAR

6 | Lieut. John Hood was standing on the port side of the U.S.S. *Maine*, which was moored in Havana Harbor on the evening of February 15, 1898. "Hardly anything was moving in the harbor, and the wind was still," Hood later remembered. "A more perfect scene of peace and rest could hardly be imagined." Then at 9:40, he saw "the whole starboard side of the deck, with its sleeping burden, burst out and fly into space, as a crater of flame came through, carrying with it missiles and objects of all kinds, steel, wood, and human."

The sinking of the *Maine*, with the loss of 252 American lives, was blamed on Spain. While the newspapers of William Randolph Hearst and Joseph Pulitzer beat the drums of war, claiming a bomb had sunk the warship, Assistant Secretary of the Navy Theodore Roosevelt decided to act. In the absence of the ill Secretary of the Navy, Roosevelt took charge. On February 25, he sent a coded cable (shown on page 46) to Adm. George Dewey in Hong Kong, ordering him to prepare the Asiatic Squadron for combat. The decoded telegram appears opposite.

Roosevelt knew that war in Cuba could be expanded into war against Spain's other possessions. Roosevelt was girding for war while President William McKinley was trying to maintain peace. There has never been definitive evidence that Spain blew up the

Original cable from Roosevelt to Dewey, encoded and signed by Roosevelt.

Maine. But McKinley could not withstand congressional and public pressure—"Remember the *Maine!*" became the outcry for vengeance. On April 20, McKinley signed a joint House and Senate resolution demanding that Spain give up Cuba or face military action by "the land and naval forces of the United States." Spain responded with a declaration of war.

Roosevelt, eager for front-line action, resigned as assistant secretary and was commissioned a lieutenant colonel of an all-volunteer cavalry regiment called the Rough Riders. On May 1, Dewey destroyed the Spanish fleet in Manila Bay. Roosevelt feared that the war would be over before he got to Cuba. But he did reach the war, and in the Battle of San Juan Hill, on July 1, he led his men up Kettle Hill, "mounted high on horseback, and charging the rifle-pits at a gallop," as a war correspondent admiringly wrote.

U.S. Navy warships sank or beached Spain's Cuban fleet and U.S. soldiers kept the city of Santiago under siege. Spanish officers had no choice but to surrender, effectively ending the war on July 17.

Impact on History: Theodore Roosevelt's telegram facilitated Dewey's victory, put America in the Pacific, and set in motion events that gave the United States an empire—Puerto Rico, the Philippines, and Guam, with Hawaii soon added. Under Roosevelt, America would build a mighty navy and would appear on the world stage as a major power. As the hero of San Juan Hill, Roosevelt marched from the war to election as Governor of New York, then as Vice President in McKinley's second term. When President McKinley was assassinated, Roosevelt, at the age of 42, became the youngest President in American history.

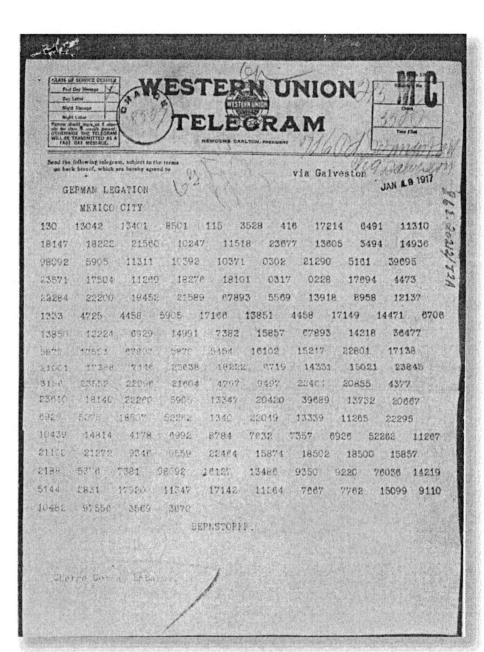

via Galveston

JAN 19 1917

GERMAN LEGATION

MEXICO CITY

130	13042	13401	8501	115	3528	416	17214	6491	11310
18147	18222	21560	10247	11518	23677	13605	3494	14936	
98092	5905	11311	10392	10371	0302	21290	5161	39695	
23571	17504	11269	18276	18101	0317	0228	17694	4473	
23284	22200	19452	21589	67893	5569	13918	8958	12137	
1333	4725	4458	5905	17166	13851	4458	17149	14471	6706
13850	12224	6929	14991	7382	15857	67893	14218	36477	
5870	17553	67893	5870	5454	16102	15217	22801	17138	
21001	17388	7446	23638	18222	6719	14331	15021	23845	
3156	23552	22096	21604	4797	9497	22464	20855	4377	
23610	18140	22260	5905	13347	20420	39689	13732	20667	
6929	5275	18507	52262	1340	22049	13339	11265	22295	
10439	14814	4178	6992	8784	7632	7357	6926	52262	11267
21100	21272	9346	9559	22464	15874	18502	18500	15857	
2188	5376	7381	98092	16127	13486	9350	9220	76036	14219
5144	2831	17920	11347	17142	11264	7667	7762	15099	9110
10482	97556	3569	3670						

BERNSTORFF.

Charge German Embassy.

Encoded telegram from Johann Heinrich von Bernstorff to Heinrich von Eckhardt,
proposing an alliance between Mexico and Germany in the event of the U.S. entering WWI.

A Telegram's Special Delivery

CREATED: JANUARY 1917
SUBJECT: WWI — GERMANY'S
PROPOSED ALLIANCE
WITH MEXICO

7 | While riding in a motorcade through the streets of Sarajevo, Serbia, on June 28, 1914, Archduke Franz Ferdinand, heir to the Austro-Hungarian throne, and his pregnant wife Sophie were shot to death by Gavrilo Princip, a member of the Black Hand, a Serbian terrorist group. When Austria-Hungary declared war on Serbia, European nations rapidly began fulfilling treaty obligations. Germany, after declaring war on Russia and France, invaded Belgium. Britain declared war on Germany. Bulgaria and Turkey allied with Germany. German troops advanced into France and threatened Paris. By the end of the year, both sides were fighting from trenches along the 350-mile Western Front that extended from Switzerland to the English Channel.

Americans hoped that the United States could stay out of the war, with its bewildering cast of nations. President Woodrow Wilson declared U.S. neutrality and, trying to explain what had happened in Europe, blamed it on the historic disorder of the Balkan countries. The causes of the war, he said, "run deep into all the obscure soils of Europe." In 1916, Wilson successfully ran for his second term with the slogan, "He kept us out of war."

Two months after the election, German Foreign Minister Arthur Zimmermann sent a "Most Secret" telegram to Johann

Heinrich von Bernstorff, the German ambassador to the United States. The telegram was to be relayed to Heinrich von Eckhardt, Germany's envoy to Mexico (see page 48). The decrypted and translated message read:

We intend to begin unrestricted submarine warfare on the first of February. We shall endeavor in spite of this to keep the United States neutral. In the event of this not succeeding, we make Mexico a proposal of an alliance on the following basis: Make war together, make peace together, generous financial support, and an understanding on our part that Mexico is to reconquer the lost territory in Texas, New Mexico, and Arizona. The settlement in detail is left to you . . . Please call the [Mexican] President's attention to the fact that the unrestricted employment of our submarines now offers the prospect of compelling England to make peace within a few months.

When British cryptanalysts began cracking the message, they realized that the telegram was an explosive message that had great potential for bringing America into the war. Thanks to British agents' success in obtaining codebooks and other secret documents involving encipher systems, code breakers had been reading German messages for some time.

The original telegram began its journey when the German Foreign Ministry gave the encoded telegram text to the American embassy in Berlin for transmission to Washington, telling the U.S. ambassador that the text contained instructions for Bernstorff regarding peace negotiations. The obliging Americans then sent the telegram to the German ambassador in Washington, via London, the usual route to Washington. The German ambassador then forwarded the telegram to his counterpart in Mexico, using Western Union, which sent it on to Mexico City via Galveston, Texas.

British codebreakers, who routinely intercepted and cracked both American and German communications, saw immediately the importance of the telegram. But to keep the U.S. government from learning that Britain could break American codes, British intelligence had to create a deception. When they showed a decryption of the telegram to American officials, the British claimed that the Germans had sent the telegram out by several channels, including Buenos Aires and Stockholm. The British assured the Americans that they had obtained the telegram from one of those channels, rather than from the American cable. The deception was still undiscovered as late as 1958, when historian Barbara W. Tuchman's book *The Zimmermann Telegram* was published.

British code breakers protected themselves by having American officials give reporters the impression that an American agent had done the job. The code breakers then intercepted German queries about the "leak"—and were relieved to learn that the Germans did not realize that their messages were regularly being cracked.

Wilson released the telegram to the press, which published the sensational news on March 1, 1917. As the British government had expected, news of the telegram intensified American hostility toward Germany. Anti-German hysteria soared days later, when a U-boat sank a British passenger ship, killing 12 civilians, including two Americans.

Impact on History: On April 2, in a war message to Congress, President Wilson cited the Zimmermann telegraph as "eloquent evidence" that "the recent course of the Imperial German Government" was "nothing less than war against the Government and people of the United States." Four days later, Congress overwhelmingly voted to go to war against Germany, launching the U.S. onto the world stage.

the entrance of the station. This man was alive but he was completely unconscious. I tried to open his eyes. I couldn't recognize that he was alive by his eyes, only by his breathing. I didn't see the shot wound but a lot of blood was smeared across his face. I didn't look exactly at him because it was dark and the sight was very shocking.

Q When was he shot?

A I couldn't say that exactly.

Q The hypodermic, then, had nothing to do with the shooting?

A No, I think this was just Muller's "humane" idea.

Q Did he have any identification papers put in his clothes?

A I cannot say, because I didn't have anything to do with this. Muller had an expert commission ready that waited for the moment to appear and to write down the police report.

Q Was it part of the plan that he was supposed to be a German or a Pole?

A He should have represented a Pole but he certainly was not a Pole. He was a German.

Q But the plan was that he should be a Pole?

A It should look like that. That is, it should look as if he was wounded at the attack. It was our order that we should shoot a few pistols when leaving the station, so

-16- (NAUJOCKS)

Page of the sworn testimony of Alfred Helmut Naujocks at Nuremberg, in which he details the events of Operation Canned Goods, which the Germans used to justify an invasion of Poland.

The Man Who Started a War

CREATED: SEPTEMBER 1945
SUBJECT: WWII—THE PLOY
GERMANY USED TO JUSTIFY
AN INVASION OF POLAND

8 | Alfred Helmut Naujocks joined the SS—*Schutzstaffel,* the "Protective Echelon," or strong-arm force, of the Nazi Party in 1931. He later became a member of the SD, *Sicherheitsdienst,* the Security Service, that served as the intelligence service of the SS. By 1939 he wore on the collar of his SD uniform the four silver pips of a *Sturmbannführer,* a storm unit leader—the equivalent of a major in the army. Sometime early in August 1939, Reinhard Heydrich, the head of the SD, personally gave Naujocks an order that would remain secret until September 12, 1945—the day Naujocks spoke to an investigator for the prosecution of the war crimes trials at Nuremberg, Germany. Naujocks, in sworn testimony in December 1945, told how he had engineered a fake incident that Adolf Hitler used to justify his attack on Poland—the act of aggression that plunged Europe into war. A page from the transcript of this testimony appears opposite and on the following page.

According to Naujocks, Heydrich "personally ordered me to simulate an attack on the [German] radio station near Gleiwitz, near the Polish border, and to make it appear that the attacking force consisted of Poles." Naujocks quoted Heydrich as saying, "Actual proof of these attacks of the Poles is needed for the foreign press, as well as for German propaganda purposes."

SECRET

point. I have not mentioned before that the injection this
man received acted deadly after 5 hours. Then, if any members
of the press were led to the place, they would always have
found a dead man and as an expert the same doctor carried out
the function that actually gave the injection, which was Heydrich's
doctor.

    Q Do you know his name?

    A If I would hear the name and if you would
perhaps give me 20 names of doctors that would come in to
question, immediately I would be able to find it.

    Q He was Heydrich's personal doctor?

    A Yes. One cannot say personal doctor; Heydrich
was a hypochondriac who ate tablets all day long and asked
for all sorts of doctors.

    Q Do you know where he lived, this doctor,
or where he had his office?

    A He was a doctor for the SS and he was a
Saxon because his pronunciation was Saxon.

    Q Where was he stationed at the time?

    A He worked in Berlin in the Gestapo office
and he worked on bacteriological things for Heydrich which I
refused later on to do in my office, when I took over the
technical department. When I was asked to carry through these

Another page of Naujock's testimony, describing the scene of the incident at the radio station and alleging that Heydrich's own doctor was called to act as coroner.

When the war crimes investigator interrogated Naujocks, he said that Heinrich Müller, head of the *Geheime Staatspolizei* (Secret State Police, abbreviated "Gestapo"), provided "12 or 13 condemned criminals" who were to be dressed in Polish uniforms and left dead on the ground at the scene of the incident to show that they had been killed while attacking. The code name for the operation was "Canned Goods," a name also jokingly applied to the dead men.

Naujocks said that Operation Canned Goods was a success: "We seized the radio station as ordered, broadcast a speech of three to four minutes over an emergency transmitter, fired some pistol shots, and left." The speech—a call to arms for Poland to strike at Germany—was made by a Polish-speaking German.

Germany used the fake attack and a score of other staged "incidents" along the border to justify the invasion of Poland at dawn on September 1, 1939. At 10 a.m., Hitler spoke to the Reichstag, the German Parliament: "I am wrongly judged if my love of peace and my patience are mistaken for weakness or even cowardice . . . This night for the first time Polish regulars fired on our own territory. Since 5:45 a.m. we have been returning the fire, and from now on bombs will be met with bombs."

Britain and France, committed to come to Poland's aid if Hitler attacked, declared war on Germany. Europe's second world war had begun.

Impact on History: Hardly anyone in the West believed Hitler's unlikely claim that Poland started the war. But Naujocks's eyewitness account revealed the ugly facts of the incident and absolutely established the truth. Also, documents such as the Naujock affidavit laid the groundwork for the prosecution of the war crimes trials at Nuremberg and provided posterity with the horrific record of Nazi rule over conquered Europe.

PREPARING OFFICE
WILL INDICATE WHETHER
Full rate
Collect | Day letter
| Night letter
Charge Department   XX
Full rate
Day letter
Night letter
Charge to
$

TELEGRAM SENT

TO BE TRANSMITTED
CONFIDENTIAL CODE
NONCONFIDENTIAL CODE
PARTAIR
PLAIN

Department of State

Washington,
August 13, 1940

AMERICAN EMBASSY
LONDON

STRICTLY CONFIDENTIAL FOR THE AMBASSADOR.

Please deliver as soon as possible the following
message from the President to the former naval person:

QUOTE I have been studying very carefully the message transmitted to me through the British Ambassador
in Washington on August 8, and I have also been considering the possibility of furnishing the assistance
in the way of releases and priorities contained in the
memorandum attached to your message.

It is my belief that it may be possible to furnish
to the British Government as immediate assistance at
least fifty destroyers, the motor torpedo boats hereto-
fore referred to; and, insofar as airplanes are concerned,
five planes of each of the categories mentioned, the latter to be furnished for war testing purposes. Such assistance, as I am sure you will understand, would only
be furnished if the American people and the Congress frankly recognized that in return therefor the national defense

Enciphered by ....

Sent by operator .... M. .... 19 ....

811.34544/1 6/12

Eavesdropping on Roosevelt and Churchill

CREATED: AUGUST 1940
SUBJECT: WWII — THE
DESTROYERS FOR BASES DEAL

9 | Europe simmered through a relatively quiet eight months called the "phony war." Then, on May 9, 1940, Hitler announced, "The decisive hour has come," and the German blitzkrieg rolled across Europe, heading for the swift conquest of Holland, Luxembourg, Belgium, and France. The next day, Winston Churchill became prime minister of Britain, replacing Neville Chamberlain who in 1938 had negotiated with Hitler and thought he had won "peace for our time."

On the afternoon of May 15, 1940, a Royal Navy courier carried a document from the desk of the new prime minister to the U.S. Embassy. In the embassy code room the document was encrypted and cabled to the White House code room, where it was decrypted and handed to President Franklin D. Roosevelt.

Roosevelt and Churchill had been secretly communicating for months. As First Lord of the Admiralty, Churchill had asked Roosevelt to pass on intelligence about U-boats spotted by U.S. Navy ships on Atlantic patrol. Roosevelt had readily complied. The director of British Navy Intelligence told Churchill that the U.S. ships "have been thoroughly unneutral" in Britain's war against German submarines. Both Roosevelt and Churchill knew that public disclosure of their connivance to violate U.S.

neutrality laws would ruin U.S.-British relations and politically hurt Roosevelt, soon to be running for a third term.

Neither realized that their secret communication was being disclosed to Germany. Working in the U.S. Embassy code room was a clerk, Tyler G. Kent, who believed that Roosevelt was "plotting with Churchill to sneak the United States into the war." Kent, openly anti-Semitic, also believed Roosevelt was a tool of Jews, as did Kent's Russian-born mistress and her pro-Nazi friend, Anna Wolkoff, who had been a maid of honor to the last czarina of Russia. Kent gave Anna documents which a photographer copied. She then passed the photographs on to a contact in the Italian Embassy in London. The Italian ambassador relayed the information to Rome. The German ambassador to Italy then sent the intelligence on to the German Foreign Ministry in Berlin.

At Bletchley Park, the nerve center of British codebreaking, German Foreign Ministry traffic was routinely intercepted and decrypted. One day in May the codebreakers were stunned to see, transmitted from Rome to Berlin, a secret Roosevelt cable that had been sent to Churchill: "It would be possible to hand over 40 or 50 destroyers of the old type, but this is subject to the special approval of Congress, which would be difficult to obtain at present."

British intelligence officers quickly singled out Kent as a suspect. For sometime, he had been seen with Anna Wolkoff, who, with her associates, had been under surveillance by MI5, the British Security Service responsible for counterintelligence operations. On May 20, an MI5 operative along with detectives from Scotland Yard's special branch and a Foreign Service officer from the U.S. Embassy burst into Tyler Kent's apartment. The detectives arrested him (MI5 had no arrest powers). A search of the apartment turned up 1,929 U.S. Embassy documents, including many Roosevelt-Churchill messages. Also found was a book containing the names of people under surveillance by the special branch and by MI5.

U.S. ambassador Joseph Kennedy waived diplomatic immunity for Kent, an American citizen and the son of an American

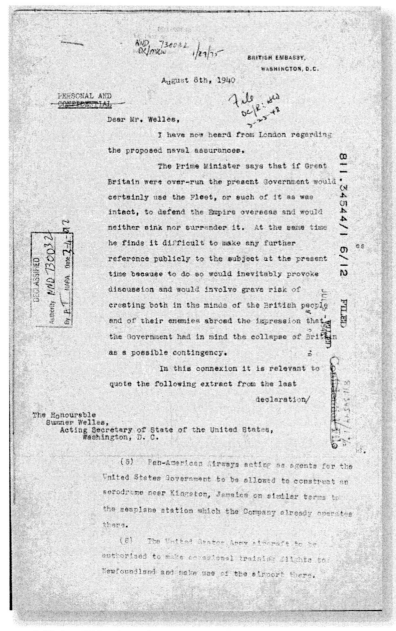

BRITISH EMBASSY,
WASHINGTON, D.C.

August 8th, 1940

PERSONAL AND
CONFIDENTIAL

Dear Mr. Welles,

I have now heard from London regarding the proposed naval assurances.

The Prime Minister says that if Great Britain were over-run the present Government would certainly use the Fleet, or such of it as was intact, to defend the Empire overseas and would neither sink nor surrender it. At the same time he finds it difficult to make any further reference publicly to the subject at the present time because to do so would inevitably provoke discussion and would involve grave risk of creating both in the minds of the British people and of their enemies abroad the impression that the Government had in mind the collapse of Britain as a possible contingency.

In this connexion it is relevant to quote the following extract from the last

declaration/

The Honourable
    Sumner Welles,
        Acting Secretary of State of the United States,
            Washington, D. C.

(5) Pan-American Airways acting as agents for the United States Government to be allowed to construct an aerodrome near Kingston, Jamaica on similar terms to the seaplane station which the Company already operates there.

(8) The United States Army aircraft to be authorised to make occasional training flights to Newfoundland and make use of the airport there.

Cable from FDR to Acting Secretary of State Summer Welles, communicating Churchill's intentions for the fleet. The Battle of Britain began less than a month later.

diplomat. Kent was held for eleven days under secret arrest and then charged with violating the Official Secrets Act, as was Anna Wolkoff, who also had been arrested on May 20.

In a confidential damage assessment, a State Department official reported that the stolen documents showed "a complete history of our diplomatic correspondence since 1938 . . . It means not only that our codes are cracked . . . but that our every diplomatic maneuver was exposed to Germany and Russia . . ." Later investigation established, however, that Kent had not seriously compromised State Department codes.

Kent's secret trial began at the Old Bailey on October 23. Brown paper was pasted on the windows and glass door panels. The only spectators were official observers. Kent was specifically charged with obtaining documents that "might be directly or indirectly useful to an enemy" and letting Wolkoff have them in her possession. He was also accused of stealing documents that were the property of the American ambassador.

Kent admitted that earlier in his career he had taken documents from the U.S. Embassy in Moscow and had hidden them away, vaguely thinking that someday he might show them to U.S. senators who shared his isolationist and anti-Semitic views. His predecessor in Moscow also had passed information to the Soviets. Kent was found guilty and given a seven-year sentence, as was Anna. When newspapers revealed Kent's arrest and conviction, U.S. and British officials played down the espionage.

Through the summer, Roosevelt worked behind the scenes with congressional leaders to get approval for what was the most important aspect of the Churchill-Roosevelt correspondence: an unprecedented swap of 50 overage destroyers in exchange for leases of British naval and air bases in the Western Hemisphere. Opposed by many members of Congress as well as U.S. Navy officials, Roosevelt persevered. The deal was accepted in principle on July 24, 1940. The first eight destroyers were given over to British crews at Halifax on September 9—three days after Germany began all-out air attacks on London in what became known as the Battle of Britain. The other ships followed rapidly.

All were crammed with provisions for British sailors on austerity rations. And the sailors found out they would be sleeping in bunks instead of hammocks.

Kent, released in September 1945, and deported to the United States, never changed his opinions. He published a weekly newspaper that attacked blacks, Jews, and the late President Roosevelt, and condemned President John F. Kennedy as a communist. Kent died in 1988.

Impact on History: After news of Kent's arrest, anti-Roosevelt rumors spread that Kent had been imprisoned to keep him quiet, allegedly because he had found evidence of a Churchill-Roosevelt conspiracy to drag the United States into the war. Had those documents been revealed in 1940, they would have become an issue in Roosevelt's campaign for a controversial third term. He won so spectacularly (449 electoral votes to 82 for Republican opponent Wendell Wilkie) that it is hard to believe the revelations would have helped to defeat him. But a substantial reaction against his secret communications might have slowed down his efforts to aid Britain—as well as his decision, during the campaign, to urge Congress to pass the nation's first peacetime conscription law, which helped America to prepare for the war that came on December 7, 1941.

– 6 –

L a n d	Zahl
A. Altreich	131.800
Ostmark	43.700
Ostgebiete	420.000
Generalgouvernement	2.284.000
Bialystok	400.000
Protektorat Böhmen und Mähren	74.200
Estland – judenfrei –	
Lettland	3.500
Litauen	34.000
Belgien	43.000
Dänemark	5.600
Frankreich / Besetztes Gebiet	165.000
Unbesetztes Gebiet	700.000
Griechenland	69.600
Niederlande	160.800
Norwegen	1.300
B. Bulgarien	48.000
England	330.000
Finnland	2.300
Irland	4.000
Italien einschl. Sardinien	58.000
Albanien	200
Kroatien	40.000
Portugal	3.000
Rumänien einschl. Bessarabien	342.000
Schweden	8.000
Schweiz	18.000
Serbien	10.000
Slowakei	88.000
Spanien	6.000
Türkei (europ. Teil)	55.500
Ungarn	742.800
UdSSR	5.000.000
Ukraine 2.994.684	
Weißrußland aus-	
schl. Bialystok 446.484	
Zusammen: über	11.000.000

*A page from the Wannsee Protocol, identifying the number of Jews
in various European nations—a step in the Nazi Final Solution.*

Planning the "Final Solution"

[
CREATED: JANUARY 1942
SUBJECT: WWII—THE
NAZI FINAL SOLUTION
]

10 | Soon after Adolf Hitler's Nazi Party rose to power in 1933, the government moved against German Jews through legislative, social, and economic actions. Anti-Semitism turned openly violent on November 9-10, 1938— *Reichskristallnacht* (Night of Broken Glass)—when storm troopers led mobs that attacked synagogues, Jewish-owned stores, and Jewish homes. Nearly a year later, when the German invasion of Poland launched Europe into World War II, the genocide of European Jews began.

During Germany's invasion of the Soviet Union in June 1941, special killing units accompanied the army, murdering supposed "enemies of the state," especially Jews. At some point in the murder campaign, Nazi leaders began to use the term "final solution" as shorthand for the extermination of Jews. But there was no central, efficient system for carrying out the genocide. To produce that system, 15 high-ranking Nazi officials assembled on January 20, 1942, in a villa alongside Lake Wannsee in an exclusive quarter of Berlin.

The meeting, chaired by *SS-Obergruppenführer* Reinhard Heydrich, head of the Security Police and the Reich Main Security Office (RSHA), produced a document known as the Wannsee Protocol, a chillingly methodical plan for wiping out Jews—

without specific language about how the mass murders would be perpetrated. The document was stamped Top Secret and only 30 copies were printed. We would not be seeing it today if the Allies had not won the war, found the protocol, and introduced it into the Nuremberg War Crimes Trial. Here are excerpts, translated from Copy No. 16:

Under proper guidance, in the course of the final solution the Jews are to be allocated for appropriate labor in the East. Able-bodied Jews, separated according to sex, will be taken in large work columns to these areas for work on roads, in the course of which action doubtless a large portion will be eliminated by natural causes.

The possible final remnant will, since it will undoubtedly consist of the most resistant portion, have to be treated accordingly, because it is the product of natural selection and would, if released, act as the seed of a new Jewish revival (see the experience of history).

The document then lists the number of Jews and their nations (this page of the Protocol reproduced on page 62). The list is preceded by this sentence: "Approximately 11 million Jews will be involved in the final solution of the European Jewish question . . ."

Following the conference, the Jews "to be allocated for appropriate labor" were deported to six death camps in Poland (Auschwitz, Treblinka, Chelmno, Belzec, Sobibor, and Majdanek). Specialists in the Holocaust estimate that more than 3 million Jews were killed by poison gas in the death camps and that about 3 million more were killed in other ways in other Nazi-controlled sites. Among the other victims were Roma (Gypsies), people with disabilities, and homosexuals.

Although extermination is not mentioned in the Wannsee Protocol, Nazi officials at the conference did talk of mass murder and the scheme for working Jews to death. We know that from the recollections of Heydrich's aide, *SS-Obersturmbannführer* Adolf Eichmann, who attended the conference as the SS expert on Jews.

After the conference, Eichmann later said, "We all had drinks . . . We sang songs. After a while we got up on the chairs and drank a toast, then on the table and then round and round—on the chairs and on the table again. Heydrich taught it to us. It was an old North German custom."

According to Eichmann, *SS-Reichsführer* Heinrich Himmler, director of state security and overseer of the death camps, never put orders about the final solution in writing, relying instead on verbal orders. One of the few written records of his true feelings dates from October 1943, when an underling wrote down what he said to a group of SS officers: "Whether or not 10,000 Russian women collapse from exhaustion while digging a tank ditch interests me only in so far as the tank ditch is completed for Germany . . . We Germans, who are the only people in the world who have a decent attitude to animals, will also adopt a decent attitude to these human animals. But it is a crime against our own blood to worry about them . . ."

Eichmann's recollections of the conference, published in *Life* magazine, came to light after Israeli intelligence agents traced him to Argentina, seized him, and took him to Israel for trial on charges that included crimes against the Jewish people and crimes against humanity. He was found guilty and hanged in 1962.

Impact on History: Eichmann claimed that "my department never gave a single annihilation order. We were responsible only for deportations." But the Wannsee Protocol revealed a high-level Nazi plan of annihilation. And testimony at his trial by survivors added explicit horrors to what was implicit in the Protocol, presenting the realities of the Holocaust to a new generation.

THE WHITE HOUSE
WASHINGTON

SECRET

MEMORANDUM FOR THE ATTORNEY GENERAL

   I have not had an opportunity to talk with you about the prosecution of the eight saboteurs landed from two German submarines nor have I recently read all the statutes which apply.

   It is my thought, however:

1. That the two American citizens are guilty of high treason. This being wartime, it is my inclination to try them by court martial. I do not see how they can offer any adequate defense. Surely they are just as guilty as it is possible to be and it seems to me that the death penalty is almost obligatory.

2. In the case of the other six, who I take it are German citizens, I understand that they came over in submarines wearing seamen's clothes -- in all probability German Naval clothes -- and that some of them at least landed on our shores in these

THE WHITE HOUSE
WASHINGTON

German Naval clothes. I think it can be proved that they formed a part of the German Military or Naval service. They were apprehended in civilian clothes. This is an absolute parallel of the case of Major Andre in the Revolution and of Nathan Hale. Both of these were hanged. Here again it is my inclination that they be tried by court martial as were Andre and Hale. Without splitting hairs, I can see no difference.

   Offenses such as these are probably more serious than any offense in criminal law. The death penalty is called for by usage and by the extreme gravity of the war aim and the very existence of our American Government.

                              F. D. R.

Memo from President Roosevelt to Attorney General Francis Biddle stating his wishes for dealing with the eight enemy saboteurs apprehended on U.S. soil.

Seeking Justice for Saboteurs

CREATED: JUNE 1942
SUBJECT: WWII — THE
APPREHENSION OF EIGHT
ENEMY SABOTEURS

11 | In an odd touch of history, Admiral Wilhelm Franz Canaris, chief of the Abwehr (German military intelligence), selected the code name Pastorius for a secret operation he set up in April 1942. Francis Daniel Pastorius was the founder of what is believed to be the first German settlement in America in 1683. Operation Pastorius was aimed at landing eight saboteurs in America.

The operation began at one of the Abwehr's spy schools, where eight former U.S. residents (two of them Americans) were trained for their mission: Travel by U-boat to American waters, take a rubber dinghy to shore, and begin a campaign of sabotage against America's defense plants and railroads.

Shortly after midnight on June 13, 1942, a U.S. Coast Guardsman, patrolling a Long Island beach near Amagansett, New York, challenged a group of men. One pulled a gun, then offered him a $250 bribe to forget what he saw. Instead, the Guardsman ran to the nearest Coast Guard station. By the time other Coast Guardsmen arrived, the men had disappeared. But searchers dug in the sand and found boxes of explosives, incendiary devices that looked like pens and pencils, and other sabotage tools. There was also a duffle bag stuffed full of German uniforms.

The next day, one of the saboteurs, George J. Dasch, identifying himself as Frank Pastorius, called the FBI in New York. His claim to be a German saboteur was dismissed as a crank call. Dasch next went to Washington and repeated his story in a call to FBI headquarters. This time he was believed. He had told his plans to a comrade, Ernest P. Burger, who also gave himself up. A manhunt began, not only for the other Long Island saboteurs but also for four others from a second U-boat that had landed near Jacksonville, Florida, on June 17. All eight were tracked down and arrested by the FBI. President Roosevelt ordered a news blackout on the saboteurs while he pondered how to dispense American justice. He sent a memo on his thoughts to Attorney General Francis Biddle (the original of this memo is reproduced on page 66):

The two Americans are guilty of treason. I do not see how they can offer any adequate defense . . . it seems to me that the death penalty is almost obligatory . . . [The German citizens] were apprehended in civilian clothes. This is an absolute parallel of the Case of Major André in the Revolution and of Nathan Hale. Both of these men were hanged. The death penalty is called for by usage and by the extreme gravity of the war aim and the very existence of our American government.

Biddle was doubtful. Cautiously challenging Roosevelt, he pointed out that the saboteurs had been caught before they committed sabotage. Later recalling the discussion, Biddle cited an analogy: "If a man buys a pistol, intending murder, that is not an attempt at murder." But Roosevelt was adamant. "I want one thing clearly understood, Francis . . . I won't hand them over to any United States Marshall armed with a writ of habeas corpus" (the constitutionally protected right against illegal detention).

On July 2, Roosevelt proclaimed that the men would be "subject to the law of war" and handed over to a military tribunal. The proclamation went on to say that the saboteurs were not to be permitted "to seek any remedy or maintain any proceeding directly or indirectly, or to have any such remedy or proceeding sought on their behalf, in the courts."

Two Army officers appointed to defend the men ignored Roosevelt's proclamation and immediately sought habeas corpus in U.S. District Court. The case swiftly went through a federal appeals court and then to a special session of the U.S. Supreme Court, which said that no presidential proclamation could limit the power of courts. But the court also said that "those who during time of war pass surreptitiously from enemy territory into our own, discarding their uniforms upon entry, for the commission of hostile acts involving destruction of life or property, have the status of unlawful combatants punishable as such by military commission."

The tribunal of seven Army generals held the secret trial which began on July 8, 1942, on the fifth floor of the Department of Justice building on Pennsylvania Avenue, with Biddle as prosecutor. Black curtains covered the windows. The trial went on until August 4. Four days later, Roosevelt announced that all eight men had been convicted and six had been executed. Roosevelt commuted the death sentences of Dasch and Burger, who had helped to convict their comrades. Dasch was sentenced to 30 years, Burger to life imprisonment. In 1948 President Truman granted executive clemency to them on condition of deportation to what was then the American Zone of Germany.

Impact on History: At the time, the saboteurs' capture and trial fueled American suspicions about foreign agents operating on U.S. soil. Even more important, however, are contemporary legal implications. In 2001, the case reappeared as a precedent for the U.S. government's declaration that prisoners taken in Afghanistan at the start of the war on terror were "unlawful enemy combatants." The government maintained that, like the 1942 saboteurs, prisoners taken during the war on terror, held at an American base on Guantanamo Bay, Cuba, could be treated outside traditional U.S. law. Repeatedly, defense attorneys and government lawyers raised questions about the Guantanamo prisoners, and most of their arguments reflected those raised in vain by defense counsel in 1942.

Soviet leader Josef Stalin was responsible for encouraging the North Koreans to invade South Korea, thus sparking the Korean War.

Stalin Approves a War

[
CREATED: APRIL 1950
SUBJECT: KOREAN WAR—SOVIET
UNION'S ROLE IN THE
INVASION OF SOUTH KOREA
]

12 | On August 29, 1945, near Hamhung, Korea, Soviet fighters fired on and forced down an American B-29 Superfortress that was dropping supplies to Allied prisoners of war still in POW camps just abandoned by Japanese guards. World War II had been over for 15 days, but unknown to the crew of the B-29, a new war had begun. It would be called the Cold War.

To the B-29 crewmen, their mercy flight was over a country called Korea, newly freed after some 40 years as a Japanese colony. To the Soviet pilots, the American warplane was flying over communist-controlled North Korea. When the Soviet Union entered the war against Japan in the last month of World War II, Red Army troops had poured down the Korean peninsula, and, as in Europe, the Soviet Union had claimed control of the territory that its soldiers had conquered.

The U.S. and Soviet governments established the 38th Parallel as the dividing line between North Korea, which became the Soviet-backed Democratic People's Republic of Korea, and South Korea, the American-backed Republic of Korea. From 1945 to 1950, the Soviet Union trained and equipped North Korea's army, and the U.S. did the same for South Korea's army. By May 1950, North Korean leader Kim

N 101.I   — 120   97

Передано —.Булганину.
1.X.50г. в 3ч.00м.

ПЕКИН СОВПОСОЛ

Для немедленной передачи МАО ЦЗЕ-ДУНУ или ЧЖОУ ЭНЬ-ЛАЮ.

Я нахожусь далеко от Москвы в отпуску и несколько ото-
... от событий в Корее. Однако, по поступающим ко мне ...
сведениям из Москвы, я вижу,что положение у корейских товарищей становится отчаянным.

Москва еще 15 сентября предупреждала корейских товарищей,
что высадка американцев в Чемульпо имеет большое значение и
преследует цель отрезать первую и вторую армейские группы
северо-корейцев от их тылов на севере. Москва предупреждала
немедленно отвести с юга хотя бы четыре дивизии, создать
фронт севернее и восточнее Сеула, постепенно отвести потом
большую часть южных войск на север и таким образом обеспечить
38 параллель. Но командование 1 и 2 армейских групп не выпол-
нили приказа Ким Ир Сена об отводе частей на север и это дало
возможность американцам отрезать войска и окружить их. В райо-
не Сеула у корейских товарищей нет каких-либо войск, способных
на сопротивление, и путь в сторону 38 параллели нужно считать
открытым.

Я думаю, что если вы по нынешней обстановке считаете воз-
можным оказать корейцам помощь войсками, то следовало бы не-
медля двинуть к 38 параллели, хотя бы пять-шесть дивизий с
тем, чтобы дать корейским товарищам возможность организовать
под прикрытием ваших войск войсковые резервы севернее 38 параллели. Китайские дивизии могли бы фигурировать, как добро-
вольные, конечно, с китайским командованием во главе.

Enciphered message sent from Red Army Gen. Terenty Shtykov to Soviet Foreign Secretary Andrey Vyshinsky telling of a meeting Shtykov had had with Sung.

- 2 -

Я ничего не сообщал и не думаю сообщать об этом корейским товарищам, но я не сомневаюсь, что они будут рады, ког-
да узнают об этом.

..ду Вашего ответа.

Привет

ФИЛИППОВ.

1 октября 1950г.

Il Sung believed he had a war machine powerful enough to invade and take over South Korea.

At the time, U.S. intelligence services did not realize how much the Soviet Union was encouraging Kim Il Sung to attack South Korea. Nor were Western observers fully aware of Chinese involvement in Kim Il Sung's plans. The Soviet and Chinese connections were not fully known until the collapse of the Soviet Union and the end of the Cold War, when Russian archives became available to historians. They now have documentary proof that Soviet leader Josef Stalin and Chinese Communist leader Mao Zedong were hidden actors in the events leading to the Korean War.

The documents showed, for example, how Kim Il Sung was being cheered on by Red Army General Terenty Shtykov, former commander of Soviet forces in North Korea and, beginning in 1948, the Soviet ambassador to North Korea. Also revealed was Kim Il Sung's secret meeting with Stalin in Moscow in April 1950.

Among the new revelations was an enciphered message that Shtykov sent to Soviet Foreign Secretary Andrey Vyshinsky on May 12, 1950. The message, marked "strictly secret, copying prohibited" and shown on pages 72-73, told of a meeting Shtykov had had with Sung, who talked with him about China's involvement in Sung's invasion plans.

Excerpts produce a new dimension to the Korean War:

Kim Il Sung reported to me that upon his return from Moscow he received a letter from Li Zhou-yuan [ambassador to China], in which he reported about a meeting that took place with Mao Zedong and [Chinese Foreign Minister] Zhou Enlai . . . Mao, turning toward Li as if asking when you intend to begin the unification of the country, without waiting for an answer, stated that . . . the unification of Korea by peaceful means is not possible; solely military means are required to unify Korea. As regards the Americans, there is no need to be afraid of them. The Americans will not enter a third world war for such a small territory.

Kim Il Sung reported further that he . . . [intended] to leave for Beijing in the morning of May 13 and asked me if the plane coming for him will be ready by this time. I answered that the plane is ready.

Kim Il Sung reported to me that [he would inform] . . . Mao Zedong . . . about unifying the country by military means and to report about the results of the discussions on this question in Moscow . . .

He stated that he doesn't have more requests for Mao about assistance, since all his requests were satisfied in Moscow and the necessary and sufficient assistance was given him there. Kim Il Sung reported to me that with regard to the question of the preparation of the operation he had given all necessary orders to the chief of the general staff, who already has begun to implement them, that his wish is to begin the operation in June. . .

North Korea had secretly moved about 90,000 combat troops to areas near the 38th Parallel. On June 25 (American time), seven North Korean infantry divisions, supported by armor and artillery brigades, and under an air cover of more than 100 Soviet-made warplanes, surged into South Korea. The Republic of Korea's 65,000-man army, with neither armor nor an air force, reeled back in retreat.

President Harry S Truman asked for an emergency meeting of the United Nations Security Council, which the Soviet Union boycotted. The council passed a resolution calling for a ceasefire and withdrawal of North Korean invaders. On June 27, Truman ordered General of the Army Douglas MacArthur, commander in chief of U.S. forces in the Far East, to launch naval and aerial attacks on "all North Korean military targets south of the 38th parallel." The "police action," as Truman called it, quickly escalated into a war, with MacArthur leading a UN Force dominated by U.S. Army soldiers and including forces from Britain, Canada, Australia, Turkey, and other UN nations.

When UN forces began to roll back the invaders, Stalin started worrying. He was wrong when he said that the United States would not defend "such a small territory." In a message to Mao and Zhou on October 1, 1950, using the code name Filippov, he

Kim Il Sung, leader of North Korea in 1950, was encouraged by the Soviet Union to invade South Korea.

said, ". . . I see that the situation of our Korean friends is getting desperate . . . I think that if in the current situation you consider it possible to send troops to assist the Koreans, then you should move at least five-six divisions toward the 38th parallel at once so as to give our Korean comrades an opportunity to organize combat reserves north of the 38th parallel under the cover of your troops. The Chinese divisions could be considered as volunteers, with Chinese in command at the head, of course."

Impact on History: Stalin's advice came at a time when China looked upon the Soviet Union as "Big Brother." His telegram predicting no U.S. intervention spurred North Korea and China, which, to the surprise of U.S. intelligence officials, entered the war, hurling "human waves" of troops against UN lines. Fighting continued into the spring of 1951, when a combat stalemate at the 38th Parallel produced negotiations that continued into the administration of President Dwight D. Eisenhower. An armistice, signed on July 27, 1953, set up the Korean Military Demarcation Line near the 38th Parallel. Soldiers of the People's Army began patrolling one side of the line and U.S. and Republic of Korea soldiers began patrolling the other. The patrols still walk that line.

No. 1873

NEW YORK TIMES COMPANY,
PETITIONER

v.

UNITED STATES OF AMERICA

No. 1885

UNITED STATES OF AMERICA,
PETITIONER

v.

THE WASHINGTON POST COMPANY, et al.

ON WRITS OF CERTIORARI
TO THE UNITED STATES COURT OF APPEALS
FOR THE SECOND CIRCUIT AND THE
UNITED STATES COURT OF APPEALS
FOR THE DISTRICT OF COLUMBIA CIRCUIT

BRIEF FOR THE UNITED STATES
(SECRET PORTION)

There have been great difficulties in the prosec
of this case. The United States does not know what mater
are in the possession of the New York Times or the Washin
Post, and neither District Court below was willing to req
disclosure of those papers, even in camera, without repre

*First page of the secret brief in which Solicitor General Erwin N.
Griswold laid out classified information that would be disclosed should the Pentagon
Papers continue to be published.*

The Pentagon Papers' Legacy

[
CREATED: OCTOBER 1971
SUBJECT: VIETNAM WAR—THE
STRUGGLE TO PREVENT PUBLICATION
OF THE PENTAGON PAPERS
]

13 | Daniel Ellsberg, a former Marine and former Department of Defense analyst who had also served for two years at the U.S. Embassy in Saigon, in 1969 was working on a top-secret study of the Vietnam War when he was seized by what he later called "an urgent sense that Nixon was about to escalate the war." To let the American public know what top officials had been keeping in locked filing cabinets, Ellsworth decided to photocopy 7,000 highly classified pages of the report and, after trying in vain to get Senators interested in what he had, gave the documents to the *New York Times*. The documents became known as the Pentagon Papers.

The *Times* began publishing the Pentagon Papers on Sunday, June 13, 1971 under the headline "Vietnam Archive: Pentagon Study Traces 3 Decades of Growing U.S. Involvement." The *Times* reported that, according to the study, President Lyndon B. Johnson had begun "planning in the spring of 1964 to wage overt war, a full year before it publicly revealed the depth of its involvement . . . " Quoted in the study was a 1967 memo from Assistant Secretary of Defense John T. McNaughton to Secretary of Defense Robert S. McNamara: "A feeling is widely and strongly held that 'the Establishment' is out of its mind. The feeling is that we are trying to impose some U.S. image on distant peoples we cannot understand (any more than we can the younger generation here at home) and that we are carrying the thing to absurd lengths. Related to this feeling is the increased polarization that is taking place in the United States with seeds of the worst split in our people in more than a century."

The *Washington Post*, which also began publishing excerpts, summarized the contents of the papers in an editorial: "The story that unfolds is not new in its essence—the calculated misleading of the public, the purposeful manipulation of public opinion, the stunning discrepancies between public pronouncements and private plans—we had bits and pieces of all that before. But not in such incredibly damning form, not with such irrefutable documentation."

The day after the first of the Pentagon Papers was published, Attorney General John Mitchell warned the *Times* not to publish any more installments. On Monday, the *Times* ignored Mitchell's warning and published the next in the series. On Tuesday, the government, claiming that publication of the papers caused "irreparable injury to the defense interests of the United States," got a federal court to issue a "prior restraint" order against the *Times*. The government also tried to stop the *Washington Post*'s presses, again using the argument that publication would endanger national security.

The *Times* appealed its restraint order to the U.S. Supreme Court, where Solicitor General Erwin N. Griswold, arguing for the government, introduced a "secret brief," describing classified information so that the justices would be convinced that continued publication of the documents would damage national security. Part of the secret brief is reproduced on page 82.

Griswold had taken examples from four "diplomatic volumes" in the 47-volume study. Griswold apparently did not realize that Ellsberg had not copied them because he knew that they contained sensitive information. Griswold's brief, describing Pentagon Papers that had not been published, had little impact on the court. In a landmark 6-to-3 decision, the Supreme Court lifted the restraining order, ruling that the government had not met the "heavy burden of showing justification for the enforcement of such a restraint." Newspapers hailed the decision, which ended one of the most important First Amendment cases in history.

Griswold's brief remained a classified document for decades. The National Security Archives, an independent, non-governmental research institute and library, obtained a copy through the Freedom of Information Act but noted, "It continues to have deletions in it to this day."

The Pentagon Papers study covered the war through 1968, ending before President Nixon's election. But Nixon agreed with the verdict of his chief of staff, H. R. Haldeman, who on the day after the *Times* began publishing the Pentagon Papers told the President what they really meant: "[Y]ou can't trust the government; you can't believe what they say; and you can't rely on their judgment; and the—the implicit infallibility of Presidents, which has been an accepted thing in America, is badly hurt by this, because it shows that people do things the President wants to do even though it's wrong, and the President can be wrong."

We know Haldeman said those words to Nixon because Nixon had bugged the Oval Office and secretly taped all his phone calls. That secret was one of many revealed along the twisting path that began with the publication of the Pentagon Papers and ended with Nixon's resignation in August 1974.

Nixon took his first step down that path on July 1, 1971. According to transcripts of his White House tapes for that day, at a meeting with his aide he exclaimed, "We're up against an enemy, a conspiracy! They're using any means. We are going to use any means. Is that clear?"

Reacting to the publication of the Pentagon Papers, the Nixon White House created a clandestine group whose members were dubbed "the Plumbers" because their mission was to track down and stop leaks. After Ellsberg was arrested and was charged with violating the Espionage Act and theft of government property, the Plumbers broke into a psychiatrist's office to find files on Ellsberg that could discredit him at his trial. When this was later revealed, the judge declared a mistrial. Ellsberg was freed.

nations or governments. The publication of this material is likely to close up channels of communication which might otherwise have some opportunity of facilitating the closing of the Vietnam war.

2. Closely related to this is the fact that there is much material in these volumes which might give offense to South Korea, to Thailand, and to South Vietnam, just as serious offense has already been given to Australia and Canada. South Korea, South Vietnam, and Australia have troops in Vietnam, and Thailand allows the use of airfields from which 65% of our sorties are launched.

For the past many months, we have been steadily withdrawing troops from Vietnam. The rate at which we can continue this withdrawal depends upon the extent to which we can continue to rely on the support of other nations, notably South Vietnam, Korea, Thailand, and Australia. If the publication of this material gives offense to these countries, and some of them are notably sensitive, the rate at which our own troops can be withdrawn will be diminished. This would be an immediate military impact, having direct bearing on the security of the United States and its citizens.

There are further references to these items in the "Special Appendix" filed in the United States Court of Appeals for the Second Circuit in the New York Times case, and in this court.

3. There are specific references to the names and activities of CIA agents still active in Southeast Asia. There are references to the activities of the National Security Agency.

— 5 —

Another page of the Griswold Brief, this particular section explaining the damage posed by the publication of the Pentagon Papers to the planned U.S. withdrawal of troops from Vietnam.

Impact on History: Publication of the Pentagon Papers led to the unprecedented resignation of a president. Two of the Plumbers were among the men who were caught on June 17, 1972, after breaking into the Democratic National Committee's headquarters in a building whose name would forever symbolize the scandal-ridden downfall of an American president: Watergate. Disgraced by revelations of congressional investigators and facing impeachment, Nixon resigned on August 8, 1974. The Pentagon Papers became an enduring emblem not only of the Vietnam War but also of Watergate and struggles over secrecy between elected officials and a free, questioning society.

République Du Niger
Fraternité - Travail - Progrès

Niamey, le 27/07/2000

MONSIEUR LE PRESIDENT,

J'AI L'HONNEUR DE ME REFERER A L'ACCORD N° 381-NI 2000,
CONCERNANT LA FOURNITURE D'URANIUM, SIGNE A NIAMEY LE 06
JUILLET 2000 ENTRE LE GOUVERNEMENT DE LA REPUBLIQUE DU NIGER
ET LE GOUVERNEMENT DE L'IRAQ PAR LEURS RESPECTIFS REPRESEN-
TANTS DELEGUES OFFICIELS.

DITE FOURNITURE EQUIVALENTE A 500 TONNES D'URANIUM PUR
PAR AN, SERA DELIVRE EN 2 PHASES.

AYANT VU ET EXAMINE LEDIT ACCORD, JE L'APPROUVE EN TOUTES
ET CHACUNE DE SES PARTIES EN VERTU DES POUVOIRS QUI ME SONT
CONFERES PAR LA CONSTITUTION DU 12 MAI 1966.

The letter that allegedly arranged the sale of uranium to Iraq from Niger.

16 Troublesome Words

CREATED: JULY 2000
SUBJECT: THE ALLEGED
SALE OF URANIUM TO
IRAQ FROM NIGER

14 | Of the 5,414 words spoken by President George W. Bush in his State of the Union address on January 29, 2003, sixteen words reverberated, taking on a life of their own. After describing Iraqi leader Saddam Hussein as a "brutal dictator, with a history of reckless aggression, with ties to terrorism, with great potential wealth," President Bush went on to say that Saddam was building a stockpile of weapons of mass destruction. Then came those ominous sixteen words: "The British government has learned that Saddam Hussein recently sought significant quantities of uranium from Africa."

The words added presidential authority to other information about Saddam that had been stated in March 2002 by Vice President Dick Cheney: "[T]here's good reason to believe that he continues to aggressively pursue the development of a nuclear weapon," and in September 2002 by National Security Adviser Condoleezza Rice: "[T]here will always be some uncertainty about how quickly he can acquire nuclear weapons. But we don't want the smoking gun to be a mushroom cloud."

Had Saddam Hussein gotten uranium from somewhere in Africa, he could have begun building a nuclear bomb. That possibility became a leading justification for an invasion of Iraq in 2003, which drastically changed America's position in the Middle East.

By the time of the invasion, many political observers were wondering exactly how those sixteen words got into the State of the Union address. The answer is both convoluted and illuminating, for it shows how a dubious document wends its way through the U.S. intelligence community, challenging analysts and policymakers to determine whether it is true, false, or partially true. The document (shown on page 84) purported to reveal an agreement for the sale of uranium to Iraq from the African nation of Niger. The document, in capital letters, topped by the letterhead of the Republic of Niger, and dated July 27, 2000, was in French, Niger's official language. Translated, it read:

MR. PRESIDENT.

I HAVE THE HONOR OF REFERRING TO ACCORD NO. 381-NI 2000, CONCERNING THE PROVISION OF URANIUM, SIGNED IN NIAMEY ON THE SIXTH OF JULY 2000 BETWEEN THE GOVERNMENT OF THE REPUBLIC OF NIGER AND THE GOVERNMENT OF IRAQ BY THEIR RESPECTIVE OFFICIAL DELEGATED REPRESENTATIVES.

SAID PROVISION EQUALLING 500 TONS OF PURE URANIUM PER YEAR WILL BE DELIVERED IN 2 PHASES.

HAVING SEEN AND EXAMINED THE SAID ACCORD, I APPROVE IT IN ALL AND EACH OF ITS REQUIREMENTS IN VIRTUE OF THE POWERS VESTING IN ME BY THE CONSITUTION OF 12 MAY 1966.

THEREFORE, I ASK THAT YOU CONSIDER THIS LETTER AS A FORMAL INSTRUMENT OF APPROVAL OF THIS ACCORD BY THE GOVERNMENT OF THE REPUBLIC OF NIGER WHICH THUS FINDS ITSELF DULY BOUND.

I WOULD LIKE TO ADD, MR. PRESIDENT, ASSURANCES OF MY HIGHEST ESTEEM.

At the bottom of the page was a seal for what appeared to be the Office of the President and the faint signature of President Mamadou Tandja.

Information about a Iraq-Niger connection had been given by *Servizio per le Informazioni e la Sicurezza Militare* (SISMI), the

Italian intelligence agency, to the CIA chief of station in the U.S. Embassy in Rome in October 2001 and then in January 2002, according to the authors of *The Italian Letter*, Peter Eisner and Knut Royce, who broke the story in 2007.

Those reports from SISMI were viewed skeptically by CIA analysts, but they led Vice President Cheney and his chief of staff, I. Lewis ("Scooter") Libby to recieve from the CIA all the intelligence on a possible Niger-Iraq link. The mission was given to the CIA's Counterproliferation Division in the Directorate of Operations. One of the intelligence officers in the division was Valerie Plame, who for a long time had worked under "non-official cover," meaning she did not have the diplomatic immunity that protects intelligence officers who operate under "official cover." An intelligence officer caught spying while under official cover is merely expelled as persona non grata. Officers like Valerie Plame who work under non-official cover face arrest, trial, and punishment if they are caught.

When Plame was told about the uranium report, she agreed with a colleague's suggestion that her husband, Joseph Wilson, go to Niger and check out the story. Wilson had been ambassador to Gabon and deputy chief of mission in Baghdad. In February 2002, he went to Niger, found no evidence of the deal, returned to America, and reported his finding to the CIA. (Later, in a *New York Times* article, Wilson would reveal his failure to find any Iraq-Niger connections. This triggered a long Washington saga involving Plame, Wilson, Libby, and other Bush administration officials.)

In September 2002, British Prime Minister Tony Blair, basing his statement on similar SISMI material, told Parliament, "We know Saddam has been trying to buy significant quantities of uranium from Africa, though we do not know whether he has been successful." Then on October 7 came a speech by President Bush. White House speechwriters had put a Niger-Iraq connection in the speech, but, finally accepting CIA advice, deleted it. In the speech, billed as a major policy address, Bush did say that Saddam was working on nuclear weapons and that if he were to "buy or steal an amount of highly enriched uranium a little larger than a single softball, he would be in a position to threaten America."

Two days after the Bush speech, Elisabetta Burba, an investigative reporter for the Italian newsweekly *Panorama*, was handed a packet of documents by a shadowy man who had been an informant for Italian, French, and Egyptian intelligence services. He said he wanted $10,000 for the documents. After carefully examining them, Burba decided that they did not look as official as they should have. One, for instance, was signed by Niger's foreign minister, Ailele Elhadj, who no longer held that position in 2000. And his name was misspelled. Burba said she had to check the documents' validity and would get back to him about payment.

Believing she might find an American official who would verify the documents, Burba took them to the U.S. Embassy in Rome, unaware that SISMI had passed along to the CIA similar documents about a year before. Burba appeared at the embassy on October 9, 2002. Ironically, the next day the House and Senate gave President Bush the authority to go to war against Iraq.

Between October 2002 and January 2003, members of the Bush administration frequently mentioned reports of Saddam's attempts to obtain uranium. As White House speechwriters began working on the President's State of the Union speech, they obtained agreement from a CIA official that they could include mention of the Niger report, providing that they attributed it to the British government, which had publicly made the accusation. Thus, the sixteen words.

When Secretary of State Colin Powell, speaking at the United Nations, made the case against Saddam Hussein in February 2003, he said that Saddam had been trying to acquire plutonium. But in his 10,000-word presentation Powell did not mention Niger. Intelligence analysts were losing whatever faith they may have had in the authenticity of the documents.

Finally, on March 7, 2003, Mohamed ElBaradei, director general of the International Atomic Energy Agency, in a presentation to the Security Council of the UN, said that the IAEA had compared "the form, format, contents, and signature" of real official Nigerian correspondence with the suspected documents. The IAEA concluded that the documents "are in fact not authentic." On March 11, the CIA said it could not dispute the IAEA's conclusion.

Impact on History: The fake Niger document, apparently fabricated to get money and not to influence policymakers, became part of the evidence cited by the Bush administration in its campaign to justify an invasion of Iraq.

TWO

Double Agents, Turncoats, and Traitors

SOMETIME AROUND 1850, ALLEN PINKERTON, A CHICAGO DEPUTY SHERIFF, established the first U.S. detective agency and named it after himself. His motto was "We Never Sleep," and the agency used an unblinking eye as its logo—the source of the expression "private eye." Pinkerton did some counterintelligence work for the Union during the Civil War. After the war, he explained the merits of the double agent: "In war, as in a game of chess, if you know the moves of your adversary in advance, it is then an easy matter to shape your own plans, and make your moves accordingly, and, of course always to your own decided advantage. So . . . I concluded that if the information intended for the rebels could first be had by us, after that, they were welcome to all the benefit they might derive from them."

Intelligence developed by a double agent can change history. As World War II began, British intelligence services were reeling from a superb double agent operation that German intelligence had run against them. But by the end of the war, the British had developed their own version of a double agent operation—a phenomenally successful espionage caper aptly code-named the Double-Cross System. Until some new genius builds a better one, the Double-Cross System remains the ultimate double agent scheme in espionage history.

During a typical double agent operation, an agent works for an intelligence service, while secretly working against this service for an opposing service, which provides false information to the agent. Double agents are usually created by threats and inducements from one of their two masters. A double agent is a potent adversary, as British intelligence officers learned when they were caught in the German sting at the beginning of World War II.

After Britain declared war on Germany on September 3, 1939, Prime Minister Neville Chamberlain hoped to rapidly end the war by negotiations. The SD (*Sicherheitsdienst*, the German Security Service) decided to play to the British yearning for peace while at the same time staging a fake anti-Hitler operation that would smoke out real dissidents. A German agent working for S. Payne Best, an officer of MI6, the British Secret Intelligence Service, infiltrated a genuine opposition group and, in traditional double-agent style, acted if he were controlled by Best while secretly working for the SD.

The agent claimed to have set up meetings for best in Holland in October 1939 with a German officer who called himself "Major Schemmel" and said he was involved in an anti-Hitler plot. Accompanying Best was H. R. Stevens of MI6. Best had been empowered to tell Schemmel that Britain would accept an end to the war and grant Germany its territorial claims up to 1938 if the German army overthrew Hitler. Schemmel said that the plotters would arrest Hitler and take over Germany. But Schemmel told Best and Stevens that the leaders of the plot wanted to speak directly with British government officials.

MI6 arranged for a plane to pick up the Germans at Venlo, near the Dutch-German border. On November 8, while Best and Stevens awaited the German delegation, a car smashed through the border checkpoint, Nazi gunmen firing at the Dutch border guards. Germans leaped from the car, grabbed the two Britons, and sped back across the border into Germany. Schemmel turned out to be Walter Schellenberg, deputy leader of the SD.

The MI6 officers were handed over to the Gestapo for interrogation and were imprisoned until the end of the war. A postwar MI6 investigation revealed that they gave up enough information to enable the Gestapo to eradicate much of the MI6 network in Europe.

Winston Churchill, who replaced Chamberlain as prime minister in May 1940, sought no deals with Germany. He enthusiastically supported the work of the Double-Cross System, a scheme to make double agents of captured German agents who had slipped into Britain. The Double-Cross System gave them a stark choice: Work for us or face the consequences.

At the heart of the system was the mixture of true and false secrets that the doubled agents transmitted by radio to a completely deceived Abwehr, the German military intelligence organization. The Germans not only accepted the false intelligence but also sometimes acted on it—fulfilling the committee's hope to "influence and perhaps change" German plans.

The idea of doubling an agent is at least as old as the spy advice Sun Tzu gave in the sixth century B.C. and as new as 21st-century warfare. General Tommy Franks, commander of U.S. military forces when the Iraq War began, revealed in 2004 that an Iraqi intelligence officer, under cover as a diplomat, asked a U.S. army officer to spy for Iraq. The American feigned agreement, thereby becoming a double agent. He gave his Iraqi handler phony documents that led Iraqi strategists to deploy forces to areas far from the real invasion route.

9th March 1812.

Dear Sir ( ) Henry's secret mission

As the Intelligencer will not publish the message & documents just laid before Cong.ᵗˢ. for the present mail, I send you a copy of the former. It is justified by the Documents, among which are the original credential & instructions from the Gov.ᵗ of Canada, and an original dispatch from the Earl of Liverpool to him approving the conduct of the secret agent. This discovery, or rather formal proof of the cooperation between the Eastern Junto & the B. Cabinet will, it is to be hoped, not only prevent future evils from that source, but expel good out of the past.

Jas. Madison

One of the "Henry letters," which President Madison used to prove to Congress
that the British had hired Capt. John Henry as a spy to foment unrest in the Union.
The letters helped spark the War of 1812.

Captain Henry's $50,000 Letters

[
CREATED: MARCH 1812
SUBJECT: THE WAR OF 1812—
CAPT. JOHN HENRY'S CAREER
]

15 | Irish-born John Henry, a former U.S. Army officer, left his home and farm in Vermont in 1806 and settled in Montreal because, he said, he "preferred a monarchial government." Canada was then a colony under the British crown. Captain Henry, as he called himself, soon was involved with Canadian politicians and their allies, the wealthy "fur barons" who controlled the nation's pelt trade. The governor general of Canada, Sir J. H. Craig, was particularly intrigued by the garrulous captain.

In March 1807, Britain and France were at war. British warships were in the Chesapeake Bay, blockading two French warships. When five sailors deserted one of the British ships, reports soon spread that they had enlisted as crew members of the U.S. Navy frigate *Chesapeake*. After the captain of the *Chesapeake* refused to allow his ship to be searched, a British warship fired on the *Chesapeake*, killing three men and wounding eighteen. An armed British party boarded the *Chesapeake* and seized four men as deserters.

The incident had been preceded by other such acts of impressment—the forcible recruitment of Americans by British seafarers. Now Britain and the United States were on the brink of war. Canadian officials, fearing invasion if the

U.S. did go to war, needed intelligence. Captain Henry was enlisted as an undercover agent and sent across the border to investigate rumors that if war came the New England states would secede from the Union and perhaps form some kind of connection with Britain.

During his three months in Vermont and Boston, Captain Henry wrote frequently to Governor Craig's civil secretary. Henry reported that discontent was widespread in New England and that if war were declared, the Massachusetts state legislature would lead a secession movement and establish a relationship with Britain. The letters passed from Craig to the British to Secretary of State in London.

Henry himself went to London, where he was snubbed by officials who viewed Canada as a colony and not an initiator of British policy. He left London, ostensibly to return to Canada, but sailed instead to Boston, and with the aid of a European conman posing as a count, obtained a letter of introduction to President James Madison. Madison, eager for proof of British perfidy, used $50,000 from his "secret service fund" to buy what became known as the "Henry letters." One of these is shown on page 94.

Madison presented the Henry letters to key members of Congress, along with a message in which Madison charged that the British had hired Henry as a secret agent to foment disaffection in Massachusetts "for the purpose of . . . destroying the Union and forming . . . a political connection with Great Britain." Henry, meanwhile, had sailed to France. Little about his subsequent life is known, though reports circulated in 1820 that he was in Italy, seeking intelligence about an affair that Queen Caroline of England was said to be having.

Impact on History: On June 1, 1812, Madison delivered to Congress a message that included accusations stemming from the Henry letters. Eleven days later, the United States declared war on Britain. The War of 1812 established America's independence from Britain. In 1814, the two nations sought a negotiated peace so that they could resume their trade.

President James Madison used the Henry letters to prove to Congress Britain's intention of "destroying the Union."

I have not changed the views expressed in my former communications. All that a large portion of the Northern people—especially in the Northwest — want to resist the oppressions of the despotism at Washington, is a _leader_. They are ripe for resistance and _it may come soon after the Presidential Election_. At all events it must come if our armies are not overcome and destroyed or dispersed. **No** people of the Anglo-Saxon blood can long endure the usurpations and tyrannies of Lincoln. Democrats are more hated by Northern Republicans than Southern Rebels and will be as much outraged and persecuted if Lincoln is re-elected. They must yield to a cruel and disgraceful despotism or fight. They feel it and know it.

I do not see that I can achieve anything by remaining longer in this Province and unless instructed to stay shall leave here by 20th inst. for Halifax and take my chances for running the blockade. If I am to stay till Spring I wish my wife to join me under flag of truce, if possible. I am afraid to risk a winter's residence in this latitude and climate.

I need not sign this. The bearer and the person to whom it is addressed can identify me.

A page of a decrypted letter which was produced as evidence at the Lincoln assassination trial. It hints at dire action—possibly an attempt at assassination—to be taken against Lincoln following the presidential election.

Lincoln's Double Agent

CREATED: OCTOBER 1864
SUBJECT: CIVIL WAR—
REVELATION OF CONFEDERATE
PLOTS AGAINST LINCOLN AND
THE NORTH

16 | The Confederate spy-and-sabotage cell in Canada (discussed previously on page 38 in "A Golden Export to Canada") received important instructions from Richmond through a covert courier system. One of the couriers was Richard Montgomery, who often carried encrypted dispatches from Confederate President Jefferson Davis. Montgomery's real employer was Lincoln's assistant Secretary of War, Charles A. Dana.

On his courier rounds, Montgomery stopped off in Washington, where the dispatches, which were usually in cipher, were copied and decrypted. One such dispatch came into the War Department on Sunday, October 16, 1864, when President Lincoln himself happened to have stopped there on his way back from a Sunday church service. Lincoln spent a great deal of time at the War Department Telegraph Office, reading and writing telegrams. Deciphered, the dispatch sent from Canada to Judah P. Benjamin, Confederate Secretary of State, said:

We again urge our gaining immediate advantage. Strain every nerve for victory. We now look upon the re-election of Lincoln as almost certain, and we need to whip the hirelings to prevent it. Besides, with Lincoln re-elected, and his armies victorious, we need not hope even for recognition [from Britain], much less the help mentioned in our last. Holcombe will explain this. Our friend shall be immediately set to work as you direct.

The answer from Richmond, signed by Benjamin, was also presented to Dana and Lincoln. Decrypted, it said:

Your letter of the 13th inst., is at hand. There is yet time enough to colonize many voters before November. A blow will shortly be stricken here. It is not quite time. Gen. Longstreet is to attack Sheridan without delay, and then move north, as far as practicable, toward unprotected points. This will be made instead of the movements before mentioned. He will endeavor to assist the Republicans in the collection of their ballots. Be watchful, and assist him.

Montgomery's dispatches proved that Confederates were using Canada as a safe haven and base of operations. Secretary of War Edwin M. Stanton pounced on the documents. He told Lincoln that they should be held for use as evidence in a stern warning to Britain, which he blamed for allowing Canada, then a British colony, to become an undeclared ally of the Confederacy.

If Dana withheld the documents, Lincoln and Dana realized, the Confederates would know that Montgomery had been intercepted. Lincoln made a suggestion: "Why not allow the messenger to depart as usual, and then capture him in Virginia somewhere, take the dispatch from him, clap him in prison, and afterward let him escape?"

Union sentries were alerted, and Montgomery was sent on his way. He was captured, his papers were seized, and he was imprisoned. He soon escaped, was fired on, and wounded.

Richard Montgomery, double agent for Abraham Lincoln and the Union Army.

Abraham Lincoln relied heavily on double agent Richard Montgomery
to feed him intelligence on Confederate activity out of Canada.

Montgomery later claimed that he had shot himself in the arm so he could show his Confederate handlers a wound as proof of his escape and desperate flight. Adding verisimilitude to the escape hoax were planted newspaper notices offering a reward for Montgomery's recapture.

Impact on History: Montgomery was a key witness at the military tribunal's trial of eight Southern sympathizers charged with aiding John Wilkes Booth in a conspiracy to assassinate President Lincoln. Montgomery's testimony, buttressed by the secret dispatches, included his allegation that Jacob Thompson, a Confederate commissioner to Canada, had said that "a proposition had been made to him to rid the world of the tyrant Lincoln, Stanton, Grant, and some others; that he knew the men who had made the proposition were bold, daring men, able to execute what they undertook . . ." Montgomery's testimony helped convict the conspirators, four of whom were hanged. Thompson, fearing prosecution, fled the country. Montgomery disappeared from history, a frequent fate of double agents.

9th March, 1918.

R E I L L Y, 2nd Lieut. Sidney George.
_____

I have made discreet enquiries re the above and find he
is an Irishman, born at Clonmel in 1874. He has resided
at St. James Palace Chambers, 22, Ryder Street, S.W., since
10th January, 1918, and was previously stopping at the Savoy
Hotel. He occupies a suite of chambers at RYDER STREET, the
number of same is 81, for which he pays £8.8.0. per week.
He is said to be very respectable and pays his bills quite
regularly, has very little correspondence which is British, and
has only been known to have two friends to visit him, viz:-
British Army Officers, names not known. It is said that he
rarely leaves his rooms before after mid-day, and usually
returns about tea time, and goes out in the evening to dinner,
about 8 to 9 p.m. He has no meals at his chambers, but is
known to lunch and dine at the Savoy or Berkeley Hotel.
He does not keep late hours, the front door of the house is
closed at 12.p.m. and he is always in before that time.
He originally took the chambers for a week or so, but has been
ill, and has said that he is expecting to be recalled to his
unit at any time. I was informed that he was recommended by
an old servant of the proprietor, and interviewed this man, but
found that the truth was not a strong point with him, so deemed
it unwise to question him directly about REILLY, in case he
should be the means of letting REILLY know that enquiries
had been made about him.

Continuing my enquiries I visited the Savoy Hotel, and
learned that REILLY arrived there on the 1st January, 1918.
It is not known from where, he signed as 2nd Lieut. Sidney
George REILLY, R.F. Air Board. He occupied a suite of rooms
No.32, with Lieut. KELLY, R.F.C. (A.B.) and Lieut. M. MAREA,
R.F.C. Lieuts. KELLY and MAREA left the Savoy on the 8th
January, 1918, the former for American University Union, PARIS,
and the latter for 39th Squadron, Shropshire. REILLY left on the

that REILLY is to be seen at the Savoy Hotel nearly
every day, and is in the habit of taking lunch or
dinner there, also that he speaks French fluently.

P.   A.L.W.

M15 surveillance report on Sidney Reilly in 1918.

Whose Ace of Spies?

CREATED: MARCH 1918
SUBJECT: SIDNEY
REILLY'S COMPLICATED
CAREER AS A SPY

17 | Sidney Reilly, according to some of his admirers and critics, was more than a double agent. At one point he was suspected of working simultaneously for the British, the anti-Bolsheviks, the Bolshevik government, and that government's secret police. He is also reportedly the inspiration for Ian Fleming's secret agent, James Bond, who emulates both Reilly's daring and romantic entanglements. Reilly was said to have "eleven passports and a wife to go with each."

So murky were the facts of Reilly's career that even Reilly's spymasters were never quite sure whether he was working for them or the opposition. Not until the year 2002 did British intelligence finally open their secret files on Reilly. One of the declassified documents ended speculation about his mysterious death in Russia in 1925: "The Bolsheviks, in order to escape the possible demands by the English for his release, murdered him."

Reilly is thought to have been born in Russia, near Odessa, as Sigmund Rosenblum, the son of a Russian woman of Polish descent and a Jewish physician. His mother was married at the time to another man, a Russian Army colonel well known in the court of the czar. Reilly sometimes gave his birth year as 1874 and sometimes as 1877.

According to one of the many versions of his early life, he left Russia for Brazil after learning of his illegitimate birth. While there, he claimed to have saved the lives of either two or three British officers, who rewarded him with a British passport, which he used to reach England. In 1898, when he married a widow named Margaret Thomas, he gave his name as Rosenblum. A year later he took the name Sidney Reilly, and kept it. He spoke English and Russian fluently, and claimed to have mastered five other languages. He zigzagged through 30-odd years of spying, mostly for Britain, covering his tracks or having them covered by someone else.

Declassified documents from the files of MI5, the British security service responsible for counterintelligence, show that he was put under surveillance in 1918, when he was an officer in the Royal Flying Corps and applying for employment in MI5. The surveillance report on page 104 provides a snapshot of a day in the life of Reilly. The report also shows that MI5 then believed that he was born in Ireland, not Russia.

Other declassified documents show that by April he was working for MI5 and in May was sent on a mission to Moscow. There, he met with Robert Bruce Lockhart, head of the British Mission to Russia. Together they plotted to overthrow the Bolsheviks, who had come into power in the revolution of 1917.

Reilly is said to have posed as Comrade Relinsky of the Cheka, the Bolshevik secret police, while simultaneously rallying anti-Bolsheviks. Reilly later claimed that he had 60,000 Russian and Latvian soldiers ready to go to war against the Bolsheviks. Whatever supporters he actually had and whatever it was that he actually did, the Cheka did uncover enough evidence to charge that Reilly and Lockhart were concocting a British plot against the regime.

In July 1918, the Bolsheviks massacred the czar and his family. A month later, an anti-Bolshevik shot and grievously wounded revolutionary leader V. I. Lenin. It was claimed at the time that Reilly was involved in that plot.

While Reilly escaped, Lockhart was arrested and subsequently exchanged for a Russian diplomat in Britain. Lockhart later wrote a bestselling book, *Memoirs of a British Agent.* The book was republished in 1974 and 1984 with an introduction by his son, Robin Bruce Lockhart, who had served in British naval intelligence during World War II. The younger Lockhart later wrote *Reilly: Ace of Spies,* an exciting and highly imaginative thriller that became a television miniseries with the same title.

After leaving the Soviet Union, Reilly continued to urge British support of a "democratic" anti-Bolshevik group that was forming among White Russian émigrés in Paris. Reilly insisted that the Bolsheviks—"the arch-enemy of the human race" and "monsters of crime and perversion"—could be overcome. In a 1921 report to the Foreign Office, Reilly predicted "a General Rising" against the Bolsheviks. The rising never came, and his handlers began to quietly wonder about Reilly. Reilly was then working for MI6, the Secret Intelligence Service responsible for conducting espionage abroad for the United Kingdom.

MI6 officers checked his reports against Soviet communications the British had intercepted and decrypted. His reports were frequently unreliable. At times, he was placed under surveillance because of suspicions that he was working either for the White Russians or for the Cheka.

To ferret out anti-Bolsheviks, Soviet intelligence officials created a secret disinformation organization known as The Trust, which appeared to be working to overthrow the Soviets. So believable was the information put out by The Trust that it lured an enemy of the Soviets out of exile. Boris Viktorovich Savinkov, a charismatic anti-czarist revolutionary who also opposed the Soviet regime, traveled to Moscow in August 1924. Savinkov was arrested and condemned to death.

In a spiral of deception, secret police agents sought out Reilly to tell him that Savinkov had indeed been condemned—but The Trust was so powerful that it had intervened and managed to get Savinkov pardoned. Reilly, oddly naïve about this deception, went to Moscow and was promptly arrested and jailed.

A cigar box given to Lockhart by Reilly, bearing the inscription:

To R.H. Bruce Lockhart
H.B.M.'s Representative in Russia in 1918
(during the Bolchevik Régime)
in remembrance
of events in Moscow in August & September of that year
from his faithful Lieutenant
Sidney Reilly

The box is the only known piece of physical evidence linking the two men.

To the outside world, Reilly simply vanished. British intelligence officials, however, managed to learn that in 1925 his guards took him for a walk in the woods and shot him, probably on the orders of Josef Stalin himself, according to the declassified documents of 2002.

Impact on History: Had Reilly and Lockhart managed to start an anti-Bolshevik counter-revolution with covert British help, the insurgency may well have succeeded. Thus would have begun an alternative 20th-century that would not haved included Stalin, the Soviet Union, or the Cold War.

Third Method

4.   For the other method shown her by DELIDAISE,
SERGUEIEW was to take what looked like an indelible copying
pencil and with it scribble on a sheet of paper so that one
side of it was completely covered. This sheet of paper was
then to be used as a carbon. It apparently left no trace on
the sheet of paper underneath.

5.   Yvonne DELIDAISE took away SERGUEIEW's experiments
in both these methods of secret writing, saying that she would
have them developed. SERGUEIEW, however, never saw the results
and can give no more information.

Fourth Method

6.   The final method of secret writing in which
SERGUEIEW was instructed was that given her for her mission
to this country. For this she was to use the pellets given
her by KLIEMANN before her departure from Paris (see para.112
1st Report). She was instructed in their use in the flat at
29 Avenue de l'Opera (see para.109 1st Report).

7.   A pellet was to be heated in a clear flame which
would not discolour it. When the pellet was melted she was to
take a wooden toothpick and dip it in the liquid. When it
was dry she would re-dip it and continue doing so until all
the liquid had been absorbed and a new pellet reformed on the
end of the stick. This could now be used as pen for her
secret writing. She would then take a sheet of paper (non-
shiny surface) and rub the paper evenly with cotton-wool.
On the side she rubbed she was to write her cover letter in
ink or pencil, preferably the former. Her letter in invisible
writing was then to be written on the same side of the paper
but at right angles to the visible text. If SERGUEIEW used
a double sheet which entailed 4 written sides, the invisible
writing was only to be done on the first and third pages.

8.   Her cover letter was to be signed "SOLANGE". It
was left to her as to whether she made use of the code for
her invisible writing, but this was considered unnecessary.

*Information about German espionage methods from MI5 interviews with Sergueiew,
which were conducted in November 1943.*

The Double Agent's Dog

CREATED: NOVEMBER 1943
SUBJECT: WWII—AN UNRELIABLE
BRITISH DOUBLE-CROSS AGENT

18 | Britain's Double-Cross System evolved into a complex scheme for misleading German intelligence about plans for D-Day. The system became an instrument of deception. But at heart Double-Cross was a double agent operation.

Of some 20 men and women who worked for the British while appearing to work for the Germans, Nathalie Sergueiew stands out. In her relationship with her case officers she personified the classic problem that arises when dealing with a double agent: When someone is living a lie, what is true and what is false?

Sergueiew, born in Russia in 1912, was taken to France when her family fled the Bolshevik Revolution in 1917. She was working as a journalist in Nazi Germany in 1937 when a fellow journalist tried unsuccessfully to recruit her to work for the Abwehr, the German military intelligence agency. When the war began two years later, however, she became an Abwehr operative, saying she had changed her mind. Later she maintained that she had wanted to work for Britain as a double agent.

After training at an Abwehr spy school, she was assigned a control officer, Emil Kliemann, and given the code name Tramp. She was sent to Spain, a neutral country, from which she could make her way to England. In Madrid, she contacted a British intelligence officer, who told her to follow Kliemann's instructions and go to England. During clandestine meetings with her British handler in Madrid, she carried her dog, Frisson. She demanded that Frisson travel with her to England, bypassing strict British animal quarantine laws, but her demand was turned down. When she left for England from Gibraltar in November 1943, she had to leave Frisson behind.

MI5, the British security service, assigned her the code name Treasure and put her into the Double-Cross system. "At first," says a digest of the MI5 files on her, "Treasure sent messages to Kliemann in secret ink or encoded letters, but later she used a radio transmitter set" for sending encrypted Morse messages. (Some of the secret tradecraft she was taught appears on page 110.) She acquired the transmitter from Kliemann during a meeting in Lisbon in March. By then, Allied officers with the highest security clearance knew D-Day was planned for early spring. Treasure passed to Kliemann information that led him "to believe that there were very few troops in South West England and that she had a boyfriend in the 14th Army (a non-existent unit invented by the Allies)."

But her real boyfriend, who had said he would smuggle Frisson into England, failed her—and Treasure had somehow learned that Frisson was dead. On May 13, three weeks before D-Day, she gave her handler, MI5 operative Mary Sherer, a shocking admission: She had been given a secret signal, which, if included in a Morse code transmission, would inform Kliemann that she had been captured and was transmitting under duress. Sherer immediately contacted her superior, Lieut. Col. Thomas Argyll Robertson, and told him about Treasure's threat, adding, "She confessed that the motive was revenge for the death of her dog."

Robertson had an MI5 communications specialist take over the transmitter and imitate Treasure's "fist," her characteristic telegraph-key technique. Robertson knew that British codebreakers could read Kliemann's own messages to his Abwehr superiors. A check of those messages showed that Treasure had not betrayed Double-Cross and that Kliemann had not detected a "fist" change. Without details, the classified report on Treasure says that Treasure entered a hospital on June 5, the day before

D-Day. Then, on June 15, Robertson met with Treasure and wrote a secret memo for MI5 files. In its matter-of-fact tone, the memo veils his outrage at her reckless behavior:

Yesterday I saw TREASURE at 39 Hill Street in the presence of Miss Sherer.

I said that I had come to deliver a very serious talk as I had, during the past few days, formed definite opinions with regard to her case. I said that we had already taken over the transmitter and were imitating her and that in future she would not be required to assist us in this way. I pointed out that my reasons for coming to this conclusion were two-fold:

1) that I had heard from Miss Sherer that TREASURE had been to Lisbon [in order to]????? and had fixed up with KLIEMANN a signal or signals which would appear in her messages indicating whether or not she was working under control, and

2) that from a reliable source it had been reported that while in Lisbon she had fixed up a means of communication with a German Intelligence Officer without this coming to our notice. I pointed out that it was quite impossible for me to place any confidence in someone who behaved in this manner.

I then said that we would pay her £5 a week as from Monday next, and that if she decided to have an operation, we would undertake to pay all expenses. At the same time we would clear up any outstanding doctors' bills. I also said that we would endeavour, although I made no promise whatever, to send her at some future date, either to her sister in Algiers or to her family in Paris, if conditions made this possible.

I pointed out, however, that if I had any cause to think that she was being indiscreet or was in any way acting contrary to the interests of the Allied cause, I would at once take severe action, and would either put her into prison or hand her over to the French authorities who would no doubt deal with her

Nathalie Sergueiew, Double-Cross agent.

pretty severely. I also said that naturally any allowance in the shape of money which I was making to her would cease. In addition, I said that we might occasionally wish to consult her over some point in connection with the [message] traffic and that I expected her to give us every assistance. I also asked her to make arrangements to leave 39 Hill Street within the next fortnight.

Before leaving, I made quite certain that she had understood what I had said and asked her if she had anything to say. She had nothing to say except that she did not want the money. I said that she would take it whether she liked it or not, and that she could do what she liked with it.

[signed] T.A. Robertson.

Impact on History: As Lieut. Col. Robertson well knew, the Double-Cross System could be destroyed if the tight controls were relaxed for even a moment. If Treasure had carried out her threat, the system might have collapsed. That would have undermined an intricate deception plan for D-Day, possibly derailing the invasion and altering the course of World War II.

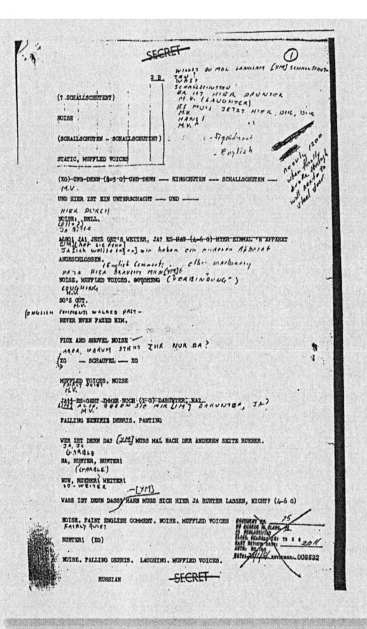

Page from the transcript of the Germans' conversations picked up when the Berlin tunnel was discovered.

The Spy in the Tunnel

[
CREATED: APRIL 1956
SUBJECT: THE COLD
WAR—EXPOSURE OF THE
BERLIN TUNNEL
]

19 | Through most of the Cold War, the divided city of Berlin was the communications center for East Germany and the other Soviet satellites in Europe. To tap into the countless Soviet phone and teleprinter lines running beneath the city, Americans and British intelligence agencies conceived a daring eavesdropping idea: Dig a tunnel from an innocent-looking building in the American sector to a cluster of cables under a street in the Soviet sector.

"The purpose of the Berlin tunnel," recalled David E. Murphy, chief of the CIA's Berlin base at the time of the dig, "was to tap the communications lines of the Soviet forces in East Germany, in Poland, and their links with Moscow, in order to provide current intelligence on those forces, and also early warning."

But even as the ultra-secret tunnel was being planned in 1953, the Soviets knew all about it. The real-time intelligence came from George Blake, an intelligence officer in MI6, the British Secret Intelligence Service, who was also a KGB agent. By strict definition, Blake was a KGB "penetration agent," or mole, rather than a double agent. He was also a "walk-in," a person who seeks out the opposition and offers to be a spy, without being recruited. By any description, Blake was an extremely valuable spy.

Born in Rotterdam as George Behne, Blake was the son of a Dutch Lutheran mother and a Jewish Egyptian father who had served in the British Army in World War I and was so patriotic that he named his son after King George V. When World War II began, Blake was in Holland finishing high school. After Germany invaded Holland in 1940, he briefly worked in the Dutch resistance movement and then made his way to England via Vichy, France and Spain. He enlisted in the Royal Navy and, because of his language skills, was assigned to the Dutch section of MI6 in London.

After the war, MI6 sent him to Hamburg, where he recruited former German naval and army officers for MI6 networks in communist East Germany. In October 1948 he was sent under diplomatic cover to Seoul, South Korea, to head the new MI6 station there. When North Korea invaded South Korea in June 1950, he was captured. While a prisoner, he took the first step on the long road of his betrayal, telling his captors that he wished to contact the Soviet Embassy in Pyongyang, North Korea. He spied, he later wrote, "for ideological reasons, never for money."

In 1953, he had been among the first prisoners released after the armistice that ended the Korean War. In England, Blake married an MI6 secretary who was the daughter of an MI6 officer.

Through the years, the KGB kept track of Blake. While he was working for MI6 in London, he was assigned a KGB case officer, Sergei Aleksandrovich Kondrashev, and given the KGB codename Diomid. They had several carefully choreographed meetings devoted to relatively routine transfers of intelligence tidbits. Then, on January 18, 1954, Blake and Kondrashev had a regular meeting, this time on the top of a London double-decker bus. Blake handed the KGB officer a packet and Kondrashev got off the bus a few stops later. In the packet was a carbon copy of the minutes of three days of CIA-MI6 meetings about the Berlin tunnel, a project called STOPWATCH by the British, and GOLD by the Americans. Blake had the carbon copy because he had been the secretary of the meetings.

*A re-creation of the Berlin Tunnel inside the International Spy Museum.
Thanks to Blake, the Soviets knew about it even before ground
had been broken for its creation.*

Blake's carbon copy, on yellow-green flimsy paper, was one of the most thorough single intelligence deliveries of the Cold War. Blake's packet included not only the names of the CIA and MI6 officials who attended the meetings but also six pages of technical information on the "plan to attack all circuits." Now the Soviets had in their hands all the details of a bold, complex CIA-MI6 operation. The KGB, wanting above all to protect Blake, held the secret tightly and decided to allow digging of the tunnel to begin without interference.

In September 1954, U.S. Army Engineers slipped into a large building in the American sector to begin excavating the basement and digging the tunnel. The building, which would conceal the dug-up dirt, looked like a warehouse, but Allied disinformation circulated about it said the building was a secret electronics intelligence station. The engineers entering and leaving the building each day were supposed to be intelligence operatives, not diggers. So they had to leave the building in clean uniforms. To keep their digging clothes secret from regular Army laundries, the engineers did their washing on site in their own washer and dryer.

The 1,476-foot tunnel was finished in February 1955 and the tapping of the cables began in May. At that point, the Soviets had to decide whether to maintain security for Blake by continuing to transmit what appeared to be normal traffic through the cables. They decided to continue.

Eavesdropping continued until about 1 a.m., on April 22, 1956, when Allied observers in their post at the warehouse saw 40 or 50 men digging exactly over the tunnel. An hour later, the men reached the tapping chamber in the tunnel. At the warehouse, Allied interpreters were producing (and recording) real-time translations of what they were hearing from microphones in the tunnel (a page of this transcript is reproduced on page 116). "How did they do it? It's fantastic!" an East German technician exclaimed. At a press conference, Soviet officials revealed the "accidental discovery" of the tunnel and protested the illegal incursion into the Soviet sector. After a few days of publicity, the true information about the tunnel entered the most secret archives of the KGB, CIA, and MI6.

At first, the CIA believed that a cable had been discovered by a repair crew sent to fix a cable shorted out by leaking water from days of heavy rain. By then, the tappers had recorded 443,000 "conversations"—368,000 by Soviets and 75,000 by East Germans—that produced 1,750 intelligence reports and secret analyses. When Blake's treachery was exposed in 1961, all those conversations came under suspicion.

Blake's double-agent career came to an end through information given to the CIA by Lieutenant Colonel Michal Goleniewski, a defector from the Polish Intelligence Service. He told the CIA that there was a spy in MI6, and British investigators tracked down the tip to Blake. He was in Lebanon, studying Arabic in a school used by Western intelligence agencies, when he was abruptly summoned to London and accused of being a longtime Soviet spy.

Blake confessed, was arrested for violating the Official Secrets Act, and was swiftly tried at the Old Bailey, where he was convicted and sentenced to 42 years in prison, "a year for each agent betrayed," according to accounts that he named— and thus doomed—all 42 British agents in the Soviet Union. In 1966, Blake escaped from prison in an elaborate breakout that included a member of the Irish Republican Army (IRA). The escape was probably financed by the KGB and carried out by IRA operatives. Blake wound up in Moscow. His autobiography, *No Other Choice,* was published in 1990. His rank as a retired KGB colonel earned him a pension and a spacious Moscow apartment.

Impact on History: U.S. intelligence officials insist that the taps provided real information that was helpful for taking the temperature of Soviet Cold War intentions in Berlin. In a 1999 evaluation of the tunnel's value, a CIA historian wrote, "Most of the useful information dealt with Soviet orders of battle and force dispositions—information that was invaluable in the days before reconnaissance satellites and other, more sophisticated means of collection became operational."

CORRECTED COPY

Assistant Secretary
of State.
JAN 14 1938
MR. ....RS.

EG
A portion of this telegram
must be closely paraphrased
before being communicated
to anyone. (A)

Hankow

Dated January 11, 1938

Rec'd 3:20 p.m., 12th

Secretary of State,

Washington.

24, January 11, 3 p.m. (GRAY)

Following for War Department from Colonel Stillwell:

(END GRAY) "Since the capture of Nanking the front
has melted away, fighting has practically ceased except
on the Tsinpu line, and the military chiefs have been at
a loss for a plan of action. The Chinese realize that
they cannot compete in a stand up fight. The Japanese
realize that they are extended dangerously and they can
see an apparent target to strike at that will give them
a decision. Both sides are in a quandary, the Japanese
hoping the Chinese will ask for peace, the Chinese hoping
for intervention by a third power but determined not to
quit.

(GRAY) On the Chinese side only the Reds have a
definite plan, the essence of which is the adoption of
guerilla warfare on a wide scale and the mobilization of
the masses. This program has a strong appeal and has
gained popular backing. (END GRAY) The Kuomintang
leaders have been forced to take notice, since they can

suggest

*A page from the confidential State Department file on the Pumpkin Papers,
this particular one from Colonel Stilwell, a military attaché
who was gathering intelligence in China.*

The Pumpkin Papers

CREATED: JANUARY 1938
SUBJECT: THE COLD WAR—
CHAMBERS-HISS CASE

20 | On the night of December 2, 1948, a pudgy, 47-year-old man led two congressional investigators through the darkness to a pumpkin patch on his farm in Westminster, Maryland. The man was Whittaker Chambers, a former *Time* magazine editor who had told the House Committee on Un-American Activities that he had been not only a member of a Communist Party cell but also a spy for the Soviet Union.

One of the other spies, he had testified, was Alger Hiss, a patrician State Department official with White House connections. Hiss filed a $75,000 libel suit against Chambers, who claimed his accusation would be confirmed by hidden documents. Chambers pointed to a large, hollowed-out pumpkin that served as a hiding place for 35-mm film wrapped in waxed paper. Some of the film images were State Department documents. Earlier, Chambers had produced 65 typed pages and four notes that he said were in Hiss's handwriting. Some of the Chambers documents had been hidden in a dumbwaiter shaft in the Baltimore home of a relative. But it was the pumpkin that fascinated the media, and the "Pumpkin Papers" became the label for all of Chambers' disclosures.

One of Chambers' hidden documents was from Col. Joseph W. Stilwell (see opposite page). Stilwell (whose name is misspelled in the document) was a military attaché, gathering intelligence in China at a crucial time. Chinese Communists, led by Mao Tse-tung, were fighting Japanese invaders while Chinese Nationalists under Chiang Kai-shek were often on the sidelines of battle. Stilwell's observations at that time would be of great interest to the Soviet supporters of Mao. The note in the upper left corner warns against direct quoting of the decoded telegram because anyone who sees it in that form could get clues to breaking the State Department GRAY code.

Chambers's charges targeted a man with a distinguished Washington career. Alger Hiss, after graduating in 1929 from Harvard Law School, served as secretary to Supreme Court Justice Oliver Wendell Holmes. In the early 1930s, Hiss joined Franklin D. Roosevelt's New Deal, first in the Department of Agriculture and then the State Department. In 1941, at the age of 40, he became a leading official in State's Office of Far Eastern Affairs. Near the end of the World War II, Hiss was put in charge of setting up the United Nations. Hiss also advised President Roosevelt at the war-time Yalta Conference, where Roosevelt, British Prime Minister Winston Churchill, and Soviet dictator Joseph Stalin met. Hiss quietly left the State Department to become, in 1947, president of the eminent Carnegie Endowment for International Peace.

The long, complex Chambers-Hiss case fueled a public frenzy in the 1940s over fears that Soviet spies had penetrated the U.S. government. Those fears were a prelude to the Reds-in-government scare trumpeted in the 1950s by Senator Joe McCarthy, whose tactics introduced the term McCarthyism.

The Pumpkin Papers also introduced a little-known member of the House Committee on Un-American Activities, California Congressman Richard M. Nixon. His face appeared in numerous newspapers as, magnifying glass in hand, he examined the films.

In 1949 Hiss was put on trial for lying to a grand jury about his meetings with Chambers. Charges of espionage were dropped. The perjury trial ended with a deadlocked jury. He was tried again, convicted this time, and in March 1951 entered a federal prison to begin a five-year sentence. He was released in November 1954.

The Chambers-Hiss case flared anew in 1996, when the National Security Agency revealed the results of a highly secret operation code-named Venona. The Venona documents—decrypted Soviet intelligence messages of the 1940s—linked Hiss to espionage. Speculation immediately arose about Hiss's wartime contacts with Donald Maclean, a British Foreign Office diplomat who had worked with Hiss on the United Nations and other issues. Maclean was one of the "Cambridge Spies" who provided high-grade intelligence to the Soviet Union.

One of the Venona documents, dated March 30, 1945, refers to an American code-named "Ales." The message notes that a Soviet agent working in the State Department accompanied President Roosevelt to the Yalta Conference in February 1945 and then flew on to Moscow. There, the message indicates, "Ales" met Andrei Vyshinsky, the Soviet Commissar for Foreign Affairs, and was cited for his aid to the Soviets. NSA analysts said that Ales could only have been Hiss, a conclusion challenged by Hiss supporters.

In 1975, through the Freedom of Information Act, Hiss obtained what had been hidden in the hollowed-out pumpkin: a roll of film that was entirely blank, along with two other rolls that seemed so innocuous that, as Hiss said, they "certainly are useless for espionage purposes." But there were still those dumbwaiter documents that referred to State Department secrets. Supporters of Hiss said there was no solid proof about the origin of those documents and there was insufficient evidence connecting Hiss to "Ales." Hiss died in 1996, still claiming he had never been a spy.

Impact on History: Hiss remains a divisive figure even today. His case also boosted Richard Nixon's career since the latter's connection with the Pumpkin Papers gave him national publicity. His anti-communism, which began with this incident, became a Nixon theme, catapulting him into the Senate in 1950 and establishing him as a major Republican figure, first as Dwight D. Eisenhower's running mate in the 1952 and 1956 presidential elections and then as a presidential candidate in 1960 and president in 1968.

THREE

Counterintelligence: Spy vs. Spy

THE OBJECT IN THE MOSCOW SUBURBAN PARK LOOKED LIKE A ROCK. NOT FAR AWAY, well hidden, was a camera, watching the "rock." It was an old story, a counterintelligence operation pitting spy against spy at a dead drop, a concealed hiding place. But this chapter of the story was unfolding in the high-tech world of 2006. The spies were using gadgets.

The "rock" was a camouflaged telecommunications device. An agent walking past the device transmitted his intelligence secrets to it by pressing a button on a handheld computer. The hidden camera was operated by the Russians' Federal Security Service (FSB), successor to the KGB of the Soviet era. A grainy film, which appeared on Russian television in January 2006, showed the fake rock. It had been opened and looked like a package with something inside: the gadget.

The film also showed clips of three men. One walked into bushes near the object with what looked like a Palm Pilot in one hand. He touched the object and walked on. A second man stopped at about the same place, lifted the hood of his car, did some work under the hood, and looked at the rock. A third man picked up the rock and walked off with it.

The FSB said the camera had caught on film three British spies who had been working under diplomatic cover at the British Embassy in Moscow. They apparently were participating in one of the oldest operations of spy tradecraft: servicing a dead drop, which allows spy and spymaster to communicate without meeting face-to-face. The film clips displayed a classic dead-drop transaction: The first man probably was activating the device and transmitting information to it; the second man may have been determining that the device had been used; the third man carried off the data-filled device. In the diplomatic furor that followed, Russia said another British official and a Russian had used the system. The Russian was arrested and reportedly confessed to espionage.

The FSB had carried out a counterintelligence operation. Counterintelligence is practiced by every country in the world to identify and neutralize any covert efforts aimed at stealing that country's secrets, including attempts to recruit its citizens to steal secrets. So counterintelligence usually becomes an effort to track down and neutralize people who have become "moles" directed by others. An operation comes down to a law enforcement agency trying to track down a human being who may or may not be working for the opposition.

To move from suspicion to proof, counterintelligence officers in democratic countries have to make a case that will stand up in a court of law. That usually means catching a spy in the act, And one of the best ways to do that is to find the dead drop and keep it under surveillance until the users show up.

The British used a successful dead drop during the Revolutionary War when Ben Franklin was in Paris, leading a secret American effort to win an alliance with France. The British Secret Service gave an american agent invisible ink and told him to write letters to a "Mr. Richards" with the spy message written between the lines in invisible ink. In what is called a timed dead drop, each Tuesday night after 9:30 the agent was to place the letters in a bottle in a hole near a certain tree in the Jardin de Tuilleries. An intelligence officer, working under diplomatic cover at the British Embassy in Paris, plucked the bottle out of the hole and replaced it with another that contained instructions to the agent. The British got a solid stream of intelligence on Franklin's activities, and the dead drop was not discovered.

The FBI used a camera to crack one of its biggest counterintelligence cases. In 1939, William G. Sebold, a California aircraft factory worker, returned to his native Germany to visit family. While there he was recruited to spy for Germany. Sebold reported this to the U.S. Consulate in Cologne and agreed to become a double agent.

Back in the United States, working under the FBI, Sebold followed German instructions and contacted two members of a German spy ring. He met with the leader of the ring and others in a room that the FBI had wired. Hidden microphones recorded conversations, and a secret movie camera filmed the spies and also a clock and calendar conveniently placed in the camera's view.

In January 1942 the FBI arrested 32 members of the ring. All the spies were tried, convicted, and sentenced to prison from 18 months to 18 years—for a total of more than 300 years. two were native-born Americans.

The FBI, as the leading U.S. federal law enforcement agency, is the nation's main domestic counterintelligence agency. The CIA, which is not a law enforcement agency, also has counterintelligence responsibilities. Both the CIA and the FBI, along with intelligence services around the world, have run investigations that led to the discovery of colleagues who had used their knowledge and skills to elude the spy seekers.

For British intelligence services, the most destructive Soviet moles were the members of the Cambridge Spy Ring. For American services, the worst traitors were Aldrich H. Ames of the CIA and Robert Hanssen of the FBI. The other spies in the accounts that follow—John Walker and Jonathan Pollard—were identified through tip-offs that let counterintelligence wrap them up.

Though much of what we know about counterintelligence comes from solved cases, many in the spy-seeking branch of espionage suspect that somewhere in the system are spies who may never be caught.

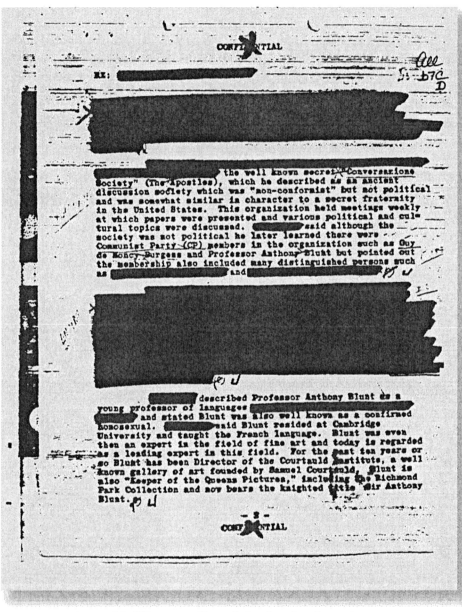

RE:

the well known secret "Conversazione Society" (The Apostles), which he described as an ancient discussion society which was "non-conformist" but not political and was somewhat similar in character to a secret fraternity in the United States. This organization held meetings weekly at which papers were presented and various political and cultural topics were discussed. ▮▮▮▮ said although the society was not political he later learned there were Communist Party (CP) members in the organization such as Guy de Moncy Burgess and Professor Anthony Blunt but pointed out the membership also included many distinguished persons such as ▮▮▮▮ and ▮▮▮▮

▮▮▮▮ described Professor Anthony Blunt as a young professor of languages ▮▮▮▮ and stated Blunt was also well known as a confirmed homosexual. ▮▮▮▮ said Blunt resided at Cambridge University and taught the French language. Blunt was even then an expert in the field of fine art and today is regarded as a leading expert in this field. For the past ten years or so Blunt has been Director of the Courtauld Institute, a well known gallery of art founded by Samuel Courtauld. Blunt is also "Keeper of the Queens Pictures," including the Richmond Park Collection and now bears the knighted title "Sir Anthony Blunt."

A page of the FBI report on Blunt, which redacts the informant's name,
but mentions "The Apostles," a Cambridge society of which the informant was a member.

The Knight Was a Spy

CREATED: JUNE 1963
SUBJECT: THE COLD WAR—
EXPOSURE OF SIR ANTHONY
BLUNT AS A SOVIET AGENT

21 | In June 1963 President Kennedy offered the chairmanship of the National Endowment for the Arts to Michael Straight, owner and editor of *New Republic* magazine. Straight was eager to accept the post. But he feared that an FBI background check would reveal that while he attended Trinity College, Cambridge, in the 1930s he consorted with Anthony Blunt, a suspected Soviet agent. Straight sought advice from historian Arthur Schlesinger, Jr., a special assistant to Kennedy. Schlesinger urged Straight to go to the FBI and tell all.

Thus began a complex counterintelligence story that ended with the exposure of Sir Anthony Blunt, the art adviser to Queen Elizabeth II, as "the Fourth Man" in the Cambridge Spy Ring. Before the revelation about Blunt, three other Cambridge alumni had been exposed as Soviet spies: Donald Maclean, Harold (Kim) Philby, and Guy Burgess, all of whom had attended Trinity and all of whom had served in high posts in British intelligence and the Foreign Service. The Cambridge Spy Ring included highly successful spies, who harvested both British and American secrets at the highest levels of government.

The FBI confidentially reported Straight's admissions about Blunt to the British Security Service, MI5. Some MI5 officers had suspected for years that Blunt was not only a spy but also a talent scout for Soviet intelligence services. MI5 counterintelligence officers had interviewed him 11 times. Now, faced with what Straight had told the FBI, and promised immunity from prosecution, Blunt not only confessed secretly but identified John Cairncross, another Cambridge alumnus, as "the Fifth Man" of the ring. Cairncross had spied for the Soviets while he was private secretary to the minister responsible for overseeing British intelligence services. Cairncross also served the Soviets while working at the super-secret British code-breaking facility, Bletchley Park, during World War II.

MI5's interrogation of Blunt still has not been declassified. Nor has the FBI revealed Straight's admissions, although Straight repeated them in his autobiography. But the FBI did respond to a Freedom of Information Act request by releasing a heavily redacted—of 120 pages, only 37 were declassified—FBI report on Blunt (a page is shown on page 130). Dates in that report coincide with the time of Straight's 1963 FBI interview. In the report, the informant, whose name is blacked out, tells of meeting Blunt and mentions "the Apostles," a Cambridge society that the informant belonged to.

The pages released in the FBI's Blunt file have many mentions of LHM, meaning "letterhead memo," a designation for documents that required special handling. One LHM is to D. M. Ladd, assistant director and head of the FBI Intelligence Division, an indication of the FBI's keen interest in the British-based spy ring. That interest stemmed from the fact that Maclean, Philby, and Burgess all had tours at the British Embassy in Washington.

Maclean was assigned as Second Secretary to the British Embassy in Washington in May 1944 and soon after became First Secretary, with access to the embassy code room. He later became the head of the American Department in the Foreign Office. Burgess was assigned Second Secretary in the embassy in August 1950 and lived at Philby's home in Washington. Philby was the British Secret Intelligence Service (MI6) liaison in Washington and, through his connections with the U.S.

intelligence community, learned of America's most secret code-breaking operation, Venona.

Burgess finally was recalled to London—ostensibly at the request of the governor of Virginia because of his repeated speeding on the Commonwealth's highways. The recall, probably arranged by Philby, occurred as a counterintelligence investigation was closing in on Burgess and Maclean. They disappeared from London on May 25, 1951, later to appear in Moscow. Philby was recalled to London on June 11 under suspicion that he had tipped off Burgess and Maclean. Later publicly accused of being the "the Third Man" in the Cambridge Spy Ring, Philby was cleared in October 1955 by Foreign Secretary (later Prime Minister) Harold Macmillan. But suspicion lingered, and the KGB helped get Philby to Moscow in 1963.

Blunt's treachery did not become publicly confirmed until November 15, 1979, when Prime Minister Margaret Thatcher, reluctantly responding to published reports, admitted in a speech in Parliament that Blunt "had been recruited by and had acted as a talent spotter for Russian intelligence before the war when he was a don at Cambridge." There was speculation that the unmasking of Sir Anthony had been long-delayed to shield the Queen and preserve Blunt's image as an important art historian. Blunt was stripped of his knighthood and, shunned by the privileged class he had served and betrayed, lived a lonely, empty life until he died in March 1983 of a heart ailment.

Impact on History: The FBI's report on Blunt gave British intelligence the evidence needed to expose him as a spy, ending the Cambridge Spy Ring saga, which had devastated British intelligence services. Blunt, a friend to the Queen, embodied the success of Soviet spy recruiters who had recruited spies from the British establishment.

Time-stamped surveillance photos of Jonathan Jay Pollard stealing and leaving with classified government documents, which he would later pass on to his Israeli handler.

The Million-Document Spy

CREATED: NOVEMBER 1985
SUBJECT: AN ISRAELI SPY
CAUGHT ON TAPE

22 | In the fall of 1979, Jonathan Jay Pollard, after two months as a naval intelligence analyst, was regarded as a security risk by a superior. Pollard was working at the Naval Intelligence Support Center in Suitland, Maryland. He was on probation, and though that should have made dismissing him easy, he was kept on as an analyst—and as a spy, stealing and copying more than one million pages of classified material, enough to fill a six-by-ten-foot room with six-foot stacks of secrets.

Navy and FBI counterintelligence agents finally ended Pollard's espionage in a hectic operation that was hampered by the strain on counterintelligence resources caused by what became known as "The Year of the Spy." Between January and October 1985, ten spies were arrested, including Navy spy John Walker and members of his ring (see page 139).

Early in Pollard's career, a polygraph test had showed that he needed professional medical help and should not be given access to highly sensitive information. But due primarily to bureaucratic inertia, he was kept at his job, for which he was cleared to handle Top Secret and Special Compartmented Information.

In November 1985, a coworker saw Pollard walk out of the building carrying documents in envelopes that showed the contents were highly classified. The coworker reported him, and Pollard was put under surveillance. A concealed camera watched his every move, producing that rarest of counterintelligence documents, a grainy surveillance image of a spy in action (see page 134). Each moment of surveillance was recorded by an unseen witness:

----

15 November 1985.10:59:11
He began shuffling papers in the drawer, then pulled out another stack and, with some difficulty, for now the brief-case was getting full, shoved it in. After much squirming and shifting about in his chair, he finally closed and locked the briefcase.

On Monday, November 18, 1985, Pollard, carrying a package containing 60 classified documents, was stopped outside the Navy facility and brought back to his office cubicle for questioning by FBI and NIS agents. During the next few days, after a series of desperate attempts to throw off the investigators and to get help from his handlers, Pollard and his wife, Anne Henderson Pollard, drove to the Israeli Embassy, followed by FBI surveillance cars. The Israelis refused to give Pollard asylum and, as he left the grounds of the embassy, he was arrested. Anne was also arrested.

Counterintelligence investigators discovered that about three times a week Pollard had put in his briefcase computer printouts, satellite photographs, and secret documents, and walked out of the Navy building without having it searched. He would drive to a place where he could not be observed—such as in a car wash—and transfer the documents to a suitcase that he reserved for his Friday or Saturday deliveries to Washington apartments, where Israelis copied the documents, which he would return on Monday.

Pollard's spying began after he met Col. Avi Sella, an Israeli combat pilot who was an operative under cover as a graduate student at New York University. Pollard told Sella he had information that could help Israel, and showed him intelligence related to Iraqi chemical weaponry. Sella handed Pollard over to a case officer,

Yosef (Yossi) Yagur, whose cover was consul for scientific affairs at the Israeli Consulate in New York.

Pollard received a monthly payment for his work, was given a Swiss bank account number, and told that $30,000 had already been deposited. Israel, Yagur said, would add $30,000 to that account every year for the next 10 years. After that, Pollard would presumably move to Israel.

Pollard pleaded guilty to charges of espionage and was sentenced to prison for life. His wife pleaded guilty to unauthorized possession of government property and to being an accessory to the possession of military documents by her husband. She was not charged with espionage. Sentenced to five years in prison, she was released in April 1990 after serving 37 months. She soon divorced Pollard.

Pollard's sentencing touched off a campaign to release him on the grounds that he had merely spied for an ally. The Israeli parliament urged his release, and Israeli prime ministers repeatedly petitioned U.S. presidents to free Pollard, claiming that he did not harm America. But assessing the damage, Secretary of Defense Caspar Weinberger said, "It is difficult for me . . . to conceive of a greater harm to national security." He said that Pollard had sold data "intentionally reserved by the United States for its own use, because to disclose it, to anyone or any nation, would cause the greatest harm to our national security."

Weinberger issued a redacted assessment of Pollard's damage. Officials said one of the most valuable documents Pollard had stolen was a compendium of frequencies used by foreign military and intelligence services. Once that was out of U.S. control, intelligence services could no longer trust the frequencies, which, after Pollard's disclosure, could be used to produce disinformation.

Impact on History: Pollard's arrest and conviction exposed the fact that Israel had been spying on the United States, and threatened a breakdown in relations between the two countries. Initially, Israeli officials claimed that the spying had been a "rogue operation," but in 1998 Israel formally acknowledged that Pollard had been its spy, and has continued to seek his release.

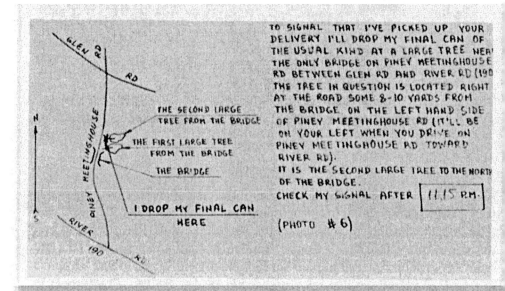

A handwritten map provided to John Walker by his Soviet handlers in May 1985, providing detailed instructions for a drop of classified materials near Poolesville, Md.

The Soviets' Key Man

CREATED: MAY 1985
SUBJECT: THE COLD WAR—A
NAVY RADIOMAN'S SALE OF
SECRETS TO THE SOVIETS

23 | When North Korean forces boarded and captured the U.S.S. *Pueblo* in January 1968, a Navy radioman half a world away realized that the loss of the ship could make him a fortune. Chief Warrant Officer John A. Walker, Jr. knew that the several KW-7 code machines aboard the *Pueblo* would soon be in the hands of Soviets, the North Koreans' allies. But the Soviets would not be able to tap into secret American communications because they did not have the unique keys needed to operate the machines. Walker had access to those keys.

The *Pueblo* had been on a secret electronic intelligence mission, listening to Korean and Soviet radio and radar frequencies. The KW-7 code machines were descendants of the Enigma, the World War II machine that Germany had relied on. U.S. and British codebreakers had been able to crack the Enigma system.

The KW-7 was more sophisticated than the Enigma because of the cipher keys, or "key lists," which contained the daily set of numbers that actuated the machine. A radioman opened a compartment on the KW-7, pressed the key card against an electronic sensor, and closed the compartment. The sensor translated the card's holes into signals that gave the machine the day's key numbers.

Messages were entered on a teletype keyboard; incoming messages were printed out electronically through the teletype. The signals went through cryptographic circuits within the box and were encrypted according to a code preset for that day by the numbers on the key card. The message was transmitted via radio as a stream of numbers. At the receiving end, the message entered another KW-7, where the message could be decrypted only if the machine had been set with a copy of the same key card.

The rules to protect the key cards were the heart of the Classified Materials System (CMS), which began with the couriers who carried keying materials, in tamperproof packages, from the National Security Agency's tightly guarded printing plant at Fort Meade, Maryland. In the U.S. Navy, the key cards' final destination was the CMS custodian, usually a Navy radioman like Walker with a "top secret-cryptographic" clearance.

Walker made contact with the Soviets sometime soon after the seizure of the *Pueblo*. He was then a watch officer and message center officer on the staff of the Submarine Force of the Atlantic Fleet in Norfolk, and was handling key cards every day and monitoring the communications of the Atlantic Fleet.

Walker retired from the Navy, but not from spying, in 1976. He set up his own spy ring consisting of his son, Yeoman Third Class Michael Walker; his brother, Lt. Comdr. Arthur J. Walker; and his friend, Chief Radioman Jerry A. Whitworth. John Walker's daughter, Laura Walker Snyder, was in the Army when he unsuccessfully attempted to recruit her, urging her to abort her pregnancy so that she could stay in the Army and become one of his spies.

Walker took a peculiar pride in his espionage work. "No member of the organization or prospective members has any of the classic problems that plague so many in this business," he once wrote to the Soviets in his best executive manner. "We have no drug problems, alcoholic problems, homosexuality. All are psychologically well-adjusted and mature. And the organization could launder funds."

From October 1982 to October 1983, Whitworth was the senior chief radioman aboard the aircraft carrier *Enterprise*. There were about 25 KW-7s aboard, and a KWR-37 modified for reception of messages from submarines. Whitworth had unlimited access to all incoming and outgoing messages.

Walker's former wife, Barbara, made a call to the FBI and tried to turn him in, but her information had sounded like ramblings and had been ignored. Then, in November 1984, urged on by Laura, she made a coherent report, and the FBI listened. Walker, then living in Norfolk, was placed under surveillance in the hope that he could be caught in the act. The moment came on May 20, 1985, when Walker was seized after leaving a plastic garbage bag full of classified documents at a dead drop in Poolesville, Maryland, after following the handwritten instructions that appear on page 138.

The 129 classified documents in the bag had been stolen by Michael Walker, who was stationed aboard the aircraft carrier *Nimitz*. Letters found in the bag and in John Walker's home linked him to Whitworth, who was arrested in California. Worried that there was not enough solid evidence to convict Whitworth, U.S. officials arranged a deal: Michael Walker would get a 25-year sentence, rather than life imprisonment, if John Walker agreed to plead guilty to espionage, accept a life sentence, and testify as a government witness at Whitworth's trial.

Whitworth was sentenced to 365 years in prison and fined $410,000. Under a formula incorporated in the sentence, it would be 60 years before Whitworth could be paroled at the age of 107. Michael Walker was paroled at age 37 in 2000 after serving 15 years.

By the time John Walker was arrested, U.S. intelligence officials estimated the Soviet Union had received and decoded more than a million messages through the material Walker had supplied.

Impact on History: If the Soviet Union and the United States had gone to war, Walker and Whitworth would have been the Soviets' hidden allies. The Director of Naval Intelligence said that the information provided by Whitworth "had war-winning implications" for the Soviets. Secretary of Defense Caspar Weinberger cited "Soviet gains in all areas of naval warfare" and said that the intelligence Walker sold to the Soviet Union "would have been 'devastating' to the United States in time of war."

I AMREADY TO MEET
AT B ON 1 OCT.
    I CANNOT READ
NORTH 13-19 SEPT.
    IF YOU WILL
MEET AT B ON ~~~~ 1 OCT.
PLS SIGNAL NORTH &
OF 20 SEPT TO CONFI.
NO MESSAGE AT PIPE.
    IF YOU CANNOT MEE.
1 OCT, SIGNAL NORTH AFTER
27 SEPT WITH MESSAGE AT
    PIPE.

The note, written by Aldrich Ames to his handlers, which FBI investigators later reassembled and regarded as their first concrete clue that Ames was a spy.

The Spy Drove a Jaguar

CREATED: SEPTEMBER 1993
SUBJECT: EXPOSURE OF ALDRICH
AMES AS A SOVIET MOLE

24 On the evening of September 9, 1993, Aldrich H. Ames, a CIA counterintelligence officer, and his wife, Rosario, left their half-million-dollar home in Arlington, Virginia, and drove their 1992 Jaguar to a parents' night at the school attended by their son in Alexandria, Virginia. They crossed the Potomac River and entered the District of Columbia, shadowed by the FBI. The car entered a cul-de-sac and turned around in a driveway. The couple then drove back to their home.

A few nights later, Ames carried out the trash. When members of an FBI surveillance team went through the Ames trash can, they found torn pieces of paper. Reassembled (shown opposite), the paper gave the FBI the first solid clue that Ames was a spy.

FBI counterintelligence experts who translated the note concluded that "B" referred to Bogota, Colombia; "North" was a signal site; and "Pipe" was a dead drop used by his handler to pass messages, instructions, and cash. Ames could not "head North" before September 20. The FBI learned that he would be out of the country on CIA business during that time.

The FBI knew about Ames' movements because months before, counterintelligence agents had successfully petitioned the secret Foreign Intelligence Surveillance Court for permission to tap Ames's phone and covertly enter his home to install cameras and electronic bugs and to tap his home computer. From a cryptic phone call, the FBI knew that the drive to the cul-de-sac was a spy procedure: Ames wanted to check for a chalk mark on a mail box used as a signal site to verify that a dead drop he had filled that day had been unloaded by one of his handlers, officers of the Russian successor to the KGB, the SVR (for *Sluzhba Vneshney Razvedki Rossii,* the Russian Federation Foreign Intelligence Service).

Ames did manage to get to Bogota, still under surveillance, in November 1993. The FBI kept watching him and gathering evidence, hoping to eventually catch him getting or receiving material from a drop. Finally, concerned that his Russian handlers were beginning to grow nervous, the FBI began to close in. Ames was arrested on February 24, 1994, the day before he was to leave for Moscow for an official CIA business meeting with Russian intelligence specialists on narcotics. Also arrested was his wife, Rosario. He had met her during his 1981–1983 tour in Mexico City, where she acted as the cultural attaché in the Columbian Embassy. She also worked covertly as "a support asset," occasionally making her apartment available for use as a safe house.

The mole hunt that ended with the arrest of Ames began in 1986, several months after Ames started spying for the Soviet Union. Sometime in 1985, CIA officials had realized that several agents in the Soviet Union had been compromised, silenced, or executed. But not until October 1986 did Directorate of Operations officials assemble a small group of mole hunters, headed by Jeanne Vertefeuille, an expert in Soviet counterintelligence. [At first, Vertefeuille's group was interested in Edward Lee Howard, a CIA case officer who had fled to Moscow in September 1985. Howard's work ruled him out as a mole. But, as a former CIA officer recalled, "We were concerned about his psychological state and that he might act precipitously and do something dumb."]

By going through countless files and tying together bits of information, Vertefeuille and her hunters found about 20 CIA employees who had broad access to sensitive Soviet operations and assets. One of the employees was Ames, a counterintelligence officer. The FBI, meanwhile, had also been investigating the loss of two Soviet intelligence officers who had been recruited by the FBI. But not until 1991 did the CIA confer with the FBI and form a joint investigative unit.

Ames was finally singled out after Sandy Grimes, one of Vertefeuille's investigators, discovered that he was regularly making large bank deposits soon after lunching with Sergei Chuvakhin, a diplomat at the Soviet Embassy—and Ames' case officer. Those meetings were known to the CIA because Ames had volunteered to cultivate and try to recruit Soviet officials in Washington.

Vertefeuille passed the suspicions about Ames to the FBI, which took over the case, codenamed Nightmover. The FBI put Ames under total surveillance, assembling the evidence needed to put him in prison for the rest of his life.

Under a plea bargain with federal prosecutors, Ames pleaded guilty to espionage and was sentenced to a life sentence without parole. He agreed to cooperate with the CIA and FBI in exchange for mercy toward Rosario, who was given a 63-month sentence that, on the condition of good behavior, could be shortened to 42 months. In prison, Ames continued to negotiate, trying to trade further cooperation for more inmate privileges. After serving her sentence, Rosario Ames returned to Colombia.

An investigation by the CIA's inspector general (IG) found that Ames was an alcoholic, notoriously sloppy officer who failed "to file accountings, contact reports and requests for foreign travel on time or at all" and "carried classified documents out of CIA facilities in shopping bags." The IG investigators professed themselves to be "dismayed at this tolerant view of Ames's professional deficiencies and the random indifference given to his assignments."

The damage Ames did was unprecedented in the CIA. During his nine years as a spy, first for the Soviet Union and then for Russia, he revealed the identities of more than 30 operatives spying for the CIA and other Western intelligence services. At least 10 betrayed Russians and East Europeans were executed. (In 1996 Congress authorized American citizenship to the widows and children of agents Ames betrayed.) Ames also disclosed more than 100 covert operations, including the existence of tunnels used to tap Soviet communications in a space facility outside Moscow and Project Absorb, a device used to count the number of nuclear warheads carried by Soviet intercontinental missiles.

A brooding Aldrich Ames in prison. Ames is the spy thought to have done the gravest damage to U.S. security in CIA history.

Impact on History: No one in the history of the CIA is known to have done more damage than Ames. He betrayed numerous CIA assets to the Soviets. At least 10 were consequently executed. He also compromised over 100 CIA operations, and his case had a profound impact on U.S. counterintelligence practices.

Dear Mr. Cherkashin:

Soon, I will send a box of documents to Mr. Degtyar. They are from certain of the most sensitive and highly compartmented projects of the U.S. intelligence community. All are originals to aid in verifying their authenticity. Please recognize for our long-term interests that there are a limited number of persons with this array of clearances. As a collection they point to me. I trust that an officer of your experience will handle them appropriately. I believe they are sufficient to justify a $100,000 payment to me.

I must warn of certain risks to my security of which you may not be aware. Your service has recently suffered some setbacks . . . details regarding payment and future contact will be sent to you personally . . . my identity and actual position in the community must be left unstated to ensure my security. I am open to common suggestions but want no specialized tradecraft. I will add 6, (you subtract 6) from stated months, days and times in both directions of our future communications.

Re-creation of the letter sent from Robert Hanssen to his spymaster in 1985, offering to resume his activities as a Soviet spy.

The FBI Mole

CREATED: OCTOBER 1985
SUBJECT: ROBERT HANSSEN'S
OFFER TO SPY FOR THE SOVIETS

25 | FBI agent Robert P. Hanssen began spying for the Soviets in 1979. A counterintelligence specialist, Hanssen used his expertise to avoid detection for more than 20 years. His Russian handlers—first the KGB and then its successor, the SVR (Foreign Intelligence Service)—never knew his name. Nor did they ever learn that he was an FBI agent. He saw no reason to identify himself, and his production was so valuable that his handlers probably never sought to identify him. He signed his name as Ramon Garcia, leading the Soviets to believe that he might be a CIA officer, since his assumed name ended in the letters *cia.*

Hanssen sold his handlers the identities of several American agents, at least two of whom were executed. The highly classified documents and computer disks that he handed over in dead drops included information about several espionage cases, U.S. nuclear war strategy, and developments in military weapons. He also reportedly informed the Russians about a tunnel dug under their Washington embassy to tap into communications. Apprised of this, Russians may have fooled eavesdroppers with disinformation.

After examining why Hanssen lasted so long as a spy, the inspector general of the Department of Justice concluded that he cloaked his espionage with an appearance of laziness and

Robert Hanssen, an FBI Special Agent turned Soviet spy, was responsible for the execu-
tion of at least two KGB officers who were acting as covert agents for U.S. intelligence.

carelessness. "During his 25 years with the FBI," the report said, "Hanssen was a mediocre agent who exhibited strong technical abilities but had weak managerial and interpersonal skills . . . While Hanssen's day-to-day behavior did not suggest that he was engaged in espionage, he continually demonstrated an unwillingness to properly handle classified information. His indiscretions and security violations were largely ignored and . . . he was allowed to remain in positions offering him broad access to highly sensitive counterintelligence information." But some analysts, including those who saw him as a mentor, admired his counterintelligence work.

Hanssen started spying in November 1979, eight months after he was assigned to a counterintelligence squad in New York City. He provided information to an officer of the GRU, the Soviet military intelligence service. When his wife, Bonnie, discovered his spying, he told her that he had confessed his espionage to a priest who belonged to Opus Dei, the conservative Roman Catholic organization pledged to "spread throughout society a profound awareness of the universal call to holiness." Hanssen said that on the advice of the priest he ended his spying and donated several thousand dollars of his GRU earnings to the Little Sisters of the Poor.

Hanssen resumed his spying in October 1985 when he sent a letter to the home of Viktor M. Degtyar, known by Hanssen to be a KGB officer under cover as a diplomat in the Soviet Embassy in Washington. Inside was another envelope, marked: DO NOT OPEN. TAKE THIS ENVELOPE UNOPENED TO VICTOR I. CHERKASHIN. Cherkashin, Hanssen knew, was the chief KGB officer under cover at the embassy. (Cherkashin was also Aldrich Ames' case officer.) In the inner envelope was a letter. Excerpts of this letter are shown on page 148.

In the letter, Hanssen named three KGB officers who were serving as double agents for the FBI. Two were executed and the third was sentenced to 16 years in prison. Hanssen's betrayal began what the inspector general's report called "catastrophic and unprecedented losses of Soviet intelligence assets," meaning agents.

As the FBI closed in on a Soviet asset in the State Department, for instance, the KGB used information from Hanssen to warn the spy, who broke off contact. This was one of several incidents that triggered a search, not for a mole, but for sources of possible leaks. Initially, those efforts—encouraged by Soviet disinformation—focused on possible breakdowns in electronic communications or even coding systems. Hanssen, an expert on FBI computer systems, frequently logged on to a highly secret database to see whether he was under investigation.

The mole hunt presumably ended with the arrest in 1994 of the CIA's Aldrich Ames. But the hemorrhaging did not stop. Further investigations led the FBI counterintelligence officers to put a CIA intelligence officer under surveillance. The FBI even asked the Justice Department to prosecute the CIA suspect. Although ultimately cleared and never prosecuted, he and his family were devastated by the ordeal.

As a devout Catholic and ultra-conservative, Hanssen bored fellow workers with his preaching. Privately, he had other sides no one in the FBI suspected. Using a closed-circuit video system he had installed in his bedroom, he videotaped himself making love with his wife—and showed the tape to a friend. In a bizarre affair, he befriended a stripper, giving her money, jewels, a Mercedes Benz, and a credit card, but never sleeping with her.

Hanssen's espionage was ultimately betrayed by a former Russian intelligence officer who sold Hanssen's KGB file to American authorities. In 2000, the FBI placed Hanssen under full-time surveillance. On Sunday, February 12, 2001, Hanssen, his wife, and children left their Virginia home and went to mass at St. Catherine of Siena Church, where FBI Director Louis Freeh also worshiped. That afternoon, Hanssen went to a Virginia park and placed a black garbage bag full of documents under a footbridge. Fellow FBI agents surrounded him and arrested him for espionage.

Hanssen confessed in exchange for the government's taking the death penalty off the table as a possible sentence and agreeing that his wife would receive a portion of his pension.

Impact on History: Like Adrich Ames, Hanssen did grave harm by providing intelligence about agents and secret projects. But his most damaging disclosure involved nuclear war: He gave away the Continuity of Government Plan, the highly secret program designed to ensure survival of the president and U.S. government operations in the event of a nuclear attack.

FOUR

A Bodyguard of Lies

"In war-time," Winston Churchill famously said, "truth is so precious that she should always be attended by a bodyguard of lies." All spying involves deception, but Churchill was speaking about the special use of deception as a weapon in war. As far back as the sixth century B.C., deception was recognized as a vital element of military operations. Writing in *The Art of War*, the Chinese military strategist Sun Tzu noted that every maneuver on the battlefield should include actions that mislead the enemy. "Even though you are competent, appear to be incompetent," he wrote. "Though effective, appear to be ineffective."

Deception, in Churchill's view, extended well beyond the battlefield, encompassing many intelligence activities aimed at manipulating, distorting, or falsifying what the enemy assumed to be reality. Britain marshaled such a large bodyguard of lies during World War II that an innocuously named unit, the London Controlling Station, had to be set up to oversee the numerous deception operations. The LCS, as it was usually referred to in secret papers, was overseen by an officer known as "the Controller of Deception."

The LCS invented and developed deception plans, which were run by several agencies. One of them was another innocuously named unit, the Special Operations Executive. The SOE was created in July, in the words of Churchill, to "set Europe ablaze" by sabotage and subversion in German-occupied countries.

One of the SOE's nastiest deceptions was the exploitation of german plain-text telegrams that went from Italy to local Nazi Party representatives in Germany, asking them to inform relatives about the deaths of solders who died in German military hospitals in Italy. British radio interceptors routinely picked up these telegrams and passed them on to the propaganda operatives of the SOE. Using the intercepted information—the dead soldier's name, the name and address of his next of kin, and the name of the hospital—SOE deceivers created a letter. Supposedly from a nurse or a comrade, the letter said that the soldier had died, not from wounds, but from a lethal injection given by a Nazi doctor who needed the man's bed for a soldier more likely to recover rapidly.

The war's most effective and long-lived trickery was the work of the Twenty Committee, which concentrated on the overall plan for the Allied invasion of Europe—D-Day. The committee's name came from its double-cross purpose and the pun produced by the Roman numeral version of 20: XX. It was also called the Double-Cross Committee and the XX Committee.

The D-Day deception plan, code-named Bodyguard, was based on the Double-Cross System, which transformed German spies into double agents. The transformation began when the agent was captured and given a choice: work for the British or be executed. Counterintelligence officers believed that they had captured every German agent sent to Britain by the Abwehr, the German military intelligence agency.

Declassified records show that 17 men were tried under the "Treachery Act" of 1940, a modern successor to the 16th-century treason-against-the-king law. The 1940 law, inspired by Churchill, covered "any act which is designed or likely to give assistance to the naval, military or air operations of the enemy, to impede such operations of His Majesty's forces, or to endanger life." The spies were convicted at secret trials and secretly buried after secret executions (16 by hanging). One man had broken a leg when he parachuted into Britain. His injury made hanging too awkward, so he was shot by a firing squad in the Tower of London, the last of many executed there over the centuries.

Among those who chose to live and work for Double Cross, many became long term star performers. They sent a stream of intelligence, for instance, about the First U.S. Army Group (FUSAG), commanded by Lt. Gen. George S. Patton. When patton arrived in southern England, he made himself conspicuous, as part of the plan. Agents then sent messages containing bits and pieces of intelligence that added up to preparations for an Allied landing, led by FUSAG, across the Strait of Dover at Calais, France.

"The First U.S. Army Group," which would appear to have about 150,000 men in 11 divisions, did not exist. To convince the Germans of its existence, the U.S. Army's heraldic design section created shoulder patches for the divisions that were supposed to be in FUSAG. To add to the verisimilitude of their reports, the Double-Cross agents sent descriptions of the patches that supposedly they had seen on the uniforms of American soldiers in pubs and along the roads of southern England, across from Calais.

The fake patches, along with authentic patches, appeared in a *National Geographic* magazine article on American military insignias. And in the German Army's French headquarters in Paris, the phony insignias marked the divisions on a wall chart used by the German staff to keep track of the U.S. forces that would be used in the Calais invasion.

To create what appeared to be a massive military buildup along the Kent coast, Allied deception specialists built tent encampments with dummy tanks and other vehicles, put dummy landing crafts in the Thames estuary, and allowed Luftwaffe reconnaissance aircraft to fly over the area so that the bogus buildup could be photographed. Realistic radio messages flowed from Patton's non-existent headquarters to his non-existent divisions. The radio traffic was easily intercepted by German monitors.

Allied aerial bombing concentrated on the Pas de Calais area right up to D-Day on June 6, 1944. The deception continued after D-Day, convincing German strategists that the Normandy invasion was a feint and that the real invasion force would soon be landing on the Calais beaches. At least 19 German divisions remained in Calais for weeks after D-Day.

A similar deception operation, based upon imaginary troops in Scotland, made the Germans believe that a major force was being assembled for an invasion of Norway, thereby keeping the German divisions in Norway. Hitler, told of the agents' reports, overruled skeptical generals who wanted to transfer divisions from Norway to coastal France.

To German intelligence officers, the agents appeared to be highly successful spies because they were transmitting intelligence that seemed valid. The Twenty Committee developed the mix of both true and false secrets that the Double-Cross agents sent to their German spymasters. Most messages were sent by Morse code transmitted on supposedly hidden radios. Some were written in invisible ink between the lines of letters sent to mail drops in Spain and Portugal.

The agents completely deceived Abwehr officers, who placed great faith in the false intelligence and the agents feeding it to them. When the Abwehr asked its British agents about coastal defenses in southeast England in 1940, the question gave British strategists an indication that Germany was planning an invasion of England in that area. Asked about British preparations for gas warfare, a Double-Cross agent sent back, in the words of Sir John Masterman, chairman of the Twenty Committee, "a glowing account of the excellence of British preparations, and implied that gas warfare would be of greater advantage to the British than to the Germans."

"By means of the double-cross system," Masterman wrote, "we actively ran and controlled the German espionage system in this country."

Britain was not the only nation running deception operations during World War II. Germany's *Englandspiel* (the Game against

England) was deadly. As for America's "First U.S. Army Group," that was a deception that George Washington would have applauded. Washington may never have told a lie in peacetime, but in war he certainly made sure he was surrounded by a bodyguard of lies.

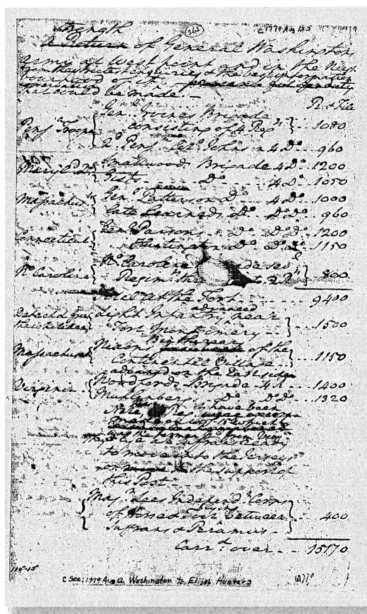

A page of Washington's letter to double agent Elijah Hunter, providing him with information on American troops to feed to the British.

George Washington's Lies

CREATED: AUGUST 1779
SUBJECT: REVOLUTIONARY WAR—
WASHINGTON'S SPY PLOT AGAINST
THE BRITISH

26 | General George Washington, confronted and outnumbered by the best-equipped and best-trained army in the world, knew from the very beginning that deception would be one of his best weapons—even though his soul recoiled at the idea. "I hate deception," he said in a letter in 1779, after years of supervising deception operations that began in his first days as commander of the Continental Army.

When he took command at Cambridge, Massachusetts, in 1776, he learned that his army had only 36 barrels of gunpowder—enough for about nine shots for each man. He sent agents into British-occupied Boston with the story that his army had *1,800* barrels. And to raise morale, he had the same reports planted among his own men.

Later in the war, when an officer offered to serve as a double agent, Washington wrote to the officer's superior, giving a glimpse of how Washington, the spymaster, mixed caution with deception: ". . . if he is really in the confidence of the enemy, as he himself believes to be the case, it will be prudent to trust him with caution and to watch his conduct with a jealous eye. I always think it necessary to be very circumspect with double spies . . . It is best to keep them in a way of knowing as little of our true circumstances as possible; and in order that they may really deceive the enemy in their reports, to endeavor in the first place to deceive them . . ."

Washington, following basic spycraft rules, did not mention the double agent's name. He was Captain Elijah Hunter, who supposedly retired from the army and posed as a Tory so he could become a double agent. Washington, who satisfied himself about Hunter's loyalty, endorsed the plan for Hunter to enter British-occupied New York City. There he became a spy for General Sir Henry Clinton, commander in chief of British forces, and Governor William Tryon.

Washington hatched a deception plan, designed to test Hunter's loyalty. Hunter was to enter Washington's camp up the Hudson River at West Point, count the troops there, and then return to Clinton with the intelligence. Washington decided to prove the double agent's value to the British by giving him a document that listed the true numbers (see page 160).

Washington knew that the British would be suspicious about Hunter's ability to get such secret information. So in his letter of instruction to Hunter (below), Washington suggests a way for Hunter to explain his possession of such knowledge to the British. The letter also mentions Lt. Col. Banastre Tarleton, a Clinton favorite. Tarleton commanded the British Legion, whose members were mostly American Tories and the fact that Hunter was able to purloin a Tarleton letter for Washington to read and return proved that Hunter had penetrated deep into British headquarters.

Sir: I rec'd your favor of the 8th. inst. with Col Tarletons letter inclosed. I now return it to you with my thanks. Inclosed you will find a return of the troops fit for duty under my immediate command. For the reasons I mentioned to you the other day I have not the least objection to our real strength being known, and it will be well for you to inform that you came by the knowledge of it from inquiry and your own observations of the troops when under arms upon which you formed an average estimate of the force of each regiment in the different

Brigades; to give your account, the greater air of probability you may observe that the Officers are very incautious in speaking of the strength of their regiments . . .

In 1777, when his army, battered after defeats at Brandywine and Germantown, was encamped near Philadelphia, Washington put together one of his most complicated deceptions. Philadelphia was occupied by the British under Gen. William Howe. Gen. Clinton occupied New York City. Washington knew that his men would be overwhelmed if the British sent troops from both New York and Philadelphia. Washington also knew that Brig. Gen. Horatio Gates' defeat of the British at Saratoga, New York, worried Howe and Clinton, for they had no idea where Gates would strike next.

Washington wanted Howe to keep his army in Philadelphia because Howe believed that Gates was heading there. And, to keep Clinton pinned down, Washington wanted Clinton to think that Gates' army was on its way to New York City. (Gates did not go to either city.)

As part of the deception, Washington ordered three generals with troops near New York to begin maneuvering as if they were preparing to invade the city. They were also told to make sure that their "secret" moves became known to "persons who you are sure will divulge" those secrets. Those persons were New York Tories, who were frequently fed false information by American agents.

For the Philadelphia part of the deception, Washington arranged to have an agent appear to become a traitor by going to Howe and offering to spy. Howe, cautious about dealing with a traitor, requested to see what the man had to offer. He gave Howe a stack of documents—some written by Washington himself, just for the deception. Among them was a paper indicating that Gates was sending 8,000 men to Washington. Howe fell for the deception.

Later in the war, wanting the British to believe he was about to attack New York from his camp in New Jersey, Washington had soldiers clear and repair roads that led to the city. A regiment marched toward Staten Island. "If we do not deceive our own men," Washington later wrote, "we will never deceive the enemy." He himself joined in the deception by asking a farmer questions

General George Washington, commander of the Continental Army during the Revolutionary War.

about Staten Island—and then, acting as if he had accidentally let information pass, he said that his words should be treated with "the most profound Secrecy." Washington knew that just the opposite would happen, for the farmer was a Tory who would quickly report the deceptive conversation to British officers.

Throughout the war, Washington arranged for fake documents to fall in the hands of known British spies. He set up the deception so that British scouts stopped his horseback couriers and grabbed the fake documents, thinking they were real. Or he had British riders stopped and their saddlebags examined. The contents of the saddlebags were then returned—along with authentic-looking documents created by Washington's deceivers.

Impact on History: Washington's masterful use of deception was critical to victory in the American Revolution. This document displays s bit of his repertoire as a general and a spymaster.

Traffic Intelligence after the 25th carried analyses similar to these:
"Carriers are quiet."

"Lack of carrier traffic usually means they are at sea."

"Carriers unheard."

(13). 25 May: The OCCUPATION FORCE, which was sailing from the Empire as well as Saipan, was making its final plans to occupy Midway. (Confidence in the success of this operation was so great that already this occupation was considered an accepted fact.)

Message of the 25th, (translated 26 May).
"OCCUPATION FORCE OPORD #8.
Comdr 1ST _____ OCCUPATION FORCE utilizing part of 2ND _____ - will occupy Midway. _____ Sutan Island.
            COMMENT: Suggest Eastern Island. This was in typical operation order form and is first one of this type received on this campaign."

Message of 25 May.
From: CinC 2nd FLEET.
"OCCUPATION FORCE OPORD #4:
After 1200 24 May, COMDESRON 4 will assign _____ DD to the _____ KAKU.
After operations of the _____ KAKU on the 24th DD will operate as directed by the _____ KAKU.
(DESDIV in DESRON 4) after above date will come under command of (SATA) at Kure and is assigned duty of screening SATA and TSURUMI.
On _____ date (74448) depart Kure.
On N-5 days be in position 26-48 N., _____ -15 E. Thence proceed to join main body of OCCUPATION FORCE."

Message of 20 May, (read on the 24th).
From: Jaluit Radio?.
"After the occupation of AF (Midway) (remainder unreadable)."

*Analysis and excerpts of intercepted Japanese radio traffic,
planning the invasion of the U.S. naval base at Midway.*

The Trick That Won Midway

[
CREATED: MAY 1942
SUBJECT: WWII—CRACKING
JAPANESE PLANS FOR AN
ATTACK ON MIDWAY
]

27 | U.S. cryptanalysts, chipping away at the Japanese Navy's most secret communications, worked during World War II in a basement room at the naval headquarters building in Pearl Harbor. The dank, dark place was known as "the dungeon." The codebreaking began with the interception of Japanese military radio traffic by eavesdropping stations around the Pacific. U.S. Navy radio operators, using special typewriters, recorded the dots and dashes of 71 phonetic Japanese characters, transmitted at speeds of 40 to 50 code groups per minute. Cryptanalysts then wrested words out of the code groups. They were aided by ancestors of today's computers—big, noisy IBM tabulating machines that sorted punch cards.

Translators put the decrypted bits into English sentences. Finally, analysts tried to fill in the gaps. On April 27, 1942, for example, a decrypt revealed that a Japanese admiral had asked for certain charts for an area that encompassed Alaska. Then came references to a place identified as Dutch Harbor, site of a U.S. naval base on the Aleutian island of Unalaska. There were also repeated mentions of "AF," a place whose identity could only be guessed at. AF could be the U.S. naval base at Midway, a coral atoll about 1,300 miles northwest of Hawaii; or even the U.S. West Coast.

Message of 19 May, (translated on the 24th).
From: 14TH AIRON.
To: Chief of Staff 1ST FLEET
       Tokyo BuPers
       All 1st Class Naval Stations, Secretary
"In the RPS(?) organization table change "to"* PTI (Imieji)
"to"* AF (Midway). (This seems to indicate next address of
14TH AIRON to be AF.)
COMMENT: "or "at", "c/o", "addressed to".
                    CI COMMENT: The 14TH AIRON is placed
                    in the Marshall Islands area, and is
                    suspected as playing a major role in
                    joint air-submarine operations from
                    the Marshall Islands Area. It is a
                    seaplane outfit and has been associated
                    with submarines in connection with both
                    AF (Midway) and K (Hawaiian) Operations.
                    It appears that this unit is one of the
                    forces which intend to actually occupy
                    Midway."

Message read on the 27th.
From: 4TH AIR ATTACK FORCE
"When will the replacements of 14th Air Patrol seaplanes
arrive Saipan. For operations require them by 3 June."

Message translated on 28 May.
"Reference the enemy engineering equipment now on Wake (there
is also some on George), request the machinery and Reserve
Construction Officer be put at my disposal for the construction
of an air base at AF. In connection with this, request that
the enemy engineers (now on Wake), about 60, be sent also."

(14).   28 May: Jap Codes were changed.

                    Traffic Intelligence contained this
analysis on the 28th.
"More traffic from issuing office."
                    CI COMMENT: This is probably last minute
                    instructions on the use of the new Code.
                    Code D1 and Cipher Table 9 were to replace
                    Code D and Cipher Table 8 on 1 May but this
                    was held off until distribution became com-
                    plete and now on 28 May the code has finally
                    been changed."

*Another page of the analysis of Japanese radio traffic planning Midway's invasion.
This page notes the abrupt change of the Japanese code, days before the planned attack.*

Midway was connected to Honolulu by an old seafloor cable that Japanese eavesdroppers could not tap. Knowing that arid Midway depended upon desalinated water, one of the dungeon dwellers had an idea. Midway's radio operators were told via the cable to send a false message. This was what they were instructed to do:

. . . send a plain language message to Com 14 [Commandant, 14th Naval District—Pearl Harbor] stating in effect, that the distillation plant had suffered a serious casualty and that fresh water was urgently needed—to which Com 14 would reply, (also in plain language), that water barges would be sent, under tow, soonest . . .

The message was also to be sent in a low-level code that the Japanese could easily read. The ruse was successful. Japanese Naval Intelligence, in a message that was heard by U.S. interceptors, reported that there was a water problem on AF. That meant that AF was Midway. This was followed by a specific location for the attack force on N Day and N Day-2—dates that the cryptanalysts had already deduced to be days in early June. The intercepted, decoded, and translated Japanese message was:

Referring to 6th Communication Units #621, as we plan to make attacks from a general northwesterly direction from N-2 to N day inclusive, please send weather three hours prior to take-off on the said day. Also, would like to be informed of enemy air activity or anything else which might be of importance. Reference to Combined Fleet #1 on the day of the attack we will endeavor to—at a point 50 miles NW of AF and move pilots off as quickly as possible.

A summary of translated intercepts (see the documents on pages 166 and 168) shows blanks, partial words, and comments. The use of OCCUPATION FORCE clearly indicates an invasion. COMDESRON and DESDIV refer to a Japanese squadron and division of destroyers (DD). SATA and TSURAUMI are oilers, part of the replenishment train accompanying the warships. Japanese aircraft carriers were named after flying creatures. So KAKU, which means crane, indicates carriers, whose names have so far eluded the codebreakers. Jaluit is an atoll in the Marshall Islands; Kure is in Japan. Both had naval bases whose radio transmissions were monitored by U.S. intelligence.

Navy strategists knew that Midway was the target of a major Japanese strike force that would form about 50 miles northwest of the atoll. Codebreakers worked tirelessly to glean more information from the intercepts. Then, at midnight on May 28, the Japanese changed the naval code, making their messages suddenly unreadable (see reference to this on the transcript on page 168).

But there was enough information to give a detailed intelligence forecast to Adm. Chester W. Nimitz, commander in chief of the Pacific Fleet: Japan would attack the Aleutians on June 3 and Midway the next day. The Midway force would include the carriers *Akagi, Kaga, Hiryu,* and *Soryu.*

Some high-ranking officers in Washington feared that Nimitz and his code breakers were falling for a Japanese deception operation. But Nimitz decided to believe his intelligence forecast and sent the carriers *Enterprise, Hornet,* and *Yorktown* to a spot in the Pacific Ocean where he hoped he could ambush the Japanese.

On June 3 the Japanese did strike the Aleutians, and on June 4, Midway. In the battle that followed, U.S. carrier aircraft sank the four Japanese carriers. The *Yorktown* was lost, but six months after the attack on Pearl Harbor, the U.S. Navy had won a major victory.

Impact on History: Midway was the decisive turning point of the war in the Pacific. Japanese losses were so high—especially among pilots and air crews—that Japan would never again launch an offensive.

eight minutes after the 3rd Canadian Division had landed on French soil.

The following is evidence in support of the successful implement-

ation by GARBO of PHASE I of FORTITUDE.

The fact that the Germans were in a receptive frame of mind to

absorb our cover plan is indicated in B.J. No. 508 of the 28.5.44 in

which the Japanese Ambassador in Berlin gave a resume of a conversation

which he had had with Hitler the previous day:-

"Speaking of the Second Front, Hitler said that he, himself,

thought that sooner or later operations for the invasion of Europe would

be undertaken. He thought that about eighty divisions had already been

assembled in England (of these divisions about eight had had actual

experience of fighting and were very good troops.) I accordingly asked

the Fuehrer if he thought that these British and American troops had

completed their preparations for landing operations and he replied in the

affirmative. I then asked him in what form he thought the Second Front

would materialize, and he told me that at the moment what he himself

thought was most probable was that after having carried out diversionary

operations in Norway, Denmark and the southern part of the west coast of

France and the French Mediterranean coast, they would establish a bridgehead

in Normandy or Brittany, and after seeing how things went would then embark

upon the establishment of a real Second Front in the channel. Germany

would like nothing better, he said, than to be given an opportunity of

coming to blows with large forces of the enemy as soon as possible. But

if the enemy adopted these methods his numerical strength would be dispersed

and he (Hitler) intended to watch for this........"

That the invasion came as a surprise is evident from the

following B.J. No. 73 dated 15.6.44:-

Extract from a despatch from the Japanese Ambassador, Berlin:

"Leaving for the moment the Anglo-American claim that the landing

... that although the Germans had   1

*A secret report on Garbo by a Double-Cross officer noting Hitler's
mistaken belief that there were 80 Allied divisions in Britain.*

The Star of Double-Cross

CREATED: NOVEMBER 1945
SUBJECT: WWII—THE CREATION
OF AN INVALUABLE BRITISH SPY

28 | Juan Pujol, a 29-year-old Spaniard who hated Spanish dictator Francisco Franco, believed that if Germany lost World War II, Franco would fall. So Pujol decided to work as a spy for the British. After offering his services and being rejected as an uneducated young man with nothing to offer, he was accepted by the Abwehr, the German military intelligence service. Pujol left Madrid in July 1941, ostensibly en route to England, carrying secret writing materials and mail drops maintained by the Abwehr.

Pujol went from one neutral country to another, crossing the border into Lisbon, where he unsuccessfully tried to contact British intelligence. He stayed in Lisbon while continuing to cleverly deceive his German handlers that he was in Britain. He concocted reports based on information culled from a copy of the *Blue Guide* to England and other reference books found in a local library. He also began creating a network of "notional agents," as figments of a spy's imagination are called.

In January 1942, still in Lisbon, he met again with British intelligence officials, who this time were impressed by his genius for fakery. They took him to Britain and enrolled him in the ranks of Double-Cross. He became the star of the deception operation that was aimed at confounding the Germans about the D-Day invasion. Pujol, who already had the German codename Arabel, was given the British codename Garbo, possibly because he was as good an actor as Greta Garbo. His case officer was Tomás (Tommy) Harris, a Spanish-speaking MI5 officer.

Together, Garbo and Harris invented 27 notional agents. Each one had a carefully crafted "legend," an invented life story that is both believable and well documented. One of the imaginary agents, for example, was a "Wren" (member of the WRNS, the Women's Royal Naval Service). Garbo said the Wren was sent to the headquarters for the Southeast Asia theater in Ceylon, where she passed information to him for the Abwehr. The Germans in turn passed the phony information to the Japanese military attaché in Berlin to be passed on to Tokyo. British intelligence officers, reading transcripts of intercepted and decrypted German radio traffic, confirmed Abwehr's acceptance of the Garbo network.

At first, Garbo contacted his German case officer in Madrid through messages in invisible ink written between the lines of handwritten letters sent to the Lisbon mail drops. He had written 315 letters before he set up a transmitter-receiver with the aid, he said, of a radio engineer who was a secret pro-Nazi.

In a secret report on Garbo, a Double-Cross officer cited an intercepted dispatch from the Japanense ambassador to Germany who quoted Hitler as believing there were about 80 Allied divisions in Britain (see page 172). In reality, there were 39 divisions, of which 8 landed on D-Day. (FORTITUDE, mentioned in the report, was the codename for the overall D-Day deception plan.)

On June 5, Garbo alerted his German contacts to stand by for an urgent radio message at 3 a.m. on June 6. This was part of a bold plan: Garbo would enhance his reputation by giving a warning that an invasion force was heading for Normandy. The 3 a.m. scheduling was crucial. By 3 a.m. D-Day would have begun and the Germans would not have the time to react. The German radio operator in Madrid failed to keep the appointment. When he learned this, Garbo transmitted his disgust at not being heard and added, "I cannot accept excuses or negligence. Were it not for my ideals I would abandon the work."

Much of Garbo's deception had been aimed at getting the Germans to believe that the invasion would be across the Strait of Dover for a landing in the Calais area. Germany kept 15 divisions there in anticipation. Then came D-Day at Normandy. Three days later, as Allied troops were fighting beyond the beachheads, Alfred Jodl, Chief of the Operations Staff High Command, responded to the pleas of his German field commanders in Normandy by releasing the Fifteenth Army in Calais to Normandy.

Meanwhile, Garbo was sending his handler in Madrid a message based on vital intelligence gathered by three trusted subagents (V372, V373, and V377). Garbo said that it was so important it should be passed to the OKW, the Wehrmacht High Command, which was one step below Hitler himself:

Request following report be urgently submitted to OKW for immediate attention. Sources do not repeat do not believe Normandy landing is main thrust of AngloAmerican invasion. V372 Liverpool reports large concentrations U.S.A. armored still held his area. V373 estimates at least 35 divisions are awaiting orders in Scottish lowlands. V377 traveled by train saw elements of 20 divisions in stretch 15 miles south of York. So far not a single soldier of FUSAG has been engaged.

See the following pages for what happened to Garbo next.

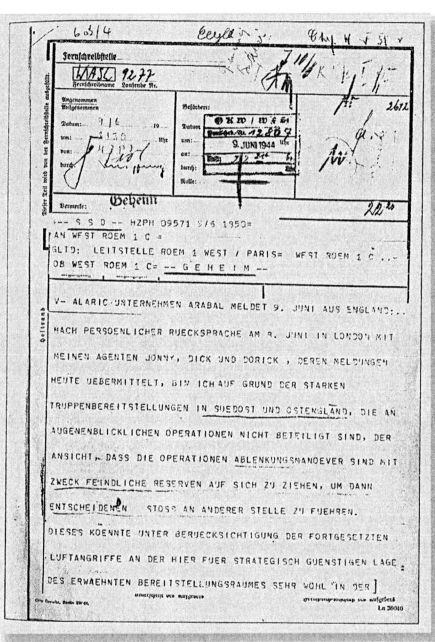

Reproduction of Garbo's message of June 9, 1944,
received and analyzed by the OKW.

"A Diversionary Maneuver"

CREATED: JUNE 1944
SUBJECT: WWII — GARBO'S
MESSAGE ABOUT THE
NORMANDY INVASION

29 | Garbo's message displayed the trust that he had earned through the work of his network of imaginary agents. Intercepts of German intelligence traffic monitored by the Double-Cross directors showed that Garbo's handlers admired his reports so much that they quoted him (as Arabel, of course) in 62 intelligence summaries.

But the British detected the movement of the German Fifteenth Army out of Calais, meaning that the German high command was not accepting the diversion scheme. The move was puzzling. Allied intelligence knew, from many intercepts, that Hitler believed Calais was the most likely site for a second, larger invasion. The deception plan, in fact, had been designed to bolster Hitler's theory. Had Hitler changed his mind?

Colonel Baron Alexis von Roenne was chief of Foreign Armies West (OKW), the high-level German intelligence organization that kept watch specifically on Allied military activity. Roenne knew that the possibility of a major invasion at Calais was backed by more evidence than Garbo's reports. There were, for example, the aerial reconnaissance photos showing landing craft, tanks, and aircraft in southern England, opposite Calais. Roenne did not know that the objects in the photos were all fakes made of rubber and plywood.

Roenne telephoned Col. Friedrich-Adolf Krummacher, chief of intelligence on Hitler's military staff, telling him that another Garbo message had reached OKW. Translated, the message said:

V-man Alaric network ARABAL reports on 9th June from England:

After personal consultation on 8th June in London with my agents Jonny, Dick and Dorick, whose reports were sent today, I am of the opinion, in view of the strong troop concentrations in South-east and Eastern England which are not taking part in the present operations, that these operations are a diversionary maneuver designed to draw off enemy reserves in order then to make a decisive attack in another place. In view of the continued air attacks on the concentration mentioned, which is a strategically favourable position for this, it may probably take place in the Pas de Calais area, particularly since in such an attack the proximity of the air bases will facilitate the operation by providing continued strong air support.

In London on June 10, intelligence officers learned through intercepts that Hitler had cancelled the movement of the Fifteenth Army out of the Calais area. The decision had been made at a midnight conference that involved the June 9 message.

Examining the original document after the war, British intelligence officers found that someone, probably Krummacher, had underlined in red the words "diversionary maneuver designed to draw off enemy reserves in order then to make a decisive attack in another place" and had added at the end of the message "confirms the view already held by us that a further attack is to be expected in another place (Belgium?)."

Jodl, the highest-ranking military officer present, had underlined "in South-East and Eastern England" and added his initial in green at the top of the message. A green marking indicated that Jodl felt it was important enough to show Hitler, and the letters *erl* (for *erledigt,* "done") in pencil indicate that the message was seen by Hitler.

In a message to Garbo on June 11, Reichsführer SS Heinrich Himmler, second only to the Führer himself, sent his "warm appreciation." The message added: "All reports received in last week from Arabel undertaking have been confirmed without exception and are to be described as especially invaluable."

Impact on History: The invasion deceptions, dispensed so superbly by the Double-Cross System and Garbo, may have prevented a costly Allied defeat. As Gen. Dwight D. Eisenhower later said, "The German Fifteenth Army, which, if committed to battle in June or July, might possibly have defeated us by sheer weight of numbers, remained inoperative throughout the critical period of the campaign . . ." Finally realizing that the Normandy invasion was no feint, Hitler released the Fifteenth. But as Eisenhower said, it was "too late to have any effect upon the course of victory."

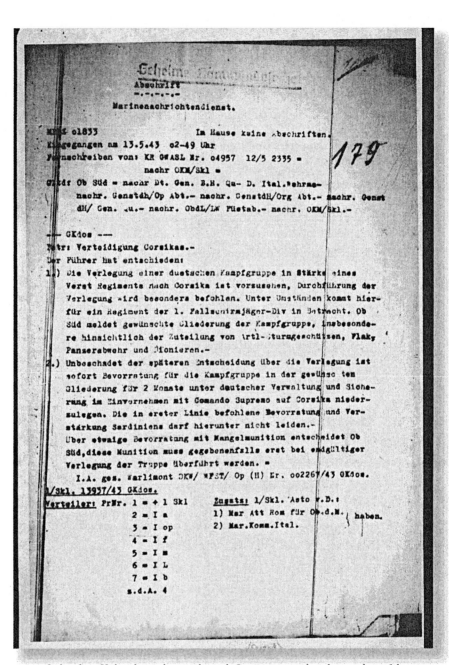

Abschrift
-.-.-.-.-

Marinenachrichtendienst.

MND. o1833   Im Hause keine Abschriften.
Eingegangen am 13.5.43 o2-49 Uhr
Fernschreiben von: KR OWASL Nr. o4957 12/5 2335 -   *179*
                nachr OKM/Skl -
Gfdr Ob Süd = nachr Dt. Gen. B.H. Qu- D. Ital.Wehrma-
        nachr. Genstdh/Op Abt.- nachr. GenstdH/Org Abt.- nachr. Genst
        dH/ Gen. Qu.- nachr. ObdL/LW Füstab.- nachr. OKM/Skl.-

--- GKdos ---

Betr: Verteidigung Corsikas.-

Der Führer hat entschieden:

1.) Die Verlegung einer duetschen Kampfgruppe in Stärke eines
    Verst Regiments nach Corsika ist vorzusehen, Durchführung der
    Verlegung wird besonders befohlen. Unter Umständen kommt hier-
    für ein Regiment der 1. Fallschirmjäger-Div in Betracht. Ob
    Süd meldet gewünschte Gliederung der Kampfgruppe, insbesonde-
    re hinsichtlich der Zuteilung von Artl-Sturmgeschützen, Flak,
    Panzerabwehr und Pionieren.-

2.) Unbeschadet der späteren Entscheidung über die Verlegung ist
    sofort Bevorratung für die Kampfgruppe in der gewünse ten
    Gliederung für 2 Monate unter deutscher Verwaltung und Siche-
    rung im Einvernehmen mit Comando Supremo auf Corsika nieder-
    zulegen. Die in erster Linie befohlene Bevorratung und Ver-
    stärkung Sardiniens darf hierunter nicht leiden.-
    Über etwaige Bevorratung mit Mangelmunition entscheidet Ob
    Süd, diese Munition muss gegebenenfalls erst bei endgültiger
    Verlegung der Truppe überführt werden. =
    I.A. gez. Warlimont OKW/ WFST/ Op (H) Nr. oo2267/43 GKdos.
1./Skl. 13957/43 GKdos.

Verteiler: PrNr. 1 = + 1 Skl   Zusatz: 1/Skl. Asto z.D.:
               2 = I a   1) Mar Att Rom für Ob.d.M. ⎫ haben.
               3 = I op   2) Mar.Komm.Ital.   ⎬
               4 = I f   ⎭
               5 = I m
               6 = I L
               7 = I b
           s.d.A. 4

Orders from Hitler about where to dispatch German troops, based on analysis of the documents planted on "Maj. William Martin," which the Germans accepted as valid.

"Mincemeat Swallowed Whole"

CREATED: MAY 1943
SUBJECT: WWII—BRITISH
PLOT USING THE "MAN WHO
NEVER WAS"

30 | Early in the morning of April 30, 1943, off the coast of Spain, the Royal Navy submarine *Seraph* surfaced. On the wave-washed deck, officers held a burial service for a man whose body they consigned to the sea. But this body was not meant to sink, for they had put a lifebelt on him and attached to his trench coat a chain linked to a briefcase. The body then drifted toward shore.

Spanish fishermen later found the body, which was claimed by Spanish military officers. From papers found on it, the corpse was identified as Maj. William Martin of the Royal Marines, assigned to Headquarters, Combined Operations. Also in his pockets were theater ticket stubs, pound notes, loose change, a bill from his London club, and love letters from his fiancée.

Spain, through diplomatic channels, notified British officials of the discovery of the body, which was buried in the Cemetery of Solitude in the Spanish town of Huelva, with "Maj. William Martin" on the tombstone. Spanish officials sent Martin's personal effects, the briefcase, and its contents to Royal Navy headquarters in London. Those contents included a top-secret letter from Sir Archibald Nye, vice chief of Britain's Imperial General Staff, to Gen. Sir Harold Alexander, the British commander in North Africa under American Gen. Dwight D. Eisenhower. The letter revealed that the Allied forces in North Africa were planning to invade Greece and Sardinia, not Sicily, as the Germans expected.

Maj. Martin was the centerpiece of Operation Mincemeat, one of the greatest deceptions of World War II, created to make the German High Command believe that the Allies were not going to strike Sicily. The corpse was that of a man who had recently died in England and was claimed by MI5. The body, scrupulously transformed into that of the imaginary Maj. Martin, had been carried to Spain in the *Seraph*. Only the officers knew about the deception.

Spanish officials assured the British that no one had seen the documents in the briefcase, an unlikely assurance. Although Spain was officially neutral, its dictator, Gen. Francisco Franco, favored Nazi Germany. Through a local agent, German intelligence officers had in fact opened the briefcase, photographed the contents, and rushed the photographs to Berlin for analysis. Nye's letter was accepted as genuine, and German strategists began to change their plans, which had focused on the expected invasion of Sicily.

On May 15, an Intelligence memo circulated among high-ranking German officers, alerting them to the discovery of enemy documents whose "genuineness" was determined to be "above suspicion." The memo went on to say, "The suggestion that they have intentionally fallen into our hands . . . is slight . . . It is possible that the enemy has no knowledge of the capture of the documents."

The memo strengthened Hitler's belief that the Allies would not invade Sicily. He ordered his generals to build up defenses in the places he favored: Orders were dispatched to move troops from the Italian mainland to Greece, Sardinia, and Corsica. Mines were laid in Greek coastal waters. Torpedo boat squadrons sped to bases near likely invasion sites. One order, dated May 13, was headed "Re: the defense of Corsica" (see page 180):

The Führer has decided:
1. Arrangements have been made for the movement of a German combat unit with the strength of a "Verst Regiment" to Corsica. The execution of this movement has been com-

manded. Use of the Regiment of the 1st Paratroopers Division should be considered. [A Verst Regiment was a strengthened regiment of about 3,500 men.]

2.   Regardless of the late decision of this [troop] movement, provisioning will be made for the combat units for two months in accordance with the Supreme Command in Corsica . . .

On July 10, when Allied troops invaded Sicily, they overpowered the diminished German forces. Italian troops offered little resistance. Gen. Eisenhower later wrote that the landings "in general did not encounter serious opposition. Shore batteries did not put up vigorous resistance . . ." There were fierce battles, but victory came by mid-August, and the Allies now held the first territory of the enemy's homeland, the threshold to Italy.

After intercepted German intelligence radio traffic showed that the Germans had fallen for the hoax, the British chiefs of staff wired to Prime Minister Winston Churchill, then in the United States: "Mincemeat Swallowed Whole."

Churchill's Chief of Staff, Gen. Hastings L. Ismay, later wrote: "The operation succeeded beyond our wildest dreams. To have spread-eagled the German defensive effort right across Europe, even to the extent of sending German vessels away from Sicily itself, was a remarkable achievement."

The mastermind of the operation was Ewen Montagu, a lawyer who served in British naval intelligence. Montagu's book about the operation, *The Man Who Never Was* (1953), was later made into a movie. The corpse's real identity was not revealed until 2003. He was Glyndwr Michael, a 34-year-old man who died, apparently a suicide, in a London warehouse. His name was placed on Major Martin's tombstone by the Commonwealth War Grave Commission.

Impact on History: The swift fall of Sicily so empowered the enemies of Dictator Benito Mussolini that he was deposed and replaced by a new government that surrendered Italy to the Allies on September 3, 1943.

Dr. Josef Goebbels, chief of Nazi Party propoganda and shown here flanking Hitler in 1935, admitted in a journal entry that Britain's black propoganda radio stations did "a very clever job."

Broadcasting Believable Lies

[
CREATED: MARCH 1944
SUBJECT: WWII—BRITISH
USE OF BLACK PROPAGANDA
]

31 | By cynical definition, the enemy spouts "propaganda," while whatever comes from our side is "news." That view makes propaganda difficult to define. But the World War II version can be seen in shades: *White* propaganda is clearly identified. (BBC had a white program with a straightforward title: "This is London calling"). *Gray* propaganda comes from a source not readily identified. (Prior to conquering France, German-produced broadcasts from unidentified radio stations aimed at panicking the French with such tactics as advising listeners to withdraw their savings from banks.) *Black* propaganda, at its best, is an undetectable lie.

Some of the finest examples of wartime black propaganda were British broadcasts pretending to be official German radio. The operation was run by the Special Operations Executive (SOE), whose main tasks were committing acts of sabotage and arming resistance groups in German-occupied Europe. The black propaganda script writers were told: "Accuracy first. We must never lie by accident, or through slovenliness, only deliberately."

Britain's black propaganda radio stations operated from transmitters in England. One pretended to be an illegal station broadcasting in Germany, supposedly presided over by *Der Chef,* who was pro-German but anti-Nazi. He interspersed music, real sports news, and anti-British tirades—Churchill is a "flat-footed bastard of a drunken old Jew"—with what sounded like coded messages to a non-existent anti-Nazi underground. One, for example, in an easily broken cipher, said, "Willy meet Jochen Friday row five parquet stalls second performance Union Theater." There were hundreds of Union Theater movie houses in Germany. And after Gestapo agents broke the code, they would presumably go scurrying around to find Willy and Jochen. Listeners believed that *Der Chef* and his undeground were real, burrowing at Germany from within. SOE propagandists hoped that the broadcasts would give some encouragement to Germans who opposed Hitler.

Der Chef spoke for the last time in November 1943, after some 700 broadcasts. Listeners heard machine-gun fire and the guttural shout of "Got you, you swine!" The "Gestapo" had finally captured *Der Chef*! The black propagandists next began to produce *Soldatensender Calais*, "Soldiers' Radio" from Calais, which was supposed to be an "official" German station. Its broadcasts included descriptions of the damage done by Allied bombers. Among its listeners was Josef Goebbels, chief of Nazi Party propaganda. On November 28, 1943, he wrote in his diary:

". . . The station does a very clever job of propaganda and from what is put on the air one can gather that the English know exactly what they have destroyed and what not."

The success of *Soldatensender Calais* was confirmed by the Bavarian Ministry of the Interior in a message addressed on March 18, 1944, to Freiherr von Eberstein, the Munich chief of the *Sicherheitsdienst,* the intelligence service of the *Schutzstaffel* (SS). Found and translated after the war, the message said:

Since October 1943 increasingly frequent references are being made by the population to the transmissions of the radio station which calls itself *Soldatensender Calais* and concerning whose nationality people are not clear. The chief effect of the station's news transmissions, which have been described as psychologically excellent, emerges from its practice of giving absolutely unexceptionable information, which has also been carried verbatim in the German News Service and mixing in with it a number of isolated, more or less tendentious items. This has caused large portions of the population to believe that *Soldatensender Calais* was a German station, perhaps one of the many Soldatensender started up in the occupied territories also without anything about them being officially communicated to the population.

That the reports of the *Soldatensender Calais* often had a sharpness otherwise nowhere to be found in the German News Service was in some cases explained by the population on the following lines: "After all they cannot present the soldier at the front with the same propaganda as they sell us at home. They have to be more honest with the soldiers at the front."

Unable to convince listeners that the broadcasters were British propagandists, German officials ordered the station jammed. But, said the official report, many people were convinced that the jammer was "an enemy jammer attacking the 'German station.'"

German civilian stations usually went off the air when Allied bombers were detected so that the aircraft could not use broadcast signals as beacons. In less than a second, British engineers could switch frequencies and begin broadcasting on the silenced station, taking it over so swiftly that the listeners would not detect the break and would think they were listening to the actual station.

What they heard was a broadcast of fake news and announcements made to sound official. Real German radio stations warned that the enemy was broadcasting fake instructions and would precede authentic announcements by saying they were official. The British black broadcasters simply did the same, adding lies and preceding them with the assurance that they were official.

Impact on History: In World War II, psychological warfare came into its own. The black propaganda produced by the SOE demonstrated how the Allies were able to penetrate a totalitarian regime's control of propaganda and reach the German population.

To Messrs Blunt,
Bingham and Successors Ltd. You are
trying to make business in Netherlands
without our assistance. We think this
rather unfair in view of our long and
successful co-operation as your sole
agent. But never mind whenever you will
come to pay a visit to the Continent you
may be assured that you will be received
with the same care and result as all
those who you sent us before. So long.

The taunting broadcast, kept secret for years, that German Major Hans Giske
sent to London on All Fools Day 1944.

The Game Against England

CREATED: APRIL 1944
SUBJECT: WWII—THE
GERMAN MANIPULATION
OF A FAILED BRITISH
ESPIONAGE PLOT

32 | For weeks during World War II, Huub Lauwer, a Dutch patriot, was one of many prospective agents of the Special Operations Executive (SOE) who endured a course in "ungentlemanly warfare"—such as killing with knife and garrote. The training took place at an estate in the heart of England's New Forest. Lauwer also learned to parachute and to send and receive radio messages by Morse code. He was to be dropped into Holland as a radio operator for a resistance cell that had been formed by the SOE. An instructor told him there was a 95 percent certainty that he would be captured. The instructor was right.

"Set Europe ablaze!" Prime Minister Winston Churchill demanded after the creation of the SOE in July 1940. The SOE's official mission was sabotage, subversion, and the formation of secret military forces in German-occupied countries. While the SOE did perform those tasks, the organization is also bitterly remembered for what happened to Lauwer and his comrades in an intelligence catastrophe.

Many in Holland believed that what happened was a deliberate, but bungled, SOE attempt at deception. But documents released soon after the war showed that the SOE had merely bungled, responding to a masterful German operation with

A WWII radio of the type Allied agents in Nazi-occupied Europe—including those of the Englandspiel debacle—used to communicate with headquarters.

the official code name *Nordpol* (North Pole). German counterintelligence officers had another name: *Englandspiel* (the Game Against England). *Englandspiel* was run jointly by the military intelligence agency Abwehr and the Gestapo. The Germans also made use of Dutch traitors called *V-männer* (short for *Vertrauensmänner*, confidential agents).

Lauwer was captured in March 1942, soon after he parachuted into Holland. Forced to transmit to Britain in a code known to his captors, he used several techniques to disclose that he was under enemy control. Radio operators in Britain were not supposed to respond when they received those secret signals. But the operators did respond, bewildering Lauwer, who wondered why the receivers wanted him to keep sending messages when they ought to have realized that he had been captured.

Other Dutch agents who were captured failed to send certain signals, assuming that the receivers in Britain would interpret the lack of those signals as a warning sign that the agent had been captured and was transmitting under duress. Lauwer, like his fellow SOE agents, had been told that he might be forced to transmit for the Germans. But, as he recalled in 2004, the agents were told that "under no circumstances should we give away our security checks. I never did." The security checks were "signatures," hidden in messages, to confirm the agent's identity. The agents were also told to transmit certain "mistakes" in their real messages and, if captured and forced to keep transmitting, they were to omit the fake mistakes.

SOE believed that a large and effective underground had been set up in Holland because control officers were reading messages like this one: "The sabotage organisation as planned is now complete. It comprises five groups containing 62 cells and totalling some 420 men. These groups are now well equipped with stores and are ready for action." That, like all the other good-news messages, was a fake.

At SOE headquarters in London, cryptographer Leo Marks began to get suspicious. He knew that as much as 20 percent of the agent messages were "indecipherable." When he noticed that few indecipherable messages appeared in the Dutch agents' traffic, Marks deduced that Germans had taken over the network and were sending false—and perfect—messages.

Marks unsuccessfully tried to convince his superiors that the Dutch network was almost certainly under German control. His warnings went unheeded because of bureaucratic squabbling.

German counterintelligence officers, aware of the time and

place of SOE deliveries by parachute and small boat, captured agent after agent and grabbed thousands of guns, containers of ammunition and explosives, and even food and currency. The Germans also shot down 11 RAF aircraft that were dropping agents or materiel.

Finally, in August 1943, two captured agents escaped, made it to Spain, and then to Britain. But a German intelligence operative, posing as a Dutch agent, sent a message to London warning that the two escapees had defected and could not be trusted. The Dutch agents were imprisoned in Britain for giving aid to the enemy. Later in 1943, when other escaped agents told what had truly happened, the British released the original two and began understanding the immensity of the German deception. Of 56 SOE agents sent to Holland, only eight survived.

When it became obvious to the Germans that the game against England was over, Abwehr Maj. Hans Giskes decided to send one last message—uncoded. On All Fools' Day 1944, a radio operator in London received the taunting transmission shown on page 188. It would remain secret for decades.

(Note: The Blunt referred to in the transmission is not Anthony Blunt [see page 130]. Major Charles Blizard, head of the SOE's Dutch section, used the codename "Blunt." He was replaced by a Major Bingham.)

SOE's failure to detect the German takeover of the Dutch network produced postwar queries from the Dutch government, which did not accept the British claim that blunders caused the disaster. Documents declassified in 2004 indicated that the SOE, knowing Dutch agents had been captured, played along in order to analyze the intelligence mindset behind the false information sent by the Germans. When the Dutch Parliament investigated the incident in 1949 and asked for British records, a high-ranking British Foreign Office advised against disclosure, saying in a secret internal memo that "a really full explanation . . . would be to the highest degree embarrassing" and "would doubtless come as a shock not only to Dutch, but also to British public opinion . . . We feel that anything less than a full explanation would evoke a flood of questions and lead to the accusation that we were trying to conceal something (as indeed we would be doing) . . ."

Impact on History: Just as the British Double-Cross System paralyzed the German intelligence in Britain, the Game Against England wiped out British intellegence in the Netherlands. As a consequence, Germans prevented the rising of a large-scale resistance and maintained firm control of this country until the Allied liberation near the end of the war.

FIVE

Espionage Accidents

DURING WORLD WAR II, POSTERS IN AMERICA AND BRITAIN CARRIED A WARNING to careless patriots: "Loose lips sink ships." In a documentary movie version of the poster, a serviceman in a bar is overheard telephoning his girlfriend about his imminent departure, complete with time and ship's name. An enemy agent overhears the conversation, goes to his secret radio transmitter, and sends off the accidental intelligence. In the next scene, the ship is blown up, presumably by an alerted enemy submarine.

The first half of the scenario was all too true. Loose lips and mislaid documents did reveal secrets during World War II. In May 1944, for example, a major general told guests at a London dinner party that D-Day would come before June 15. He was overheard by shocked Army officers who promptly reported the incident. The general was demoted and packed off to the United States, as was a Navy captain who had talked too much at another party.

In a bizarre mishap that occurred during the planning for D-Day, a U.S. Army sergeant accidentally sent a package of documents, some containing the target date and site of the invasion, to his sister. The family was of German descent and the sister lived in a German section of Chicago. When the package broke open in a Chicago post office, postal authorities saw Top Secret stamped on documents and called the FBI. Investigators cleared the soldier of espionage, though he was confined to his quarters until after D-Day. The FBI put everyone who had seen the papers under surveillance. On June 6, D-Day dawned with its secrets intact.

CIA officer Aldrich H. Ames, on his way to meet an agent, left his briefcase on a New York subway car. The briefcase's secrets included the name of the agent. The FBI recovered the briefcase, but counterintelligence officers had to wonder whether its contents had been compromised. Ames would later give the FBI a much greater source of worry by becoming a master spy for the Soviet Union (page 142).

Sometimes an accident is not an accident. General George Washington frequently let fake documents carelessly fall into the hands of British agents. His protégé, Marquis de Lafayette, used the technique during the siege of Yorktown in 1781. James Armistead, a slave who spied for Lafayette, became a double agent by slipping through the enemy lines and offering to spy for the British. He was told to go back and gather information on the location of American units. When Armistead returned to the British camp, he handed a British officer the crumpled paper, saying that he had found it on the side of a road. It was an order written by Lafayette to another general, telling him to move his men. The order was a fake, but the British reacted to it as if it were real.

And sometimes even declassified secret documents quietly regain their classified status. Researchers going through document folders in the gray boxes at the Archives are occasionally surprised to discover that an expected document isn't there. Instead, there is an inserted card that says "Access restricted. The item identified below has been withdrawn from this file." No explanation.

The mysterious disappearances were first discovered by an intelligence historian who noticed that documents he had copied years before had been withdrawn. The mystery was finally solved in 2006 by the National Security Archive, a private, independent, non-governmental organization located at George Washington University. The Archive reported that the CIA and other federal agencies had secretly reclassified more than 55,000 pages of previously declassified records. That sounded like 55,000 espionage accidents. But officials explained that sensitive documents were inadvertently (not accidentally) released during a "bulk declassification" under a President Clinton program designed to regularly release outdated secret documents.

Many of the pulled documents had already been published, including some that appear in the State Department's historical series, *Foreign Relations of the United States.* One of the "reclassified" documents was a CIA intelligence report, sent to President Truman on October 12, 1950, that said Chinese intervention in the Korean War was "not probable in 1950." Twelve days later, Chinese troops crossed the border into North Korea. The contents of the declassified report had been known for years before it was reclassified in October 2001. So officially, the 1950 report is once again a secret document.

"So-called 'espionage accidents,'" says a retired CIA case officer, "are more often colossal gaffes or blunders that may result in agents being compromised and in some cases lives lost. The descriptor 'accident' may understate the significance of the act. Blunders are not an option in human intelligence operations, but they do happen and often with terrible consequences."

General Robert E. Lee, commander of the Army of Northern Virginia.

Lee's Lost Order

CREATED: SEPTEMBER 1862
SUBJECT: CIVIL WAR—THE
ACCIDENTAL EXPOSURE OF
TOP-SECRET CONFEDERATE
BATTLE PLANS

33 | Company F of the 27th Indiana Regiment encamped in a meadow near Frederick, Maryland, on the morning of September 12, 1862. The regiment was part of Gen. George McClellan's Union Army, on the march in pursuit of Gen. Robert E. Lee's Army of Northern Virginia. Lee had invaded Maryland, drawing the Union Army from Washington and toward what he hoped to be a decisive battle. Lee had set down his strategy in Special Orders No. 191, which was marked "Confidential." Seven copies of the letter were sent out by courier to the army's major commands.

On the afternoon of September 13, Union Army Corporal Barton W. Mitchell was strolling around the meadow, talking to Private John Campbell, when Mitchell spotted something lying in the meadow clover.

He picked up three cigars wrapped in a piece of paper bearing the words *Confidential* and *Hd Qrs Army of Northern Va Sept 9th 1862 Special Order No. 191*. The paper was addressed to Maj. Gen. D. H. Hill. Mitchell, recognizing that he had picked up an important document, put it in the hands of his first sergeant, who sent it up the army chain of command until it reached Gen. McClellan. Excitedly, he telegraphed President Lincoln: "I think Lee has made a gross mistake . . . I have all

Special orders from General Lee to his major commands, which fell into enemy hands.
The result was the Battle of Antietam, the bloodiest battle in American history.

enemy at Harpers Ferry & vicinity.

VI Genl. Walker with his division, after accomplishing the object in which he is now engaged will cross the Potomac at Cheeks Ford, ascend its right bank to Lovettsville take possession of London heights if practicable by Friday morning Keys Ford on his left and the road between the end of the mountain and the Potomac on his right. He will as far as practicable co-operate with Genl. McLaws & Genl. Jackson in intercepting the retreat of the enemy

VII Genl. D. H. Hills division will form the rear guard of the army, pursuing the road taken by the main body. The reserve arty. Ordnance & supply trains will precede Genl. Hill.

VIII Genl. Stuart will detach a squadron of cavy. to accompany the commands of Genls. Longstreet, Jackson & McLaws & with the main body of the cavy. will cover the route of the army & bring up all stragglers that may have been left behind.

IX The commands of Genls. Jackson, McLaws & Walker after accomplishing the objects for which they have been detached will join the main body of the army at Boonsboro or Hagerstown

X Each Regt. on the march will habitually carry its axes in the Regt. ordnance wagons, for the use of the men at their encampments to procure wood &c.

By command of Genl. R. E. Lee
R. H. Chilton
A. A. Genl.

the plans of the Rebels and will catch them in their own trap if my men are equal to the emergency."

But it would be McClellan who was not equal to the find, an extraordinary intelligence coup of the Civil War. He held in his hand detailed battle plans (see reproductions of the originals on the preceding pages) that had come directly from Lee:

The Army will resume its march to-morrow, taking the Hagerstown road. General Jackson's command will form the advance, and after passing Middletown, with such portions as he may select, take the route toward Sharpsburg, cross the Potomac at the most convenient point, and by Friday night take possession of the Baltimore and Ohio Railroad, capture such of the enemy as may be at Martinsburg, and intercept such as may attempt to escape from Harper's Ferry.

General Longstreet's command will pursue the same road as far as Boonsboro', where it will halt with the reserve, supply, and baggage trains of the army.

General McLaws with his own division and that of General R. H. Anderson, will follow General Longstreet; on reaching Middletown he will take the route to Harper's Ferry, and by Friday morning possess himself of the Maryland Heights and endeavor to capture the enemy at Harper's Ferry and vicinity.

General D.H. Hill's division will form the rearguard of the army, pursuing the road taken by the main body. The reserve artillery, ordnance, and supply trains, etc., will precede General Hill.

By command of General R.E. Lee.

McClellan, who had about 56,000 troops, estimated that Lee had 120,000 men (three times the actual count). As usual,

McClellan moved slowly and cautiously, hardly exploiting his knowledge of Lee's strategy.

The armies clashed at Sharpsburg, along Antietam Creek, in a battle that began early on the morning of September 17. By the end of that bloodiest day in American military history, at least 5,750 men were dead and 17,300 wounded. Union Maj. Gen. Joseph Hooker later wrote that "every stalk of corn in the northern and greater part of the field was cut as closely as could have been done with a knife, and the slain lay in rows precicely [sic] as they had stood in their ranks a few moments before."

That night, Lee ordered campfires to be lit along a ridge as camouflage, and he and his survivors slipped away in the darkness.

Not until 1886 did Corporal Mitchell receive credit for finding the lost order. He had gone from the clover meadow to the killing fields of Antietam. Wounded in battle, he never recovered. He died in 1868.

Impact on History: Possession of Lee's order gave McClellan the chance to strike at Lee's defeated, reeling army in a move that could have won the war. McClellan missed the chance, but Antietam was the victory that Lincoln believed he needed in order to declare his Emancipation Proclamation: As of January 1, 1863, slaves would be "forever free" in all states still in rebellion.

General Judson Kilpatrick, who brainstormed and led the raid on Richmond that resulted in the slaying of Col. Ulric Dahlgren and the disclosure of the Dahlgren Papers.

Papers from a Corpse

CREATED: FEBRUARY 1864
SUBJECT: CIVIL WAR—EXPOSURE
OF AN ILL-FATED UNION EXPE-
DITION AND THE DISCOVERY
OF THE DAHLGREN PAPERS

34 | In February 1864, when the armies of North and South were in hibernation along opposite banks of the Rapidan River, Brigadier Gen. Judson Kilpatrick, a rash, 28-year-old cavalryman, presented a bold plan to President Lincoln. Kilpatrick proposed leading a raid into Richmond to free Union soldiers from prisons so horrible that men were dying at a rate of about 50 a day. Lincoln approved the raid, leaving the details to Kilpatrick and his superiors.

On February 28, Kilpatrick rode out of his camp at Stevensburg, Virginia, leading 4,000 mounted men southward to Richmond, about 80 miles away. Another 500 cavalrymen swung southwest to enter Richmond from the west. That force was led by Col. Ulric Dahlgren, the 21-year-old son of Rear Adm. John Dahlgren, a friend of Lincoln.

Dahlgren rode with a crutch strapped to his saddle. He had been wounded in a skirmish in Maryland after the battle of Gettysburg in July 1863, and his right leg had been amputated below the knee. He was to link up with Kilpatrick in Richmond, freeing men from one prison while Kilpatrick liberated inmates at another, larger prison.

The raid was a disaster. Sleet and snow pelted the riders. A runaway slave who was supposed to guide Dahlgren failed to

Head Qrs. Army of No Va.
1st April 1864

Major General George G. Meade
Comdg Army of the Potomac

General:

I am instructed to bring to your notice two papers found upon the body of Colonel U. Dahlgren, who was killed while commanding a part of the Federal Cavalry during the late expedition of Genl. Kilpatrick. To enable you to understand the subject fully, I have the honor to enclose photographic copies of the papers referred to, one of which is an address to his officers & men bearing the official signature of Col. Dahlgren, and the other not signed, contains more detailed explanations of the purpose of the expedition, and more specific instructions as to its execution.

In the former this passage occurs: "We hope to release the prisoners from Belle Island

*Letter from General Robert E. Lee to General George G. Meade,
referring to and excerpting the Dahlgren papers and inquiring whether
the U.S. government had sanctioned the plot.*

first, and having seen them fairly started, we will cross the James River into Richmond, destroying the bridges after us, and exhorting the released prisoners to destroy and burn the hateful city and do not allow the Rebel Leader Davis and his traitorous crew to escape. The prisoners must render great assistance, as you cannot leave your tanks too far, or become too much scattered, or you will be lost."

Among the instructions contained in the second paper are the following:

"The bridges once secured and the prisoners loose and over the River, the bridges will be secured and the City destroyed - The men must keep together and well in hand, and once in the City, it must be destroyed and Jeff Davis and Cabinet killed, Pioneers will go along with Combustible material"

In obedience to my instructions, I beg leave respectfully to inquire whether the lead him to a river ford. Believing the ex-slave had deliberately misled him, Dahlgren ordered him hanged from a nearby tree. Kilpatrick and his men made it to the outskirts of Richmond on March 1 and were fired on while waiting for Dahlgren. When Dahlgren did not appear, Kilpatrick's force retreated, pursued by Confederate cavalry. The puruit ended when Kilpatrick's force reached a main Union Army unit.

Dahlgren and his men rode for three days and nights—"only stopping long enough to feed our horses," a trooper remembered. Then, cut off from Kilpatrick, Dahlgren ordered the men to halt and build fires. Confederates, their approach muffled by the snow, ambushed the raiders. A volley wounded several men and killed Dahlgren. In the chaos that followed, some men escaped, but most of them were captured and taken to one of the prisons they had hoped to liberate.

A 13-year-old "Local Defense" boy, at the scene of the ambush, rushed to Dahlgren's body and made an accidental discovery that has raised questions in the North and South ever since. The boy, searching Dahlgren's bloodied uniform, found a cigar case, some papers, and a memorandum book containing other loose papers. He handed the papers to his military leader, a school-master, who scanned the documents and then took them on to Richmond—and to history.

The Dahlgren Papers, as they became known, were published in the *Richmond Daily Dispatch* on March 5, 1864. The *Dispatch* gave a vivid account of the ambush, ending it with this sentence: "The body of Dahlgren also fell into their hands, and on his person was found the papers which we publish below, disclosing the diabolical schemes which the party had in view in making the late, and to them, disastrous raid."

The first of the papers, labeled "Address to the Officers and Men," was a copy of a stirring speech Dahlgren made to his men: "You have been selected from brigades and regiments as a picked command to attempt a desperate undertaking . . . which will cause the prayers of our fellow soldiers, now confined in loath-some prisons, to follow you and yours wherever you may go . . ."

The published speech was followed by a note: "The following special orders were written on a similar sheet of paper, and on detached slips, the whole disclosing the diabolical plans of the leaders of the expedition":

SPECIAL ORDERS AND INSTRUCTIONS.
Guides — Pioneers (with oakum, turpentine, and torpedoes)—
Signal Officer—Quartermaster—Commissary:
Scouts and pickets—men in rebel uniform:

These will remain on the north bank and move down with the force on the south bank, not getting ahead of them; and if the communication can be kept up without giving alarm, it must be done; but everything depends upon a surprise, and no one must be allowed to pass ahead of the column. Information must be gathered in regard to the crossings of the river, so that should we be repulsed on the south side we will know where to recross at the nearest point. All mills must be burned, and the canal destroyed; and also everything which can be used by the rebels must be destroyed, including the boats on the river.--Should a ferry boat be seized, and can be worked, have it moved down. Keep the force on the south side posted of any important movement of the enemy, and in case of danger some of the scouts must swim the river and bring us information. As we approach the city, the party must take great care that they do not get ahead of the other party on the south side, and must conceal themselves and watch our movements. We will try and secure the bridge to the city (one mile below Belle Isle,) and release the prisoners at the same time. If we do not succeed, they must then dash down, and we will try and carry the bridge from each side.

When necessary, the men must be filed through the woods and along the river bank. The bridges once secured, and the prisoners loose and over the river, the bridges will be secured and the city destroyed. The men must keep together and well in band, and once in the city it must be destroyed, and Jeff Davis and Cabinet killed.

Pioneers will go along with combustible material. The officer must use his discretion about the time of assisting us. Horses and cattle, which we do not need immediately, must be shot rather than left. Everything on the Canal and elsewhere, of service to the rebels, must be destroyed. As Gen. Custer may follow me, be careful not to give a false alarm.

The signal officer must be prepared to communicate at night by rockets, and in other things pertaining to his department. The Quartermasters and Commissaries must be on the look-out for their departments, and see that there are no delays on their account.

The engineer officer will follow to survey the road as we pass over it, &c.

The pioneers must be prepared to construct a bridge or destroy one. They must have plants of oakum and turpentine for burning, which will be rolled in soaked balls and given to the men to burn when we get in the city. Torpedoes will only be used by the pioneers for destroying the main bridges, &c. They must be prepared to destroy railroads. Men will branch off to the right with a few pioneers and destroy the bridges and railroads south of Richmond, and then join us at the city. They must be well prepared with torpedoes, &c. The line of Falling Creek is probably the best to work along, or, as they approach the city, Goode's Creek; so that no reinforcements can come up on any cars. No one must be allowed to pass ahead for fear of communicating news. Rejoin the command with all haste, and, if cut off, cross the river above Richmond and rejoin us. Men will stop at Bellona Arsenal and totally destroy it, and anything else but hospitals; then follow on and rejoin the command at Richmond with all haste, and, if cut off, cross the river and rejoin us. As Gen. Custer may follow me, be careful and not give a false alarm.

Near the end of the newspaper story was this: "We understand that the body of this cold blooded leader of the Yankee raiders, who contemplated the capture and destruction of this city, will be brought to Richmond.—The object in bringing it here, we were unable to learn."

The object seemed to be vengeance. Dahlgren's body had already been desecrated. His wooden leg had been taken away as a souvenir. Someone cut off a finger to steal a ring. When his body was put on display in Richmond, his uniform was gone; the corpse wore a white shirt and what seemed to be the trousers of a Confederate soldier. After being viewed, the body, under the orders of President Jefferson Davis, was buried in an unmarked grave.

News of Dahlgren's "special orders" swept through the South, enflaming civilians and soldiers and rousing demands for revenge. Gen Robert E. Lee intervened to prevent the execution of Dahlgren's captured men.

Shown on pages 206-207 of this chapter is a letter from Lee to Gen. Meade, quoting passages from the Dahlgren papers and requesting to know whether the U.S. Government and Dahlgren's superior officers had authorized such a plot. The treatment of Dahlgren's body infuriated Northerners, who also called for revenge. Lincoln and Union Army generals emphatically denied there were any plans to assassinate Southern leaders or torch Richmond. In the North, the "special orders" were judged a forgery perpetrated to fire up a people tiring of war. In the South, the forgery claims were denounced. The claims and counter-claims have never ceased.

Impact on History: The Dahlgren Papers undoubtedly produced a change in the ways of waging war, eventually leading to the concept of "total war" in the 20th century. No longer did gentlemanly officers fight with civility. No longer were civilians exempt from what became the doctrine of total war, as expressed by Gen. William Tecumseh Sherman, who in November 1864 began his flaming March to the Sea. The Union Army, he said, was now "not only fighting hostile armies, but a hostile people, and must make old and young, rich and poor, feel the hard hand of war."

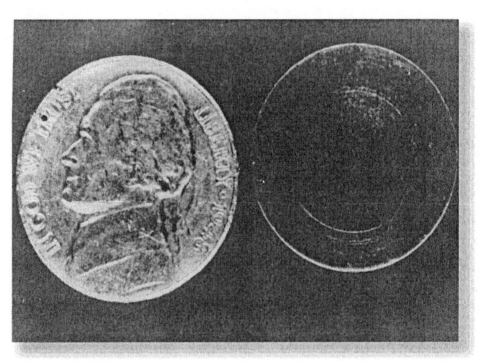

An FBI file photo of the hollow nickel that held a ciphered message.

The Hollow Nickel

CREATED: JUNE 1953
SUBJECT: THE COLD WAR—
ACCIDENTAL DISCOVERY OF AN
INGENIOUS SOVIET DEAD DROP

35 | Some espionage mistakes are drawn-out affairs. This accident starts with a newspaper boy in Brooklyn in 1953 and ends on a bridge in Berlin in 1962.

On the evening of June 22, 1953, a *Brooklyn Eagle* delivery boy was making the rounds of his customers, collecting payments. One of the customers did not have change to pay him for her papers. She handed him a dollar bill, and he went across the hall to see if anyone there could break it. The two women in the apartment went through their pocketbooks and found enough change. When the transaction was over, the newsboy had a few coins. One, a nickel, seemed oddly light. As he was balancing it on a finger, the coin fell to the floor—and came apart. Inside one of the pieces was a tiny photo of rows of numbers (shown, with the decipher, on the following pages).

The boy related the incident to a friend who happened to be the daughter of a New York City police officer, who told a detective, who told the FBI, who got the coin and photo from the boy. Only three days before the delivery boy was handed the hollow nickel, Ethel and Julius Rosenberg had been executed for espionage in Sing Sing Prison, 30 miles up the Hudson from New York. They had been convicted of giving U.S. atomic secrets to the Soviets during World War II. Soviet espionage was very much on the public mind.

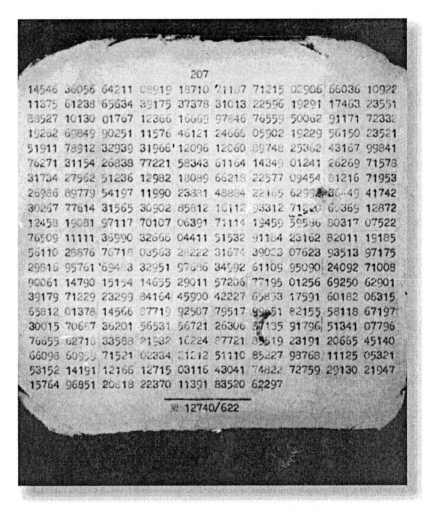

*The coded message that fell out of the hollow nickel, and (right) the completed
decoded message, later determined to be to a Soviet spy in the U.S. from his handler.*

1) WE CONGRATULATE YOU ON A SAFE ARRIVAL. WE CONFIRM
THE RECEIPT OF YOUR LETTER TO THE ADDRESS "V REPEAT V"
AND THE READING OF LETTER NUMBER 1. 2) FOR ORGANIZATION
OF COVER, WE GAVE INSTRUCTIONS TO TRANSMIT TO YOU THREE
THOUSAND IN LOCAL (CURRENCY). CONSULT WITH US PRIOR TO
INVESTING IT IN ANY KIND OF BUSINESS, ADVISING THE CHARACTER
OF THIS BUSINESS. 3) ACCORDING TO YOUR REQUEST, WE WILL
TRANSMIT THE FORMULA FOR THE PREPARATION OF SOFT FILM
AND NEWS SEPARATELY, TOGETHER WITH (YOUR) MOTHER'S
LETTER. 4) IT IS TOO EARLY TO SEND YOU THE GAMMAS
(MEANING HERE UNKNOWN, LITERALLY MUSICAL EXERCISES).
ENCIPHER SHORT LETTERS, BUT THE LONGER ONES MAKE
WITH INSERTIONS. ALL THE DATA ABOUT YOURSELF, PLACE
OF WORK, ADDRESS, ETC., MUST NOT BE TRANSMITTED IN ONE
CIPHER MESSAGE. TRANSMIT INSERTIONS SEPARATELY.
5) THE PACKAGE WAS DELIVERED TO YOUR WIFE PERSONALLY.
EVERYTHING IS ALL RIGHT WITH THE FAMILY. WE WISH YOU
SUCCESS. GREETINGS FROM THE COMRADES. NUMBER 1,
3RD OF DECEMBER.

The FBI quickly concluded that the message in photo form was the product of microphotography, which could reduce all the writing on a typical book page to an image the size of the dot at the end of this sentence. The process required special photographic equipment and was used mostly by spies. The hollow nickel was a clue to a spy network because microdot messages were usually produced in the headquarters of the spymaster and sent to his spies. Cryptanalysts went to work on the rows of numbers. The FBI Crime Laboratory, which had files on all typewriters manufactured in the United States, discovered that the numbers had been typed by a foreign-made typewriter.

The coin itself was made of two coins. The face was a 1948 Jefferson nickel with a tiny hole in the R of TRUST for insertion of a probe to pop the nickel open. The other side was from another nickel, which the FBI found to have been minted sometime between 1942 and 1945, when a wartime shortage of nickel forced the mint to use a copper-silver alloy.

Neither of the women who had found change for the newspaper boy could tell FBI agents how the hollow nickel had wound up in one of their pocketbooks. After a considerable amount of frustrating legwork, the investigators filed away the case of the hollow nickel. But they did not forget it.

A break finally came in May 1957, when KGB Lieut. Col. Reino Hayhanen defected and sought sanctuary in America. During his five years as a spy in the United States, he said, he lived under the stolen identity of an American of Finnish descent. He had a case officer, codenamed Mikhail, in New York City. To contact Mikhail, Hayhanen stuck a red thumbtack into a signboard near the Tavern on the Green in Central Park. If he suspected he was under surveillance, he stuck a white thumbtack on the board. To keep dangerous face-to-face meetings at a minimum, he and Mikhail used dead drops, such as lampposts, phone booths, hollowed-out bolts—and hollowed-out coins.

With the aid of Hayhanen, the FBI cracked the microdot message, which apparently had been sent to him shortly after he arrived in the United States.

"Mikhail," under diplomatic cover in the Soviet United Nations Delegation, was replaced by "Mark," who had slipped across the Canadian border in the late 1940s and had been spying ever since. Clues from Hayhanen led the FBI to a Brooklyn photographic studio operated under the name Emil R. Goldfus. Hayhanen identified him as "Mark." He was in fact Rudolf Ivanovich Abel, a KGB master spy.

The FBI described Abel's studio and hotel room as "virtual museums of modern espionage equipment," containing shortwave radios, cipher pads, equipment for producing microdots, and an array of hollowed objects, including a shaving brush and a pair of cuff links.

Through his trial testimony, Hayhanen helped to convict Abel of espionage in 1957. He was sentenced to prison for 30 years. Abel remained in prison until 1962, when he was exchanged for U-2 pilot Gary Powers, who had been shot down over the Soviet Union on May 1, 1960, and after a show trial was sentenced to 10 years for spying. On Feb. 10, 1962, in a spy swap arranged by their respective nations, Powers and Abel walked to freedom from each side of the Glienicker Bridge that symbolically spanned East and West Berlin.

Impact on History: The Abel-Powers spy swap gave the Soviet Union and the United States a precedent for similar prisoner exchanges that eased Cold War tensions. The Glienicker Bridge became known as the Spy Bridge, symbolizing the conflict and occasional concessions that marked East-West relations.

SIX

In Defense
of the Realm

In 1914, to guide Britons through the Great War, Parliament passed the Defence of the Realm Act, which told people what they could not do in time of war. Following the British example, the United States in 1917 passed the Espionage Act, which was aimed not only at spies but at anyone who impeded the war effort. Both laws showed that even a democratic nation had the right to demand extraordinary obedience during a war—an idea that would continue in the Cold War and the present-day war on terror.

The British legislation gave the government the power to punish critics of the war and to control civilian behavior. A "No Treating Order," for example, prohibited pub patrons from buying alcoholic drinks for others. The government banned a novel that was considered anti-war and prosecuted the book's British publisher. The American law forbade anyone to "willfully make or convey false reports or false statements with intent to interfere with the operation or success of the military or naval forces of the United States or to promote the success of its enemies and whoever, when the United States is at war." Socialist leader Eugene V. Debs denounced the Espionage Act, was tried under that law, and was sentenced to 10 years in prison.

The idea that a nation needed to defend itself even from its own citizens stemmed from the age-old belief that nations, including democracies like America and Britain, could take extreme actions to preserve themselves. The actions might be wars or secret agreements with other nations. Those covertly negotiated agreements could be so secret that they could not be told to the state's own citizens. Nor did the state reveal its own secret breaking of its own laws.

When World War II ended, Allied intelligence services began a search for Germans who would be useful in the East-West struggle that quickly became the Cold War. One of the Nazis recruited by the Office of Strategic Services (OSS), wartime predecessor of the CIA, for example, was an intelligence officer in the SD, *Sicherheitsdienst*, the Security Service. "To avoid any accusation that we are working with a Nazi reactionary," an OSS officer wrote in a secret memo, ". . . I believe that we should keep our contact with him as indirect as possible . . ."

Between 1945 and 1955, according to a National Archives report to Congress, 765 scientists, engineers, and technicians were allowed into the United States under secret arrangements that bypassed U.S. immigration and war-crimes laws. The report said that "at least half, and perhaps as many as 80 percent, of the imported specialists were former Nazi Party members." Most of them went to work on the development of guided missiles and intercontinental ballistic missiles.

A secret treaty is another form of national defense. The U.S. Constitution takes treaties seriously, making them part of "the supreme law of the land" after they are approved by two-thirds of the Senate. Treaties historically draw on the skills of State Department diplomats. But since 1947, much of the critical decisions on the foreign relations of the United States have come from recommendations of the National Security Council (NSC), which operates in secrecy for the president.

Harry S Truman, the first president served by the NSC, said after he retired that he never approved any "cloak and dagger operations." But his first NSC report—Top Secret like all significant NSC documents—authorized "covert action" to influence the Italian elections so that communists would not gain control of that nation. Later NSC authorizations made covert action an instrument of national policy.

The NSC document that defined the modern defense of the realm was NSC 68, which was presented to Truman in April 1950. "The issues that face us are momentous, involving the fulfillment or destruction not only of this Republic but of civilization itself," the report said. To defend America, the NSC recommended that the nation "encourage and promote the gradual retraction of undue Russian power and influence" by measures "covert or overt." NSC 68 was declassified in 1977, according to the Department of State. But a historian could not get background papers on it until 1998.

As the following documents show, defense of the realm and covert actions may mean the secret defense of a queen in 1586 or defense of a Soviet satellite regime in 1981.

The cipher sent to the imprisoned Mary, Queen of Scots by Anthony Babington,
supplying details of a plot to free her and assassinate Queen Elizabeth I.

The Beer Barrel Letters

[
CREATED: JULY 1586
SUBJECT: ASSASSINATION PLOT
AGAINST QUEEN ELIZABETH I
]

36 | Sir Francis Walsingham was more than the spymaster of Queen Elizabeth I. He was also master of counterintelligence and covert operations, particularly those aimed at ridding Elizabeth of her most dangerous enemy, Mary, Queen of Scots. In 1584, at a time when loyalty to monarch and nation were intertwined, the Queen's Privy Council gave Walsingham a new weapon—the Bond of Association, an ancestor of the Defence of the Realm Act: She was to be defended "against all Estates, Dignities, and earthly Powers." And anyone who intended to harm her "or claim succession to the Crown by the untimely death of Her Majesty" would be executed.

If Walsingham could prove that Mary was plotting to assassinate Elizabeth and claim her crown, then, under the Bond of Association, Mary could be tried and put to death. Walsingham knew that he would get his proof just by waiting for the right moment and the right plot. Plots naturally swirled around Mary, a Catholic Queen driven from her throne in Scotland and held by Elizabeth since 1567 as a royal prisoner. To many English Catholics, she was their legitimate queen, a belief endorsed by England's foes, Catholic France and Catholic Spain.

In December 1585, Gilbert Clifford, a suspect in an anti-Elizabeth conspiracy, agreed, under threat of death, to become a double agent for Walsingham. Following instructions, Clifford told another member of the plot, a French diplomat, that he had found a foolproof way to communicate with Mary, who was confined to Chartley Hall, a moated and battlemented mansion in Staffordshire. Clifford said he had arranged with a brewer to smuggle letters to and from Mary in a waterproof packet slipped inside the stopper of the barrel of beer delivered weekly to Chartley. Another double agent informed Mary of the beer-barrel delivery system, which she promptly began using by writing encrypted letters to supporters in Spain and France. All letters, of course, were intercepted and read by Walsingham's men, who included a "Decypherer."

One of Mary's devoted followers was Anthony Babington, a 25-year-old Catholic from a noble family. On July 6, 1586, he wrote a letter about what would be called the Babington Plot. In the letter he said that he would lead a band of men to free her. He also wrote that he knew six noble gentlemen "who for the zeal they bear to the Catholic cause and your Majesty's service will undertake that tragical execution"—the assassination of Queen Elizabeth.

Babington signed the encrypted letter (shown on page 222) and later, after being forced to confess by Walsingham, acknowledged writing it.

Mary replied in a long letter in which she praised Babington for his work and asked for details about plans for the envisioned invasion—by "the Low Countries, Spain and France"—that would put her on the throne. "Fail not to burn this present quickly," she added at the end of the letter. However, the alleged copy sent on to Babington also contained a highly incriminating postscript that asked for the names of the six gentlemen who were to assassinate Elizabeth. There is little doubt that Walsingham's expert cryptanalyst and forger, Thomas Phelippes, decrypted the original letter, made a copy, and added the incriminating postscript.

Walsingham's agents and double agents easily found the conspirators. On September 13 and 14, Babington and six others were placed on trial and sentenced to be hanged, drawn and quartered, the punishment for high treason. Two days later, seven other conspirators were tried and given the same sentence. On September 20, the first seven were individually dragged to a gallows, hanged, then taken down while still alive and disemboweled. Queen Elizabeth, supposedly shocked by the savagery of the sentence, ordered that the remaining conspirators be hanged until dead.

Walsingham now had all the evidence he needed to put Mary on trial and convict her of plotting the assassination. She denied knowing Babington and accused Walsingham of forging her incriminating letter to Babington. She was convicted on October 25 and was sentenced to death. Elizabeth, reluctant to kill a royal person, delayed authorizing the execution. Under pressure from the Privy Council, she finally signed Mary's death warrant and on February 8, 1587, Mary, Queen of Scots, was beheaded.

Impact on History: The execution of Mary, a Stuart, assured Elizabeth's continued reign, known as England's glorious age. The Tudor dynasty ended when Elizabeth died in 1603. She was succeeded by Mary's son, known as James I of England, VI of Scotland.

SIR EDWARD GREY TO M. CAMBON.

(Sykes-Picot Agreement).

Foreign Office, May 16, 1916.

Your Excellency,

I have the honour to acknowledge the receipt of Your Excellency's note of the 9th instant, stating that the French Government accept the limits of a future Arab State, or Confederation of States, and of those parts of Syria where French interests predominate, together with certain conditions attached thereto, such as they result from recent discussions in London and Petrograd on the subject.

I have the honour to inform Your Excellency in reply that the acceptance of the whole project, as it now stands, will involve the abdication of considerable British interests, but since His Majesty's Government recognise the advantage to the general cause of the Allies entailed in producing a more favourable internal political situation in Turkey, they are ready to accept the arrangement now arrived at, provided that the co-operation of the Arabs is secured, and that the Arabs fulfil the conditions and obtain the towns of Homs, Hama, Damascus, and Aleppo.

It is accordingly understood between the French and British Governments --

1. That France and Great Britain are prepared to recognise and uphold an independent Arab State, or a Confederation of Arab States, in the areas (a) and (b) marked on the annexed map, under the suzerainty of an Arab chief. That in area (a) France, and in area (b) Great Britain, shall have priority of right of enterprise and local loans. That in area (a) France, and in area (b) Great Britain, shall alone supply advisers or foreign functionaries at the request of the Arab State

The first page of the Sykes-Picot Agreement, which divided the Middle East into French and British "spheres of influence."

A Map for the Mideast

CREATED: MAY 1916
SUBJECT: BRITISH AND
FRENCH DIVISION OF
THE MIDDLE EAST

37 | T. E. Lawrence, who would become the legendary Lawrence of Arabia, was a young British military intelligence officer in Egypt in 1916 when diplomats of Britain and France were secretly drawing a new map of the Middle East. They were looking toward an Allied victory in the Great War, which would end the Ottoman Empire's reign over the region. Lawrence, stoking an Arab revolt against the Ottoman Turks, had promised the Arab leaders that after the war Britain would give them their own nation. He did not know about the new map, however.

The map showed "spheres" of British and French influence. There was no Arab nation on the map, though the agreement mentioned "an independent Arab State" under British or French "protection." Lawrence's Arabs kept fighting the Turks, knowing nothing of the map and the agreement. When the secret was exposed in 1917, the Arab distrust of the West took root.

The secret was revealed by Vladimir Ilich Lenin, leader of the Russian Revolution of 1917. The document, made public to embarrass the Allies, showed that Russia had later been added as a receiver of a part of the Ottoman Empire. But Russia's pullout from the war meant that Lenin's Bolsheviks would not share in the victory.

The accord was known as the Sykes-Picot Agreement, after the diplomats who signed it on May 16, 1916: Mark Sykes for Britain and François-Georges Picot for France. Britain received an area near Haifa, control of Palestine and Jordan, along with areas around the Persian Gulf and Baghdad; France was handed part of Turkey, territory encompassing Syria and Lebanon, and northern Iraq. Jerusalem was to be governed by an international administration. The two nations would determine the borders of countries in the region. Here are excerpts from the agreement (the first page of which is shown on page 226):

It is accordingly understood between the French and British governments:

That France and great Britain are prepared to recognize and protect an independent Arab State or a confederation of Arab states (a) and (b) marked on the annexed map, under the suzerainty of an Arab chief. That in area (a) France, and in area (b) great Britain, shall have priority of right of enterprise and local loans. That in area (a) France, and in area (b) great Britain, shall alone supply advisers or foreign functionaries at the request of the Arab state or confederation of Arab states.

That in the blue area France, and in the red area great Britain, shall be allowed to establish such direct or indirect administration or control as they desire and as they may think fit to arrange with the Arab state or confederation of Arab states.

That in the brown area there shall be established an international administration, the form of which is to be decided upon after consultation with Russia, and subsequently in consultation with the other allies, and the representatives of the sheriff of mecca.

That great Britain be accorded (1) the ports of Haifa and acre, (2) guarantee of a given supply of water from the tigres and euphrates in area (a) for area (b) . . .

That Haifa shall be a free port as regards the trade of France, her dominions and protectorates, and there shall be no discrimination in port charges or facilities as regards french shipping and french goods. There shall be freedom of transit for french goods through Haifa and by the British railway through the brown area.

That in area (a) the Baghdad railway shall not be extended southwards beyond Mosul, and in area (b) northwards beyond Samarra, until a railway connecting Baghdad and aleppo via the euphrates valley has been completed, and then only with the concurrence of the two governments.

The British and french government, as the protectors of the Arab state, shall agree that they will not themselves acquire and will not consent to a third power acquiring territorial possessions in the Arabian peninsula . . .

It is agreed that measures to control the importation of arms into the Arab territories will be considered by the two governments . . .

Sykes had also been secretly negotiating with representatives of the Zionist movement, founded to create a homeland for Jews. British acceptance of the negotiations came in the form of a letter from the British foreign secretary, Arthur James Lord Balfour, to Lord Rothschild, a Zionist leader. The Balfour Declaration was made public at about the same time as Lenin's disclosure of the-Sykes-Picot Agreement, adding to the distrust of Arab leaders who had not been consulted.

Impact on History: The Sykes-Picot Agreement became the basis for the postwar Allied conferences that finally settled the parceling out of the Ottoman Empire along the lines desired by Britain and France. The Sykes-Picot map is at the root of the disputed, war-torn geography of today's Middle East.

Joseph Patrick Kennedy, U.S. ambassador to Britian during the outset of WWII, strongly believed that Britain would fall to Germany, an unpopular view with leaders who felt American aid could turn the tide of the war.

An Ambassador's Doubts

CREATED: NOVEMBER 1939
SUBJECT: WWII—PREDICTIONS
THAT BRITAIN WAS BOUND TO FALL
TO THE GERMANS

38 | Joseph Patrick Kennedy, a supporter of Franklin D. Roosevelt's 1932 bid for the presidency, was an ambitious Boston millionaire appointed by Roosevelt to be chairman of the new Security and Exchange Commission. Kennedy's success at running that commission, and later the Federal Maritime Commission, led to his being given a reward. In December 1937 Roosevelt selected him to be ambassador to the Court of St. James, the honorific title for U. S. ambassador to Britain.

Britain at first welcomed Kennedy, a brash, all-American envoy in contrast to the usual stuffy diplomat. But, after war began in September 1939, Kennedy lost popularity, except in the British class that favored appeasing Hitler rather than going to war against him. When war came, Kennedy began assuring Roosevelt that Britain yearned for peace (see one such letter on pages 232-33).

After the German blitzkrieg swept across Europe in 1940 and Britain stood alone, Kennedy predicted a British defeat. But now Winston Churchill was prime minister—and a growing friendship was developing between him and Roosevelt. While Kennedy's reports grew more pessimistic and isolationist, Churchill was telling Roosevelt that Britain could be saved by American aid.

Roosevelt reached out to William J. Donovan, a favorite Republican, to provide a new view of the war. Donovan was a

London, November 3, 1939

Dear Mr. President,

I thought you would be interested in getting some
of the leaflets that were dropped by the British Air
Force in Germany; you might like them for a scrap book.
Strangely enough, at the minute they are very scarce in
England. I guess they took all they had on their flying
expeditions. I suppose you have heard the story about
one of the airmen who returned a couple of hours after
his colleagues on one of these leaflet-dropping parties
and the Commander said to him, "Where have you been all
this time?" "Well," said the young airman, "things were
so quiet over there, I started tucking them under the
doors." The purpose of this being to demonstrate their
complete disregard of the German anti-aircraft fire.

Make no mistake, there is a very definite under-
current in this country for peace and I think that it
is going to make itself felt by pressure on the Government to set forth definitely their war aims, because the
group who are anxious for peace feel that when those aims
are set forth, it will be apparent to the world, and
particularly to the English and French, that they are
fighting for something they probably never can attain.
It is by no means a popular war and although everybody
hates Hitler, they still don't want to be finished
economically, financially, politically and socially,
which they are beginning to suspect will be their fate
if the war goes on very long. My own impression is that
if the war stays in the state it is now, this under-
current will get stronger and stronger here. Of course,
it is impossible to set forth in despatches or in cables
just what I sense from my close observation of the
Treasury's position and my talks with the top-side
people, but perhaps I will have a chance to tell you
that personally.

The President,
    The White House.

*One of Joseph Patrick Kennedy's early letters to Roosevelt, in which he sets forth
a British yearning for peace. His increasingly defeatist attitude towards Britain's fate
in the war would eventually estrange him from Roosevelt and Churchill.*

-2-

One of the things I have particularly in mind is
your slant on the Churchill situation. Remember, Churchill
has in America a couple of very close friends who definitely are not on our team. This is a very important aspect of the situation, if by any chance there is a change
of Government in this Country.

There have been a great number of things done for
important interests in America during the last two months
right here in London, and they will be important to know
when we consider what the political criticisms are likely
to be over the course of 1940.

I am enclosing a letter from Lord Beaverbrook and we
are sending by the same pouch a couple of pictures that he
is sending you. He was terribly impressed by his talks
with you and he definitely considers that only one man
can save the world, not only in attaining peace, but in
planning for the future, and that man is yourself. If he
had his way, he would like to turn over the British Empire
to you to straighten out. I think I know what your answer
would be -- that you have troubles yourself straightening
out the one you've got. At any rate, at the minute, you
are a combination of the Holy Ghost and Jack Dempsey.

Incidentally, Beaverbrook told me that in his conversations with you, you were most complimentary in discussing
me and I am deeply grateful to you for this. One's influence in this Country is primarily dependent on how they
think one stands with the President.

There isn't much political news nowadays to be elicited
from any of the Cabinet Ministers, because there just isn't
any news. Until Germany indicates some new line of action,
things will be very dead here.

With my warmest regards to you all, I am,

Sincerely yours,

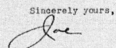

William J. Donovan believed that American support could save Britain, and he set in motion the aid the British needed to hold out against Germany during the Blitz.

prominent Wall Street lawyer and a World War I hero who had received the Medal of Honor. In July 1940 Roosevelt sent Donovan to Britain, a move that Kennedy strongly opposed. Churchill met him, set up an audience with King George VI and Queen Elizabeth, and arranged for Donovan to be briefed by ranking British military and intelligence officials. As a British historian later wrote, Donovan "helped set in motion the wheels leading to the development of initial intelligence cooperation between the two countries."

The trip convinced Donovan that with American aid Britain could hold out against Germany. His report undoubtedly helped convince Roosevelt to go through with the unprecedented deal that swapped 50 aging U.S. destroyers for the rights to several British bases in the Western Hemisphere.

German bombs were falling on London every night while Kennedy, fuming over the Roosevelt-Churchill partnership, continued to insist that Britain was doomed. "The Blitz," as Britons called it, had begun in September 1940 and would continue until May 1941. By mid-October more than 250,000 Londoners had been bombed out of their homes. In America, radio and newsreel coverage of the Blitz produced a wave of sympathy for the undaunted Britons and revulsion toward Germany's relentless bombing.

The Blitz, however, only intensified Kennedy's pessimistic reports. In November, publication of an interview with two American journalists effectively ended his ambassadorial career. "Democracy is finished in England," he said, adding that Britain was not fighting for democracy anyway. "That's the bunk. She's fighting for self-preservation, just as we will if it comes to us . . ." Kennedy stepped down as ambassador, and back in the United States he campaigned against America's escalating aid to Britain.

Roosevelt, in a letter written in February 1941, summed up Kennedy's philosophy: ". . . He has a positive horror of any changes in the present methods of life in America. To him, the future of a small capitalistic class is safer under a Hitler than under a Churchill. This is sub-conscious on his part and he does not admit it."

Impact on History: The importance of this document lies in the effects it *didn't* have. Kennedy's advocacy of appeasement fell on deaf ears in Washington, and Roosevelt's approval of the lend-lease program helped Britain hang on until the United States formally entered the war. Moreover, Donovan's mission for Roosevelt launched his career in intelligence. He became the head of the wartime Office of Strategic Services and saw the need for a peacetime intelligence agency. The CIA, which originally was staffed by many OSS veterans, became his legacy.

or seven million Poles in the United States. As I said
in Tehran, in general I am in favor of the Curzon line.
Most Poles, like the Chinese, want to save face.

Stalin:

(interrupting) Who will save face, the Poles in Poland
or the emigre Poles?

President:

The Poles would like East Prussia and part of Germany.
It would make it easier for me at home if the Soviet
Government could give something to Poland. I raised the
question of giving them Lvov at Tehran. It has now been
suggested that the oil lands in the southwest of Lvov
might be given them. I am not making a definite statement but I hope that Marshal Stalin can make a gesture
in this direction.

But the most important matter is that of a permanent
government for Poland. Opinion in the United States is
against recognition of the Lublin government on the
ground that it represents a small portion of the Polish
people. What people want is the creation of a government
of national unity to settle their internal differences.
A government which would represent all five major parties
(names them) is what is wanted. It may interest Marshal
Stalin that I do not know any of the London or of the
Lublin government. Mikolajczyk came to Washington and
I was greatly impressed by him. I felt that he was an
honest man.

The main suggestion I want to make is that there be
created an ad interim government which will have the
support of the majority of the Polish people. There are
many ways of creating such a government. One of the
many suggestions is the possibility of creating a
presidency council made up of a small number of men who
would be the controlling force ad interim to set up a
more permanent government. I make this suggestion as
from the distance of three thousand miles. Sometimes
distance is an advantage. We want a Poland that will be
thoroughly friendly to the Soviet for years to come.
This is essential.

Stalin:

(interrupting) Friendly not only to the Soviet but all
three allies.

                                                    President:

The page of the transcript from Yalta in which FDR broaches the sensitive subject
of Poland amid continual interruptions from Stalin.

Secret Notes at Yalta

CREATED: FEBRUARY 1945
SUBJECT: THE BIG THREE
AT YALTA—DISCUSSION
OF POLAND

39 | U.S. President Franklin Delano Roosevelt, British Prime Minister Winston Churchill, and Soviet Premier Josef Stalin—the Big Three, headlines called them—met at the Black Sea resort of Yalta, in the Crimea in February 1945 to plan the postwar world that would come before the year ended.

They made decisions on the creation of the United Nations and the trial of Nazi war criminals. Roosevelt and Churchill got from Stalin the promise to join the war against Japan after the end of the war in Europe. In exchange, the Soviet Union was promised the Kuril Islands and the southern part of Sakhalin Island, as well as an occupation zone in Korea (which became North Korea). Stalin also won restoration of the former Russian port of Dairen in China and joint control with China of Manchurian railroads.

China, which was not represented at the conference, later protested in vain that the Big Three had made pronouncements about Chinese territory without consulting China. Similarly, decisions were made about Poland without the presence of any Poles.

Claiming rights earned by Red Army conquest, the Soviet Union had taken over Poland, ruling through a communist puppet regime called the Lublin government after the name of a Polish town. The United States and Britain, opposing the

Soviets, supported Poland's democratic government-in-exile, then in London, waiting to return and govern.

The decision on Poland appeared in the public text of the Yalta conference: "A new situation has been created in Poland as a result of her complete liberation by the Red Army . . . The Provisional Government which is now functioning in Poland should therefore be reorganized on a broader democratic basis with the inclusion of democratic leaders from Poland itself and from Poles abroad." A Polish Provisional Government of National Unity would at some unspecified date hold "free and unfettered elections as soon as possible on the basis of universal suffrage and secret ballot."

The public text revealed the decisions reached by the Big Three, but notes that could enlighten historians about the background of the decision-making remained classified until

The Big Three at Yalta—Winston Churchill, Franklin D. Roosevelt, and Josef Stalin.

1998. They were finally declassified through the Freedom of Information Act (FOIA), which since 1967 has been responsible for making such once-secret documents public.

"I would like to bring up Poland," President Roosevelt says in the Top Secret notes on the Yalta meeting. "There are six or seven million Poles in the United States." He mentions favoring the Curzon Line, named for the British foreign secretary who had proposed an armistice line during the Russo-Polish War of 1919–20. Roosevelt goes on for a few more words. Then Stalin interrupts (see the document on page 236).

Another FOIA document was a letter that Roosevelt wrote to Stalin at Yalta. The letter said that "we cannot recognize the Lublin Government as now composed . . ." Yet, the Polish puppet state was soon recognized and the promised elections never happened. When Adm. William Leahy, Roosevelt's principal aide, saw what the Big Three had decided on Poland, he told Roosevelt that it was "so elastic that the Russians can stretch it all the way from Yalta to Washington without technically breaking it." Roosevelt replied, "I know, Bill—I know it. But it's the best I can do for Poland at this time."

Some members of the government-in-exile did join with the Lublin government to form the Polish Government of National Unity. The United States and Britain recognized the new Poland, which in 1952 became a Soviet-style "people's democracy." Three years later, Poland joined the Warsaw Pact, which confronted the North Atlantic Treaty Organization (NATO) in a Europe divided by what Churchill called the Iron Curtain. It would be a long time before Poland became Poland again.

Impact on History: Although critics of Roosevelt use "Yalta" as shorthand for what they see as his decision to hand Eastern Europe over to Stalin, in fact the secret Yalta notes show the United States and Britain joining in opposition to the Soviet Union, especially over Poland. And in this alignment is the origin of the Cold War.

ЦК КПСС

Обстановка *в ПНР* продолжает оставаться напряженной. Забастовочное движение приобретает общегосударственный масштаб.

Учитывая складывающуюся обстановку, Министерство обороны просит для создания группировки войск на случай оказания военной помощи *ПНР* разрешить в первую очередь привести с 18.00 29.8 в полную боевую готовность *три* танковые *(ПрибВО-1, БВО-2) и одну* мотострелковую *(ПрикВО)* дивизии.

На доукомплектование этих дивизий призвать из народного хозяйства до *25* тыс. военнообязанных и *6* тыс. автомобилей, в том числе *3 тыс.* на замену машин, убывших из этих войск на уборку урожая, без которых дивизии не смогут полностью поднять свои подвижные запасы. Необходимость доукомплектования дивизий за счет ресурсов народного хозяйства вызывается тем, что они в мирное время содержатся в сокращенном составе и для успешного выполнения задач *при вводе их на территорию ПНР* требуется предварительно провести с ними боевое слаживание в течение *5-7* суток.

При дальнейшем обострении обстановки *в Польше* потребуется доукомплектовать также дивизии постоянной готовности *Прибалтийского, Белорусского, Прикарпатского* военных округов до штатов военного времени, а при выступлении *на стороне контрреволюционных сил основных сил Войска Польского* увеличить группировку наших войск еще на *пять-семь* дивизий. Для этих целей разрешить Министерству обороны спланировать призыв еще до *75 тыс.* военнообязанных и *9 тыс.* автомобилей.

Всего в этом случае потребуется призвать из народного хозяйства *до 100 тыс.* военнообязанных и *15 тыс.* автомобилей.

Проект постановления ЦК КПСС прилагается.

М. СУСЛОВ   А. ГРОМЫКО   Ю. АНДРОПОВ   Д. УСТИНОВ   К. ЧЕРНЕНКО

" *28* "   августа 1980 г.

A Soviet document laying out a plan for a military invasion of Poland in 1980-1981. The "non-invasion" eventually led to the end of the Cold War.

A Package in the Snow

CREATED: AUGUST 1980
SUBJECT: THE COLD WAR—THE SOVIET
"NON-INVASION" OF POLAND

40 Poland's "people's democracy" awoke to a real democratic movement in August 1980 when a workers' trade union called Solidarity suddenly confronted the government. When an electrician named Lech Walesa led a Solidarity strike at the Lenin Shipyard in Gdansk, the government began making plans to impose martial law.

The Soviet Union reacted by increasing the combat readiness of the forces nearest to the Polish border. The Kremlin created a top-level commission whose chairman was Mikhail A. Suslov, senior party ideologist. Also on the commission were KGB chief Yuri V. Andropov, Foreign Minister Andrei A. Gromyko, and Defense Minister Dmitrii F. Ustinov.

On September 19, 1980 Admiral Stansfield Turner, Director of Central Intelligence and head of the Central Intelligence Agency, alerted President Jimmy Carter: "Soviet military activity in the last few days leads me to believe that the Soviet leadership is preparing to intervene in Poland, if the Polish situation is not brought under control in a manner satisfactory to Moscow." The crisis kept dragging on, but the tension continued unabated.

By December 1, the Soviets were on the brink of moving troops into Poland in the guise of war game maneuvers. On

December 2 Turner wrote Carter, "I believe the Soviets are readying their forces for military intervention . . ."

The next day, Carter made a rare use of the "hot line," the direct teletype link between the White House and the Kremlin. In his hot-line message, Carter said, ". . . I have to state our relationship would be most adversely affected if force was used to impose a solution upon the Polish nation."

One of the Polish Army officers deeply involved in dealing with the intervention decision was Colonel Ryszard Kuklinski, seemingly a dedicated communist. But since 1972, Kuklinski had been risking his life by providing the CIA with intelligence on Polish and Soviet military plans. Now, throughout the crisis, he was giving the United States detailed information about what was going on behind the doors of Poland's defense ministry. Increasingly, Soviet officers were there, pushing for a crackdown on Solidarity.

Stormy weather obscured U.S. satellite views of any troop movements. Whatever information Carter got was coming from Kuklinski. On the night of December 2, he drove to a certain streetlamp on a certain Warsaw street, stopped his car, got out and dropped a tightly wrapped cellophane package. Earlier that day, a CIA officer, operating under diplomatic cover, had seen a chalk mark on a mailbox, a signal that Kuklinski had information to deliver. About half an hour after Kuklinski made his drop, the officer pulled up to the same spot, got out of his car, and dug the package out of the snow. The CIA officer then translated Kuklinski's message and sent it on to CIA headquarters:

Dear Friends,

On the instruction of Defense Minister Jaruzelski, Gen. Hupalowki and Col. Puchala agreed in the General Staff of the U.S.S.R. Armed Forces in Moscow to a plan for introducing (under the pretext of exercises) the troops of the Soviet Army, the Army of East Germany, and the Czech Army to Poland. From prepared plans which were presented to them for viewing and partial copying, it is apparent that three armies consisting of 15 Soviet Army divisions, one army composed of two Czech divisions and the staff of one army and one division from East Germany are to be sent to Poland. Altogether, the group of intervening forces in the first phase will consist of eighteen divisions. An additional four divisions are to be attached to the armies of Czechoslovakia and East Germany (the Polish 5th and 11th Armored and the 4th and 12th Mechanized Divisions.) Readiness to cross the Polish borders has been set for 8 December. At the present time, representatives of the "fraternal armies" in civilian disguise are carrying out reconnaissance of marching routes, training areas and regions of future actions. The Czechs and East Germans are to operate in the Western part of the county, while the Central and eastern parts of Poland fall to the troops of the Soviet Army . . .

A summary of the message was hand-carried to the White House with a note that said, "The following information was received from a long-time reliable source who has proven access to it."

Carter issued a public warning that the Soviets were preparing to intervene. There was no troop movement. Among policy buffs, the event became known as the Soviet Non-Invasion of Poland. Soviet leaders had backed off, even though they had not hesitated to send in the Red Army to crush uprisings in East Germany and Czechoslovakia. In retrospect, the Kremlin's failure to do the same against Poland was an early signal that the Soviet Union was heading toward collapse.

Months passed. The Soviets ran a war game about the imposing of martial law on Poland, a menacing move but not an aggressive act. In November 1981 Kuklinski warned that a declaration of martial law, without Soviet intervention, was imminent. Fearing that he had been detected, he asked the CIA to get him out of Poland. The CIA produced a classic

Colonel Ryszard Kuklinski of the Polish Army risked life and limb to provide the CIA with intelligence on Soviet and Polish military activity in Poland.

covert or "black" exfiltration operation, smuggling Kuklinski, his wife, and their two sons to West Germany inside a shipping box in a van with diplomatic plates. Later, the CIA exfiltrated the girlfriend of one of the sons.

Martial law was imposed in December 1981. As Kuklinski had predicted, there was no Soviet intervention. Walesa and other Solidarity leaders were arrested. But resistance to the communist government continued. In June 1989 the free elections promised by the Yalta Conference so long before finally were held. Solidarity's winning candidates formed Eastern Europe's first non-communist government.

Kuklinski, while serving as a Polish Army Lieutenant Colonel on the Polish General Staff, had covertly provided the CIA with 40,265 pages of top secret documents. Under assumed identities, out of fear of Polish government retaliation, he and his wife and two sons settled in America. He suffered a massive stroke and died on February 11, 2004. Memorial ceremonies were held at Arlington Military Cemetery. CIA Director George Tenet and the Polish ambassador to the United States eulogized him, as did Zbigniew Brzezinski, President Carter's former National Security Advisor.

Kuklinski's ashes were flown to Poland and buried in the Powaski Military Cemetery with full military honors. The Polish government, declaring that he had acted out of patriotic motives, cleared him of charges of treason and desertion, for which he had been sentenced to death.

Impact on History: Kuklinski's message gave President Carter seemingly solid information on Soviet plans. Carter's warnings against a threatened Soviet intervention in Poland revealed to the world that the Soviet Union was on the verge of using armed force to put down dissent, as it had done in Czechoslovakia in 1968.

SEVEN

The Secret State

In World War I, the U.S. Army set up a secret "experimentation station" on the campus of American University, which was then in a relatively undeveloped area of northwest Washington, D.C. The use of poison gas in the trenches of France led to the creation of the station, whose work included investigating the production of poison-gas artillery shells.

Eventually, the site of the experiment station became part of Spring Valley, a large neighborhood of about 1,200 expensive homes. In 1993, a building contractor in Spring Valley unearthed a burial ground of poison-gas artillery shells. Anxious home owners, after learning about the forgotten World War I station, asked the National Archives for an Army map showing the layout of the camp. The National Archives reported that the map was still secret and had to be declassified. Some secrets die hard. (The map and other documents were eventually revealed, and the Army finally finished digging up the shells in 2007.)

When a nation makes a secret treaty with another nation, the secrecy is based on the idea that there exists a confidential relationship between the two nations. When a nation keeps secrets from its citizens, the reason given is national security. By that thinking, secrets protect the citizens. But if a secret endures beyond its protective years, the result can be a warping of history.

Samuel Eliot Morison, who wrote the definitive 15-volume history of the U.S. Navy in World War II, did not know about Navy code-breaking when he wrote his richly detailed account of the Battle of Midway, published in Volume V in 1949. Morison attributed the U.S. victory, a turning point in the Pacific war, to Adm. Chester W. Nimitz's use of "various bits of information from a variety of sources." In a tenth-anniversary article in 1952, Morison still made no reference to the intercepts and code breaking. Not until 1967, in Walter Lord's book *Incredible Victory* did the public begin to learn about the code-breakers' role in the battle.

Secrecy about Midway, like secrecy about the British Double Cross system and other intelligence operations during World War II, cloaked aspects of history for a generation. That is one of the costs of secrecy in a democracy. "A popular Government without popular information or the means of acquiring it," President James Madison said in 1822, "is but a Prologue to a Farce or a Tragedy or perhaps both. Knowledge will forever govern ignorance, and a people who mean to be their own Governors, must arm themselves with the power knowledge gives."

There are others, as the late Senator Daniel Patrick Moynihan discovered when he was chairman of the Commission on Protecting and Reducing Government Secrecy. The commission's final report, issued in March 1997, found that "excessive secrecy has significant consequences for the national interest when policy makers are not fully informed" because "the government is not held accountable for its actions" and "the public cannot engage fully in informed debate." When the commission was formed in 1994, the U. S. government had more than 1.5 billion pages of classified material that was 25 years old or, like documents about the Spring Valley poison-gas shells, even older. By the year 2000, there was enough classified material to, as Moynihan put it, "stack up as high as 441 Washington Monuments."

Moynihan, a New York Democrat, reported that the U.S. government was creating about 400,000 new documents a year at the highest level alone—Top Secret. Those two words are stamped on documents containing information "which if inappropriately disclosed would cause exceptionally grave damage to the national security of the United States." The other basic categories are Secret (information whose disclosure "would cause serious damage" to national security) and Confidential (disclosure would simply "cause damage" to national security).

There is also a category called "Sensitive Compartmented Information" (SCI), a "security device" designated to give special protection to certain information, restricting who can see it. For SCI or for knowledge of a Special Access Program (SAP), you need special "SCI Access" or "SAP approval." SCI is usually designated with a codeword, which is itself classified. The SCI device sharply increases the importance of the secret being protected because it was "derived from special sources and methods." That phrase is applied to extremely sensitive secrets that came from such "sources" as telephone conversations, electronic surveillance, codebreaking, and satellite imagery.

During the Cold War, for example, the codeword GAMMA GUPY referred to the National Security Agency's ability to eavesdrop on the conversations of Soviet leaders using the radio-telephones in their cars. Only a relatively few intelligence officers would even know that codeword. When the topics of those conversations were revealed to those with a need to know, the source would still not be disclosed.

Officially, only the President and about 20 people he designates have the power to apply the Top Secret classification. But this power has been passed on to more than 1,000 "original classifiers." Some two million government officials and one million industrial contractors possess "derivative classification" authority that enables them to wield the Top Secret stamp. In 2006, the executive branch designated more than 235,000 items as Top Secret. There were also 374,244 "derivative" designations. And these numbers do not include the countless images—each a specifically secret document—produced each day by satellites and drones tracking military and intelligence targets.

"Secrecy," said Moynihan, "can be a source of dangerous ignorance." As an example, he pointed to the handling of the secrecy surrounding Venona, the operation for breaking Soviet codes that began in 1946. Information about Venona was known by the FBI since 1948 but not passed to the CIA until 1952.

"Soviet cables," Moynihan wrote, "indicated that the Office of Strategic Services (OSS) in World War II had been thoroughly infiltrated with Communists. As the CIA was widely regarded as the successor to the OSS, the Army and the FBI apparently were simply not willing to entrust it with their secrets." Even President Truman does not seem to have been told about Venona, though his ignorance of it has been questioned by some, who note the exits of Hiss and White from their government posts during Truman's tenure.

In a scrupulously researched book, *Venona: Soviet Espionage and the American Response, 1939-1957*, Robert Louis Benson and Michael Warner write that Truman repeatedly denounced charges of espionage and treason against such Democratic administration officials as Alger Hiss and Harry Dexter White, even though they "appear under cover names in decrypted messages translated before he left office." Benson and Warner found no evidence that Truman was told about Venona.

Thanks to Moynihan's efforts, details of Venona were released. "This," he said, "is a history of intellectual dedication that Americans have a right to know about. And to celebrate."

The commission's work led to the creation of a system for unveiling secrets: Any classified document more than 25 years old would be automatically declassified unless the government interceded with claims that certain documents had to be kept secret in the interest of national security.

About 460 million declassified pages of federal records have been made publicly accessible since that system went into effect in 1996. But millions of pages remain secret. At the Ronald Reagan Library, for example, there are over nine million pages of classified records nearing or already 25 years old. That huge pile is being examined for "declassification review" by three archivists. In this presidential realm and elsewhere in the nation's archives, America's secret past is still eluding the curious citizens of the present.

Meriwether Lewis, Thomas Jefferson's personal secretary and joint leader of the expedition to explore the West.

A Secret Request to Congress

CREATED: JANUARY 1803
SUBJECT: EXPLORATION
OF THE AMERICAN WEST

41 | Reconnaissance—the obtaining of intelligence by trained eyewitnesses—is one of the oldest espionage skills. And reconnaissance as a military and intelligence mission was at the heart of Lewis and Clark's "Corps of Discovery," which went forth in 1804. The expedition was inspired by President Thomas Jefferson, who had been thinking about western exploration since the end of the Revolutionary War.

In 1783 Jefferson wrote of suspicions that the British would send a seemingly scientific expedition to the unexplored territory and "pretend it is only to promote knowledge." He had similar suspicions two years later, when he was America's minister to France. After hearing about French plans for an expedition to the Pacific Northwest, Jefferson mockingly wrote, "They give out that the object is merely for the improvement of our knowledge."

Jefferson's suspicions about French intentions momentarily abated in 1793 when he and the American Philosophical Society picked a French botanist named André Michaux to lead a western expedition. Michaux, whose exploration would pass through Spanish possessions, got as far as Kentucky before Jefferson somehow learned that the botanist was a French spy. That abruptly ended the expedition.

Confidential.

Gentlemen of the Senate and of the House of Representatives.

As the continuance of the act for establishing trading houses with the Indian tribes will be under the consideration of the legislature at it's present session, I think it my duty to communicate the views which have guided me in the execution of that act; in order that you may decide on the policy of continuing it, in the present or any other form, or to discontinue it altogether if that shall, on the whole, seem most for the public good.

The Indian tribes residing within the limits of the US. have for a considerable time been growing more & more uneasy at the constant diminution of the territory they occupy, altho' effected by their own voluntary sales: and the policy has long been gaining strength with them of refusing absolutely all further sale on any conditions. insomuch that at this time, it hazards their friendship, and excites dangerous jealousies & perturbations in their minds to make any overture for the purchase of the smallest portions of their land. a very few tribes only are not yet distinctely in these dispositions. In order peaceably to counteract this policy of theirs, and to provide an extension of territory which the rapid increase of our numbers will call for, two measures are deemed expedient. First, to encourage them to abandon hunting, to apply to the raising stock, to agriculture and domestic manufacture, and thereby prove to themselves that less land & labour will maintain them in this, better than in their former mode of living. the extensive forests necessary in the hunting life, will then become useless, & they will see advantage in exchanging them for the means of improving their farms & of increasing their domestic comforts. Secondly to multiply trading houses among them & place within their reach those things which will contribute more to their domestic comfort than the possession of extensive, but uncultivated wilds. experience & reflection will develope to them the wisdom of exchanging what they can spare & we want, for what we can spare and they want. in leading them thus to agriculture, to

Thomas Jefferson's secret request to Congress to fund an expedition to explore the unknown West, led by Meriwether Lewis and William Clark.

our nation seems to owe to the same object, as well as to it's own interests, to explore this, the only line of easy communication across the continent, and so directly
traversing our own part of it. the interests of commerce, place the principal object
within the constitutional powers and care of Congress, and that it should incidentally advance the geographical knowledge of our own continent, cannot but be an additional gratification.
the nation claiming the territory, regarding this as a literary pursuit, which it is
in the habit of permitting within it's dominions, would not be disposed to view it
with jealousy, even if the expiring state of it's interests there did not render it a
matter of indifference.   the appropriation of two thousand five hundred dollars
'for the purpose of extending the external commerce of the US.' while understood and
considered by the Executive as giving the legislative sanction, would cover the undertaking from notice, and prevent the obstructions which interested individuals
might otherwise previously prepare in it's way.

Th: Jefferson

Jan. 18. 1803

255

By the end of 1802, the western boundary of the United States was the Mississippi River. All the territory beyond the Mississippi, much of it occupied by Indian tribes, was claimed by Britain, Spain, and France. (Spain still held the Louisiana Territory west of the Mississippi but had deeded it to France.)

Jefferson, who had long wanted to explore that unknown West, decided to ask Congress to appropriate $2,500 for a western expedition. When Jefferson showed a draft of his request to Secretary of the Treasury Albert Gallatin, he advised the President not to make his request public because the expedition would trespass and might provoke nations that claimed the land. So on January 18, 1803, Jefferson sent a secret message to Congress (shown on pages 254-55).

Confidential is a relatively low secrecy classification today, but in the 19th century the word meant that private information was being bestowed with *confidence* in the keeper of the information. Jefferson's confidential message began with remarks about dealing with Indian problems. He also obliquely referred to the British colony of Canada, noting that "numerous tribes . . . furnish great supplies of furs and peltry to the trade of another nation, carried on in a high latitude." And near the end of the message Jefferson added a phrase—"the purpose of extending the external commerce of the US"—as a diplomatic way of saying that there was more to the expedition than scientific exploration. The House and Senate authorized the appropriation in a secret session.

In the spring of 1803, Napoleon, about to go to war against Britain, decided to give up his American holdings. His foreign minister offered to sell the Louisiana Territory to America, which purchased the vast realm for $15 million, adding to the nation what would become all or part of 15 states. On July 3, Jefferson learned that the deal had been completed. Now the expedition would be across American-owned land.

Jefferson had chosen his personal secretary, Capt. Meriwether Lewis, to lead the expedition. The co-leader would be William Clark, who had served in the Army with Lewis. The objective of the expedition was still not generally known in March 1804, when Lewis and Clark were in St. Louis to celebrate the formal transfer of the Louisiana Territory to the U.S. But Gen. James Wilkinson, as commanding general of the U.S. Army, knew the details and revealed the plans of the expedition to Spain. He was a covert agent of Spain with the code name Agent 13, and he lived a life of persistent treachery.

Agent 13 and Spain saw the Lewis and Clark expedition as a military intelligence mission, as well they might. Capt. Meriwether Lewis was an officer on active duty and Clark, an Army veteran, would become a brigadier general commanding the territory's militia. Of the 50 men who in 1804 traveled up the Missouri River to the Mandan villages, 36 were soldiers. Jefferson had developed a cipher for secret communication with Lewis. If Lewis ever used the cipher, no enciphered messages were ever found.

Impact on History: Jefferson and the nation learned enough about the West to see its inestimable value. In time, the intelligence aspect of the great expedition was eclipsed by its legacy: the establishment of relations between the U. S. government and Indian tribes, the strengthening of the U.S. claim to the Oregon Territory, and fulfillment of Lewis's vow to "advance the information of the succeeding generation."

Cover of the 1920 German version of the Protocols,
said to be the first printed edition outside of Russia.

An Enduring Lie

[
CREATED: 1903
SUBJECT: CREATION OF
THE PROTOCOLS OF ZION
]

42 How and when *The Protocols of the Elders of Zion* was created is unknown. Parts of the notoriously anti-Semitic tract were published in a Russian newspaper in 1903. Two years later, the *Protocols* appeared as an appendix to *The Great in the Small: The Coming of the Anti-Christ and the Rule of Satan on Earth,* written by Russian writer and mystic Sergei Nilus. Still a mystery is the author of the original counterfeit document that launched what has been called the most widely distributed anti-Semitic publication of modern times—and the most infamous political fabrication of the 20th century.

The overwhelming evidence points to Pyotr Rachovsky, chief of the foreign branch of the Russian czars' secret police known as *Okhrana* (Protection Section) from March 1885 to November 1902. According to a CIA study of *Okhrana* documents discovered in 1957, Rachovsky was a "born intriguer" who "delighted" in fabricating documents. That made him the leading suspect in the fabrication of the *Protocols.* (The CIA's Counterintelligence Staff was interested in the files in the belief that they would yield insights into the czarist roots of Russian "intelligence culture.")

Publication of the fabrication reflected Rachovsky's exploitation of anti-Semitism as a tool for convincing the czar and his supporters that discontent in Russia was fostered not by domestic repression but by a worldwide Jewish conspiracy.

Whether or not Rachovsky was the author, the *Protocols* did emerge from czarist Russia in the early 20th century and have been spreading hatred of Jews ever since. The 24 chapters, or protocols, purport to be records of meetings of Zionist elders who make plans for Jews to rule the world by secretly manipulating the economy.

The *Protocols* appeared in the United States in 1920 when automobile pioneer Henry Ford ordered its text to be published as a series in his newspaper, *The Dearborn Independent*. The series was republished as a book, *The International Jew*, which was translated into more than a dozen languages, including German. Adolf Hitler cited the *Protocols* in his autobiography, *Mein Kampf*, as proof of his warnings about a global Jewish conspiracy.

Literary sleuths trace the *Protocols* format to *The Dialogue in Hell Between Machiavelli and Montesquieu* by Maurice Joly, which was published in 1864 in Brussels as a veiled attack on Napoleon III (as Machiavelli) for his attacks on liberty's champions (such as Montesquieu). French police arrested Joly and suppressed the book. *Okhrana* agents used the dialogue style as a structure for the *Protocols*.

The fabrication—and plagiarism—was revealed in *The Times* of London in 1921 by Robert Graves, a writer and classical scholar. Graves met a Russian in Constantinople (now Istanbul) who had bought the Joly book from a former *Okhrana* officer. Graves found that about 50 paragraphs in the *Protocols* "are simply paraphrases" of passages in the Joly book.

The *Protocols* became a propaganda tool during the Russian Revolution of 1905-1906, which was supported by many liberal Russian Jews. "It is said by some Russians," Graves wrote, "that the manuscript of the Protocols was communicated to the Tsar early in 1905." More importantly, "they have done harm by persuading all sorts of mostly well-to-do people that every recent manifestation of discontent on the part of the poor is an unnatural phenomenon, a factitious agitation caused by a secret society of Jews."

When Nazis circulated a German-language edition of the *Protocols* in Switzerland in 1935, a Swiss court declared the *Protocols* "libelous . . . obvious forgeries," and "ridiculous nonsense." Still, the libel continues today.

Impact on History: "Many school textbooks throughout the Arab and Islamic world teach the *Protocols* as fact," Holocaust Museum researchers report. "Countless political speeches, editorials, and even children's cartoons are derived from the *Protocols*. In 2002, Egypt's government-sponsored television aired a miniseries based on the *Protocols*, an event condemned by the U.S. State Department. The Palestinian organization Hamas draws in part on the *Protocols* to justify its terrorism against Israeli civilians." And "a typical Internet search yields several hundred thousand sites that disseminate, sell, or debate the *Protocols* or expose them as a fraud."

Le Bordereau

The bordereau, giving away critical French intelligence,
that Alfred Dreyfus was accused of writing and passing to the Germans.

The Dreyfus Affair

CREATED: SEPTEMBER 1894
SUBJECT: IMPLICATION OF CAPT.
ALFRED DREYFUS AS A SPY

43 | Marie Basitian, a cleaning woman at the German Embassy in Paris in 1894, was also a lowly agent of the *Section de Statistiques et de Reconnaissances Militaires*, a French Army general staff unit concerned with foreign intelligence and counterintelligence. The woman's assignment was to pass to her French handler the contents of embassy wastepaper baskets. One of her finds was a letter in which the embassy's principal intelligence officer, Lt. Col. Maximilien von Schwartzkoppen, referred to French war plans obtained from "that scoundrel D."

Then, in September 1894, the chief of French counterintelligence, Col. Jean-Conrad Sandherr, received a *bordereau* (see opposite page), or covering memorandum, handwritten on onionskin paper. He got it from his deputy, Major Hubert Joseph Henry, Marie Basitian's case officer.

Here, in translation, is how the bordereau began:

Having received no news that you wish to see me, I am nevertheless sending, sir, some interesting information:

1. A note on the hydraulic brake on the 120 [millimeter cannon] and the way the part has worked

2. A note on covering troops (some modification will be made by the new plan.)
3. A note on a modification of artillery formations
4. A note concerning Madagascar
5. The draft of the firing manual for field artillery
(March 14, 1894)

The last document is extremely difficult to procure, and I am able to have it at my disposal for only a very few days. The War Ministry has sent a fixed number of copies to the regiment, and the regiment is responsible for them. Every officer holding a copy must return it after maneuvers. If, therefore, you take from it whatever interests you and then keep it at my disposal, I will call for it. Unless you would like me to have it copied in extenso and send you the copy.

I am leaving on maneuvers.

On the morning of October 15, 1894, Capt. Alfred Dreyfus entered the War Ministry in Paris. Dreyfus, who was Jewish, had attended the *École Polytechnique* before entering the Army. At the age of 35 he seemed destined for a brilliant military career. But, given the virulent anti-Semitism in the French Army, he faced a formidable obstacle.

He had been given the puzzling order to wear civilian clothes that day. Once inside the ministry he was led by an officer into the office of the chief of the general staff. A senior officer approached Dreyfus and said, "The general is coming. While we wait, I have a letter to write, and since my finger is sore, would you write it for me?" As soon as Dreyfus finished writing the letter, the officer took one look at it and shouted, "In the name of the law, I arrest you! You are accused of the crime of high treason!" Dreyfus was immediately taken to prison and placed in solitary confinement. Thus began the Dreyfus Affair, a scandal that rocked France.

A military court martial tried Dreyfus behind closed doors in December 1894. The only evidence against him was the bordereau. Dubiously qualified experts testified that Dreyfus had written the bordereau even though the writing differed from the writing sample that Dreyfus had unwittingly produced on the day of his arrest.

After the trial, as the judges were pondering their verdict, a French Army intelligence officer presented to the judges a dossier of forged or ambiguous documents collected to show Dreyfus' guilt. Neither Dreyfus nor his lawyer knew about the dossier.

Convinced by the secret dossier, the judges convicted Dreyfus of treason and sentenced him to life in prison. On January 5, 1898, in the inner courtyard of the French Military College, before hundreds of troops, Dreyfus was formally degraded: His buttons, insignia, decorations, and ribbons were torn from his uniform, and his sword broken in two. Dreyfus raised his right hand and shouted, "I swear and declare that you are degrading an innocent man. Vive la France!"

He was held for a month in France and then sent to the notorious penal colony of Devil's Island in French Guiana. During nightmares in his solitary cell, he cried out, "My only crime is to have been born a Jew." He seemed destined to die on the island.

Two years after Dreyfus was sent off in disgrace, Lieut. Col. Georges Picquart became chief of army intelligence. Picquart reopened the case, starting with the bordereau. Picquart was convinced that the man who wrote the bordereau was Maj. Ferdinand Walsin-Esterhazy, a veteran of the papal army and the French Foreign Legion who had worked in the general staff offices translating German documents. Picquart gathered enough evidence to have Esterhazy court martialed in 1898. He was acquitted. Picquart was sent to Tunisia and later "discharged for gross misconduct in the service." Official knowledge of Dreyfus's innocence led to a cover-up that reached to the highest levels of the Army.

In 1898 novelist Émile Zola wrote *J'Accuse*, an open letter to the French president charging the Army with having framed Dreyfus. Pressure grew for a reexamination of the case. Dreyfus was brought back to France for a new court martial. His second conviction on rigged evidence shook France, setting off demonstrations that ended with his being pardoned by the President of the Republic. Esterhazy fled to exile in England, where he later confessed that, deep in debt, he had earned money by spying for Germany.

Dreyfus fought for reinstatement, which he finally won in 1906. He was restored to the rank of major and made a knight in the Legion of Honor. He retired in 1907, but volunteered to serve in World War I. His son, Pierre, was an artillery captain at the front and was awarded the Croix de Guerre.

Capt. Alfred Dreyfus being formally degraded and his sword broken in half at the French Military College before hundreds of troops.

Impact on History: The Dreyfus Affair convulsed France for years, exposing the anti-Semitism that had long simmered throughout the nation. In 1898, reacting to the Dreyfus case, the Catholic paper *La Croix du Midi* asserted the legitimacy of anti-Semitism: "the primary effort of the indigenous Frenchman to reconquer his native soil." In 2006, a state ceremony at the courtyard where he had been degraded marked the centennial of Dreyfus' reinstatement in the army.

On the day of the murder, van Dendreschd visited Trotsky with
an article he had written containing statistical data on France, and was
invited by Trotsky into his office. On this occasion van Dendreschd was
armed with a pistol (Alpine climber's pick) inside of his raincoat, a 45-
caliber pistol hung between his shoulder blades and a dagger sewed in the
lining of his coat. When the opportunity presented he struck Trotsky
with the pistol, and was prevented from being slain by the guards through
the efforts of Mrs. Trotsky.

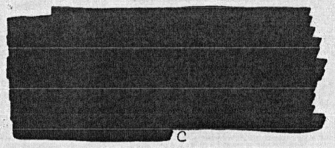

Additional information obtained regarding van Dendreschd's background and activities reflects that he left France on September 2, 1939
on the S. S. Ile de France, arriving in New York six or seven days later;
that he proceeded to Mexico by train about a month later, entering Mexico
about the middle of October, 1939. Van Dendreschd speaks good Spanish,
excellent French and, due to his good command of English, appeared to
have resided for some time in the United States. Sylvia Agyloff resides
at 50 Livingston Street, Brooklyn, New York, and it was through her that
van Dendreschd gained entree to Trotsky's home, since she was quite well
acquainted with Trotsky's wife.

On June 12, 1940, van Dendreschd as Frank Jacson obtained visa
#328 from the American Consul General's Office in Mexico City for a
transient trip through the United States to Montreal, Canada. His

*A redacted page from the 909-page report the FBI compiled on Ramón Mercader,
Leon Trotsky's assassin. This page provides in detail the events of Trotsky's murder.*

The FBI and Trotsky

[
CREATED: SEPTEMBER 1940
SUBJECT: ASSASSINATION
OF LEON TROTSKY
]

44 | Leon Trotsky, born Lev Davidovich Bronstein, had joined Lenin in the Russian Revolution of 1917, had organized the Red Army, and seemed destined to become Lenin's successor. But in the power struggle after Lenin's death in 1924, Joseph Stalin outmaneuvered Trotsky and forced him into exile, first in Turkey, then in France, then in Norway, which expelled him during an uproar over Soviet claims that he was plotting to kill Stalin.

The President of Mexico, through the intercession of the painter Diego Rivera, offered Trotsky asylum, and in January 1937 Trotsky arrived in Mexico, where he took up residence in a well-guarded suburban villa. Stalin had targeted him for assassination. But the NKVD—the secret police organization that preceded the KGB—was in turmoil due to Stalin's purges, delaying the assassination until 1940.

The task was given to Leonid Eitingon, an NKVD officer who picked David Alfaro Siqueiros, a Spanish Civil War veteran, popular muralist, and left-wing radical, as the assassin. On May 23, 1940, Siqueiros, in the disguise of a Mexican Army officer, led a band of men who stormed the villa, killed a sentry, sprayed a patio and rooms with machine gun fire, and left behind incendiaries and a bomb, all set to go off. The incendiaries did flare up, but the bomb did not explode. Siqueiros left, thinking he had killed Trotsky. But Trotsky had survived, with a slight wound in his right leg. Siqueiros, arrested and given bail, went to Chile at the invitation of the poet Pablo Neruda.

Eitingon began organizing another assassination plot. This one would reach over the border into New York City and involve members of the Communist Party of the United States. The FBI had been keeping watch over American communists and were aware of their ties to Moscow. But the FBI did not know about this new plot to kill Trotsky.

Eitingon ordered Ramón Mercader, a shadowy young man of many names, to renew his romance with Sylvia Ageloff, a New York social worker Ramón had met at a Trotskyite gathering in Paris. Ramón was the son of Caridad Mercader, a Spanish communist with whom Eitingon had been romantically involved during the Spanish Civil War. The NKVD collected the passports of casualties of the International Brigades—volunteers from many countries who were killed fighting the fascists under Gen. Francisco Franco. The passports later came in handy for creating false identities for operatives like Ramón.

The FBI knew Ramón as van Dendreschd or Jacques Mornard van den Dreschd, the name on the passport from the NKVD's Spanish Civil War collection. Eventually, the FBI would accumulate more than 900 pages on van Dendreschd, Sylvia Ageloff, and others involved in what happened in August 1940.

In the summer of 1940 Ramón had renewed his romance with Sylvia, who had gone to Mexico to become a volunteer secretary for Trotsky. Introduced by the trusted Sylvia, Ramón got to know the guards in the Trotsky villa and met Trotsky himself. The two men made a date for Trotsky to look at a manuscript Ramón had written. The date was August 20, 1940.

Ramón had expected to kill Trotsky with a single blow. But before he could accomplish his purpose, Trotsky screamed, bringing in guards and Trotsky's wife, who grappled with Ramón. The FBI file contains a vivid account of the assassination (see page 268).

In his confession, Ramón told of striking Trotsky and—"the man screamed in such a way that I will never forget it as long as I live. His scream was Aaaaaa! . . . very long, infinitely long, and it still seems to me as if that scream were piercing my brain . . ."

Trotsky died of his wounds on August 21. Ramón was arrested, tried, convicted, and sentenced to 20 years in prison. An FBI agent under diplomatic cover at the U.S. Embassy in Mexico City interviewed Trotsky before he died and Ramón before his trial. The interviews went into the copious FBI file on the Trotsky murder, a file that grew to 909 pages, many of them blacked-out.

When U.S. code breakers of the Venona project succeeded in decrypting Soviet espionage messages of the 1940s, they found references to futile plans to free from prison a man with the cover name "Gnome"—Ramón, the assassin. His mother, Caridad Mercader, appears in Venona messages with the code name "Klava."

Ramón served almost his entire sentence. When he was freed he returned to Moscow. In a ceremony witnessed by his mother, he was given a medal and a gold wristwatch.

Impact on History: The FBI investigation of Trotsky's assassination showed the link between the Soviet Union and zealous Communist Party members in the United States, a revelation that foreshadowed the intelligence produced by the Venona project. Stalin's secret police showed its reach, setting up a murder far from Moscow.

Franklin D. Roosevelt, first President to authorize the use of wire-tapping for purposes of "domestic security."

Tap, Tap, Tap

CREATED: MAY 1940
SUBJECT: AUTHORIZATION
OF WIRE-TAPPING

45 | Roy Olmstead, a former Seattle police officer, became known as the "king of the bootleggers" of Puget Sound. He ran a fleet of ships that carried liquor from Canada to islands where speedboats were loaded to hurry whiskey to waiting trucks and cars owned by Olmstead. The enterprise was earning $2 million a year in the Roaring Twenties, when Olmstead became a major target for agents of the Department of Justice's Bureau of Investigation.

To enforce the Prohibition law against the sale or import of alcoholic beverages, federal agents were using a new weapon against bootleggers: the telephone tap. Records of the taps were used as evidence in the conviction of Olmstead and 20 others in 1926. Olmstead, sentenced to four years in prison and fined $8,000, appealed, saying that obtaining evidence by wiretaps was unconstitutional. He argued that his right to privacy and protection against self-incrimination, under Fourth and Fifth Amendments, had been violated. The Supreme Court disagreed, ruling by a 5-4 majority that the taps did not violate the Constitution.

Justice Louis Brandeis dissented, saying that the invasion of privacy by wiretapping was even worse than tampering with the mail. "Whenever a telephone line is tapped," he wrote, "the privacy of the persons at both ends of the line is invaded, and all

PSF : Justice j'folder

Jackson

THE WHITE HOUSE

WASHINGTON

CONFIDENTIAL

May 21, 1940.

MEMORANDUM FOR

THE ATTORNEY GENERAL

I have agreed with the broad purpose of the Supreme Court decision relating to wire-tapping in investigations. The Court is undoubtedly sound both in regard to the use of evidence secured over tapped wires in the prosecution of citizens in criminal cases; and is also right in its opinion that under ordinary and normal circumstances wire-tapping by Government agents should not be carried on for the excellent reason that it is almost bound to lead to abuse of civil rights.

However, I am convinced that the Supreme Court never intended any dictum in the particular case which it decided to apply to grave matters involving the defense of the nation.

It is, of course, well known that certain other nations have been

Franklin D. Roosevelt's 1940 executive order, authorizing the use of wire-tapping to monitor espionage by foreign agents.

THE WHITE HOUSE
WASHINGTON

-2-

engaged in the organization of propaganda of so-called "fifth columns"
in other countries and in preparation
for sabotage, as well as in actual
sabotage.

It is too late to do anything
about it after sabotage, assassinations and "fifth column" activities
are completed.

You are, therefore, authorized
and directed in such cases as you
may approve, after investigation of
the need in each case, to authorize
the necessary investigating agents
that they are at liberty to secure
information by listening devices
direct to the conversation or other
communications of persons suspected
of subversive activities against
the Government of the United States,
including suspected spies. You are
requested furthermore to limit these
investigations so conducted to a
minimum and to limit them insofar
as possible to aliens.

F. D. R.

conversations between them upon any subject . . . may be over-heard. Moreover, the tapping of one man's telephone line involves the tapping of the telephone of every other person whom he may call, or who may call him. As a means of espionage, writs of assistance and general warrants are but puny instruments of tyranny and oppression when compared with wire tapping."

After the repeal of Prohibition in 1933, Congress, reflecting Brandeis's dissent, passed, and President Franklin D. Roosevelt signed, the 1934 Communications Act, which outlawed nonconsensual wiretapping. The law was upheld by the Supreme Court in 1939.

That was the status of legal wiretapping in 1940 when President Roosevelt wrote a letter on the subject to Attorney General Robert Jackson (see pages 274-75). Roosevelt's order narrowed the use of wiretaps to listening in on espionage by foreign agents. But the uses of wiretapping quickly broadened. President Harry S Truman, presiding over the beginning of the Cold War, approved the tapping of phones in cases involving "domestic security."

The need to keep watch over espionage suspects steadily grew, leading to the enactment of the Foreign Intelligence Surveillance Act, which became law in 1978. Authority to secretly allow wiretaps (and the planting of electronic bugs) was given to the clandestine Foreign Intelligence Surveillance Court, which convenes in an electronically secure room in the Department of Justice building in Washington.

By then, FBI use of wiretapping was rampant and became notorious when the tapping of Dr. Martin Luther King, Jr., became known. From 1963, when Attorney General Bobby Kennedy approved the tap, until his assassination in 1968, the FBI was listening to King's phone calls. Tapping became an accepted form of intelligence-gathering.

Forty-five days after the attacks of September 11, 2001, came the USA Patriot Act, the sweeping national security law that expanded the power of law-enforcement agencies to search telephone and email records and electronically gather intelligence in the U.S. (The name of the act is an acronym for "Uniting and Strengthening America by Providing Appropriate Tools Required to Intercept and Obstruct Terrorism.")

What began as President Roosevelt's executive order in 1940 by the next century became a 342-page law that not only extended the boundaries of wiretapping to include terrorist suspects but also amended 15 different federal statutes covering disparate issues that include surveillance of internet use.

"The progress of science in furnishing the government with means of espionage is not likely to stop with wire-tapping," Justice Brandeis warned in 1928. "Ways may some day be developed by which the government, without removing papers from secret drawers, can reproduce them in court, and by which it will be enabled to expose to a jury the most intimate occurrences of the home."

Impact on History: By citing national security needs to justify wiretapping, President Roosevelt established a standard still in use in the 21st century. In 2007, it was revealed that the Bush administration had bypassed the Patriot Act and, on its own, extended secret wiretaps, an Executive Branch action that remains contentious at the time of this writing.

Albert Einstein fled Nazi Germany in 1938 and immigrated to the U.S.
He soon became involved in efforts to expand the U.S.'s experimentation with
uranium, which he knew could lead to the creation of atomic weaponry.

Bombs of a New Type

CREATED: AUGUST 1939
SUBJECT: WWII — RESEARCH
FOR ATOMIC WEAPONRY

46 | By 1939, physicists in both Germany and Japan were exploring the possibility of using atomic energy to make a bomb. British atomic scientists, in a secret government-sponsored project, were working toward production of weapons-grade fissionable material.

Leo Szilard, a Hungarian-born physicist who had been a colleague of Albert Einstein in Germany, moved to England in 1933, fleeing Nazi persecution. He moved to America in 1938. As war in Europe loomed, he became concerned that American physicists were not seeing an atomic bomb as a possible product of newly discovered uranium fission.

Einstein was an American celebrity. The director of the Kaiser Wilhelm Physical Institute in Berlin in 1914, he had been awarded the 1921 Nobel Prize for his contribution to theoretical physics. In 1933, with the Nazis in control of Germany, Einstein knew that, as a Jew, he had to leave. He was welcomed by the Institute for Advanced Study at Princeton, became an American citizen, and was well publicized as the nation's greatest genius.

Sometime in July 1939, Szilard and another Hungarian-born physicist, Eugene Wigner, visited Einstein at his vacation cabin in Long Island. Szilard asked Einstein to send a letter to the Queen Mother of Belgium, warning that she should do all

Albert Einstein
Old Grove Rd.
Nassau Point
Peconic, Long Island

August 2nd, 1939

F.D. Roosevelt,
President of the United States,
White House
Washington, D.C.

Sir:

Some recent work by E.Fermi and L. Szilard, which has been communicated to me in manuscript, leads me to expect that the element uranium may be turned into a new and important source of energy in the immediate future. Certain aspects of the situation which has arisen seem
to call for watchfulness and, if necessary, quick action on the part
of the Administration. I believe therefore that it is my duty to bring
to your attention the following facts and recommendations:

In the course of the last four months it has been made probable -
through the work of Joliot in France as well as Fermi and Szilard in
America - that it may become possible to set up a nuclear chain reaction
in a large mass of uranium,by which vast amounts of power and large quantities of new radium-like elements would be generated. Now it appears
almost certain that this could be achieved in the immediate future.

This new phenomenon would also lead to the construction of bombs,
and it is conceivable - though much less certain - that extremely powerful bombs of a new type may thus be constructed. A single bomb of this
type, carried by boat and exploded in a port, might very well destroy
the whole port together with some of the surrounding territory. However,
such bombs might very well prove to be too heavy for transportation by
air.

*Albert Einstein's letter to FDR, telling of the potential potency of weapons created using
uranium and recommending that the U.S. step up its research on the element.*

-2-

The United States has only very poor ores of uranium in moderate quantities. There is some good ore in Canada and the former Czechoslovakia, while the most important source of uranium is Belgian Congo.

In view of this situation you may think it desirable to have some permanent contact maintained between the Administration and the group of physicists working on chain reactions in America. One possible way of achieving this might be for you to entrust with this task a person who has your confidence and who could perhaps serve in an inofficial capacity. His task might comprise the following:

a) to approach Government Departments, keep them informed of the further development, and put forward recommendations for Government action, giving particular attention to the problem of securing a supply of uranium ore for the United States;

b) to speed up the experimental work,which is at present being carried on within the limits of the budgets of University laboratories, by providing funds, if such funds be required, through his contacts with private persons who are willing to make contributions for this cause, and perhaps also by obtaining the co-operation of industrial laboratories which have the necessary equipment.

I understand that Germany has actually stopped the sale of uranium from the Czechoslovakian mines which she has taken over. That she should have taken such early action might perhaps be understood on the ground that the son of the German Under-Secretary of State, von Weizsäcker, is attached to the Kaiser-Wilhelm-Institut in Berlin where some of the American work on uranium is now being repeated.

Yours very truly,

(Albert Einstein)

she could to prevent Nazi Germany from getting uranium from the Belgian Congo. Einstein preferred writing to his friend, the Belgian ambassador to the United States.

Szilard later met with Alexander Sachs, an economist who was an adviser to his longtime friend, President Franklin D. Roosevelt. Sachs said that if Szilard could get Einstein to write a letter to Roosevelt, Sachs would personally deliver it to the President. Szilard wrote a draft, which he sent to Einstein, following up with a visit, this time with another Hungarian physicist, Edward Teller. After much discussion and several drafts, Einstein approved a version (shown on pages 280-81), which was sent to President Roosevelt on August 2, 1939. A month later, World War II began. Sachs did not meet with Roosevelt to discuss the letter until October 11.

Eight days later, Roosevelt replied in a "My dear Professor" letter: "I found this data of such import that I have convened a Board consisting of the head of the Bureau of Standards and a chosen representative of the Army and Navy to thoroughly investigate the possibilities of your suggestion regarding the element of uranium." The physicists' grapevine, however, did not pick up any sign of an American atomic program.

On March 7, 1940, Einstein and Szilard collaborated on a second, more urgent letter to Roosevelt. It began: "Since the outbreak of the war, interest in uranium has intensified in Germany. I have now learned that research there is carried out in great secrecy."

Secret work also began in the United States. In June 1940 Roosevelt approved the creation of the National Defense Research Committee, chaired by Vannevar Bush, president of the Carnegie Foundation. Bush stopped publication of articles on uranium research and forbade committee membership to foreign-born scientists, thus denying knowledge to many physicists.

What would become the top secret Manhattan Project began a month before the Japanese attack on Pearl Harbor, when a scientific committee reported that a powerful bomb could be produced by a critical mass of between 2 and 100 kilograms of uranium-235. Roosevelt approved the recommendation on January 19, 1942, with a handwritten note to Bush: "V. B. OK-returned-I think you had best keep this in your own safe FDR."

Impact on History: Einstein was not directly involved in the development of the bomb. However, his letter certainly led to the building of the nuclear bomb and ushered in the atomic age.

of more time to decode the message. The Secretary asked why he had specified one o'clock. The Ambassador replied that he did not know but that that was his instruction.

The Secretary said that anyway he was receiving the message at two o'clock.

After the Secretary had read two or three pages he asked the Ambassador whether this document was presented under instructions of the Japanese Government. The Ambassador replied that it was. The Secretary as soon as he had finished reading the document turned to the Japanese Ambassador and said,

"I must say that in all my conversations with you (the Japanese Ambassador) during the last nine months I have never uttered one word of untruth. This is borne out absolutely by the record. In all my fifty years of public service I have never seen a document that was more crowded with infamous falsehoods and distortions—infamous falsehoods and distortions on a scale so huge that I never imagined until today that any Government on this planet was capable of uttering them."

The Ambassador and Mr. Kurusu then took their leave without making any comment.

A copy of the paper which was handed to the Secretary by the Japanese Ambassador is attached.[13]

J[OSEPH] W. B[ALLANTINE]

711.94/2594¼

Memorandum Handed by the Japanese Ambassador (Nomura) to the Secretary of State at 2:20 P. M. on December 7, 1941

1. The Government of Japan, prompted by a genuine desire to come to an amicable understanding with the Government of the United States in order that the two countries by their joint efforts may secure the peace of the Pacific Area and thereby contribute toward the realization of world peace, has continued negotiations with the utmost sincerity since April last with the Government of the United States regarding the adjustment and advancement of Japanese-American relations and the stabilization of the Pacific Area.

The Japanese Government has the honor to state frankly its views concerning the claims the American Government has persistently maintained as well as the measures the United States and Great Britain have taken toward Japan during these eight months.

2. It is the immutable policy of the Japanese Government to insure the stability of East Asia and to promote world peace and

---

A page from an official State Department document recording the outraged reaction of Secretary of State Cordell Hull to the Japanese response to America's proposal for peaceful settlement. The attack on Pearl Harbor was by then already underway.

The Magic Messages

CREATED: DECEMBER 1941
SUBJECT: WWII—FINAL
FAILED PEACE PROPOSAL
TO JAPAN

47 | On November 26, 1941, a huge Japanese fleet—six aircraft carriers screened by two battleships, three cruisers, and nine destroyers—departed Hitokappu Bay in the Kurile Islands, and headed toward Hawaii, maintaining radio silence. The Japanese military government had not yet approved the "Hawaiian Operation," an attack on the U.S. Pacific Fleet at Pearl Harbor, because peace negotiations were underway between the two nations. Coincidentally, U.S. Secretary of State Cordell Hull had handed the Japanese America's "suggestions for a comprehensive peaceful settlement" on the very day the Japanese fleet left Hitokappu Bay.

Hull, awaiting Japan's reply to his offer of a peaceful settlement, had an advantage called "Magic:" American codebreakers could read intercepted Japanese diplomatic messages sent by radio.

The Purple Code (named for a Japanese code machine known as Purple) was first broken in the fall of 1940 by a U.S. military cryptologist team directed by William Friedman, chief cryptanalyst of the Army's Signal Intelligence Service. Friedman referred to his staff as "magicians." This apparently is the origin of the term "Magic" that was used for Purple-derived intelligence.

Some Japanese military codes had also been broken, but the radio silence kept Americans in the dark about the six-carrier strike force. On December 2, the fleet got the signal—*"Climb Mount Niitaka"*—that meant the government had authorized the attack on Pearl Harbor. The message was sent in a code not yet cracked by U.S. codebreakers. American intelligence officers knew that the Japanese Navy was on the move, but they believed the destination was British Malaysia and the Netherland Indies.

Washington officials had warned Pearl Harbor commanders that Japan was on an aggressive path, though that did not imply an attack on U.S. forces. At airfields around the island of Oahu, some 250 Navy, Marine, and Army Air Corps planes were parked in neat lines to make it easier to guard them against sabotage.

In Washington, the Japanese ambassador, Admiral Kichisaboru Nomura, and Japanese special emissary Saboru Kurusu continued their talks. Then, on December 6, they got instructions from Tokyo. An American cryptographic unit, using the Purple code, decrypted the intercepted message. Translated, it read:

From: Tokyo
To: Washington
December 6, 1941 Purple
#909 Re my #644 (a).
1. The Government has deliberated deeply on the American proposal of the 26th of November and as a result we have drawn up a memorandum for the United States contained in my separate message #902 (in English).
2. This separate message is a very long one. I will send it in fourteen parts and I imagine you will receive it tomorrow. However, I am not sure. The situation is extremely delicate, and when you receive it I want you please to keep it secret for the time being.
3. Concerning the time of presenting this memorandum to the United States, I will wire you in a separate message. However, I want you in the meantime to put it in nicely drafted form and make every preparation to present it to the Americans just as soon as you receive instructions.

On December 6, a decryption unit also intercepted the first 13 parts of the "very long" Japanese reply to the American proposal. The message ended with a declaration that negotiations were to be broken off at 1 p.m. Washington time (7:30 a.m. Hawaii time). To U.S. officials, this amounted to a threat of imminent war. New warnings went out to Pearl Harbor, but the belief persisted that Japan was aiming south at Malaysia or the Netherland Indies, which Germany had handed over to Japan after the fall of Holland.

When the Japanese ambassador asked for an appointment at 1:45 p.m., Secretary Hull knew, from his reading of the intercept, that war was imminent. The Japanese representatives did not arrive until 2:05. Hull made them wait until 2:20. By then he had been given the first reports on the attack on Pearl Harbor.

The Japanese envoy handed over the rejection of the American offer of November 26. Hull read the Japanese document, and, according to the official State Department account, "with the greatest indignation" uttered the damning statement on the State Department transcript that is shown on page 284.

During those Washington moments, the attack on Pearl Harbor had begun. The toll would be 2,403 Americans killed and 1,178 wounded.

Impact on History: Modern U.S. code breaking and radio interception skills developed before World War II and were sharpened during the war and throughout the Cold War as the intelligence product became increasingly highly valued by American government and military leaders. This led to the establishment of the U.S. National Security Agency (NSA) at Fort Meade outside Baltimore, Maryland, the world's leading and largest electronic intelligence organization.

Mr. HOOVER,

       Exceptional circumstances impel us to infc
of the activities of the so-called director of the S
Intelligence in this country. This "Soviet" intell
officer genuinely occupies a very high post in the G
enjoys to a vast extent the confidence of the Soviet
but in fact, as we know very accurately, works for J
while his wife (works) for Germany. Thus, under cove
of the USSR, he is a dangerous enemy of the USSR and
The vast organisation of permanent staff [KADROVYE]
the NKVD under his command in the U.S.A. does not su
thanks to the treachery of their director, they are
inflicting frightful harm on their own country. In
false position is also their whole network of agents
whom are many U.S. citizens, and finally BROWDER him
has immediate contact with them. BROWDER passes on
very important information about the U.S.A., thinkin
this goes to MOSCOW, but, as you see, it all goes to
Japanese and Germans. ⊕ The "Director" of the Soviet
here is ZUBILIN, Vasilij, 2nd secretary in the embas
USSR, his real name is ZARUBIN, V., deputy head of t
Intelligence Directorate [UPRAVLENIE] of the NKVD.
deals with getting agents into and out of the U.S.A.
organises secret radio-stations and manufactures for
His closest assistants are:
1. His wife, directs political intelligence here,
network of agents in almost all ministries including
Department. She sends false information to the NKV
everything of value passes on to the Germans through
Boris MOROZ (HOLLYWOOD). Put her under observation
very quickly uncover the whole of her network.
2. KLARIN, Pavel, vice-consul in NEW YORK. Has a
work of agents among Russian emigrés, meets them almo
brings agents into the U.S.A. illegally. Many of hi
work in very high posts in American organisations, tl
Russian.
3. KhEJFETs - vice-consul in SAN FRANCISCO, deals
political and military intelligence on the West Coast
has a large network of agents in the ports and war fa
collects very valuable strategic material, which is t
ZUBILIN to Japan. Has a radio station in the consul
He himself is a great coward, on arrest will quickly
all the agents to save himself and remain in this cou
4. KVASNIKOV, works as an engineer in AMTORG, is ZU
assistant for technical intelligence, through SEMENOV
works in AMTORG, is robbing the whole of the war indu
America. SEMENOV has his agents in all the industri
of the U.S.A. in all aviation and chemical war facto

Translation of the anonymous letter sent to J. Edgar Hoover in August 1943, accusing various individuals of spying for the Soviet Union from within the U.S. government.

The Golden Age of Soviet Espionage

CREATED: AUGUST 1943
SUBJECT: COLD WAR—THE
VENONA OPERATION

48 One of the longest and most complex of all U.S. spy stories has the codename Venona. The story unfolds through many years: In 1937, during the Spanish Civil War, when an American in the Abraham Lincoln Brigade is recruited to become a spy for the Soviet Union. In 1941, when the body of a defector—a senior Soviet military intelligence officer—is found in a Washington hotel room. On August 7, 1943 when J. Edgar Hoover, director of the FBI, gets in the mail an anonymous letter (shown opposite) typed on a Cyrillic typewriter. In 1945, when a code clerk in the Soviet Embassy in Ottawa defects to Canadian authorities and tells them about a spy ring stealing U.S. atomic secrets. In 1948, when a former courier of U.S. government secrets publicly testifies about her spying to a congressional committee.

The recruited spy was Steve Nelson, a leader of the Communist Party of the United States (CPUSA). His California home was bugged by the FBI, which was probing espionage activity in the CPUSA. The dead Soviet spy was Walter Krivitsky, who wrote *Saturday Evening Post* articles exposing Soviet espionage and whose death was quietly investigated by the FBI because he had once said: "If they ever try to prove I took my own life, don't believe it." Unofficially, investigators believed he was murdered by his erstwhile colleagues. The Soviet clerk was Igor T.

BRIDE

~~TOP SECRET~~

USSR

Ref. No: 3/NBF/T943 (of 11/6/1957)

Issued: ████ 26/3/1958

Copy No. 205

2nd RE-ISSUE

"ALBERT" TO OBTAIN INFORMATION ABOUT PLANS FOR THE
SAN FRANCISCO CONFERENCE (1945)

From: MOSCOW

To: NEW YORK

No: 195   3 Mar. 45

At the forthcoming meeting with ALBERT[i] pass on to him on our behalf
the following task:

Jointly with ROBERT[ii] take all requisite steps to obtain in good time
and pass on to us information about the composition of the delegation to the
forthcoming conference[iii] which[a] is in BABYLON[VAVILON][iv] [5 groups
unrecovered]; what tactics the delegation intends to adopt, whom it is counting
on for support, what blocs have been prepared already and [0% formed], how far
there will be a united line for the representatives of the Anglo-Saxon world
and so on. As the information comes in pass it on to the Centre[v] by telegraph without delay.

No. 1300   VIKTOR[vi]
3rd March

Note: [a] I.e. the delegation.

Comments: [i] ALBERT : Unidentified cover-name.
          [ii] ROBERT : Nathan Gregory SILVERMASTER.
          [iii] The United Nations Conference at SAN FRANCISCO opened on
                25th April 1945.
          [iv] BABYLON: SAN FRANCISCO.
          [v] Centre : I.e. the MOSCOW Headquarters of the writer's
                organization, viz. the MGB.
          [vi] VIKTOR : Lt. Gen. P.M. FITIN.

Distribution

3/NBF/T948

~~TOP SECRET~~

BRIDE

*Two Venona decrypts, the one above referring to the founding of the UN, and the one
opposite referencing "Antenna," or Julius Rosenberg, who was convicted of espionage.*

Reissue(T282)

From: NEW YORK

To: MOSCOW

No: 1053

26 July 1944

To VIKTOR[i].

In July ANTENNA[ii] was sent by the firm for ten days to
work in CARTHAGE [KARFAGEN][iii]. There he visited his school
friend Max ELITCHER[a], who works in the Bureau of Standards as
head of the fire control section for warships [which mount guns]
[b] of over five-inch calibre. He has access to extremely valuable materials on guns.

Five years ago Max ELITCHER [MAKS E.] graduated from the
Electro-Technical Department of the City College of NEW YORK.
He has a Master of Science degree. Since finishing college he
has been working at the Bureau of Standards. He is a FELLOW
COUNTRYMAN [ZEMLYaK][iv]. He entered the FELLOW COUNTRYMEN's
organization [ZEMLYaChESTVO] after finishing his studies.

By ANTENNA he is characterized as a loyal, reliable,
level-headed and able man. Married, his wife is a FELLOW COUN-
TRYWOMAN [ZEMLYaChKA]. She is a psychologist by profession,
she works at the War Department.

Max ELITCHER is an excellent amateur photographer and has
all the necessary equipment for taking photographs.

Please check ELITCHER and communicate your consent to his
clearance [OFORMLENIE].

No. 594
26 July   MAJ[v]

Notes: [a] Given in Roman alphabet.
       [b] Inserted by translator.
Comments:
       [i]   VIKTOR: Lt. Gen. P. M. FITIN.
       [ii]   ANTENNA: Julius ROSENBERG.
       [iii] KARFAGEN: WASHINGTON, D. C.
       [iv]   ZEMLYaK: Member of the Communist Party.
       [v]   MAJ: i.e. MAY, Stepan APRESYaN.

28 April 1975

Gouzenko, whose espionage revelations to the Canadian Royal Mounted Police were shared with the FBI.

The former courier was Elizabeth Bentley, who first confessed her espionage to the FBI in 1945. She produced the first leak about the codebreaking project called Venona, but her slip did not gain public currency. In 1948, she told a federal grand jury that an aide to President Roosevelt had learned that American codebreakers had nearly cracked "the Russian secret code." The presidential aide was almost certainly economist Laughlin Currie, who was named as a member of a Soviet "espionage ring" in a letter to a Truman aide in November 1945.

All five pieces of the puzzle come together to reveal the magnitude of Soviet espionage in America. The anonymous letter to Hoover, postmarked Washington, was mailed from a mailbox near the Soviet Embassy.

The letter, whose existence was not revealed publicly until 1995, was written in Russian. It began: "Exceptional circumstances impel us to inform you of the activities of the so-called director of the Soviet Intelligence in this country. This 'Soviet' intelligence officer genuinely occupies a very high post in the GPU (now NKVD) and enjoys to a vast extent the confidence of the Soviet Government, but in fact, as we know very accurately, works for Japan itself while his wife works for Germany. Thus, under cover of the USSR, he is a dangerous enemy of the USSR and the U.S.A."

The letter named Vassili Mikhailovich Zubilin, second secretary of the Soviet Embassy in Washington, as the "dangerous enemy," and his wife, Elizabeta Yurevna Zubilin, as running a network of agents who worked for the U.S. government. (U.S. investigators were never able to verify the charge that the Zubilins spied for Japan and Germany.)

Other names included Soviet intelligence officers under diplomatic cover. One of them was attached to the Soviet Embassy in Mexico City and aided in the assassination of Leon Trotsky. An American named in the letter, Boris Morros, a Hollywood producer and music director, would reveal in 1957 that he had been a double agent under FBI control for 12 years.

The author of the letter was never identified, though investigators speculated that it may have been Vasili Mironov, Zarubin's assistant. The letter contained the confession that Zarubin and Mironov (his real name was Markov), killed 10,000 Poles while serving in Russian-occupied Poland. Mironov/Markov later was committed to a psychiatric clinic in the Soviet Union. Zaubin and several other Soviet diplomats mentioned in the letter must have somehow learned about it because they left the United States in the summer of 1944.

The letter further revealed the breadth of Soviet espionage in the United States and almost certainly spurred the FBI's participation in a secret program begun in 1943 by the Army's Signals Security Agency (SSA), predecessor of the National Security Agency. SSA cryptanalysts were working to decrypt Soviet telegrams that had been intercepted as they were radioed from Soviet diplomatic facilities in the United States to Moscow in the 1940s. The project eventually got the codename Venona. In 1948 FBI special agent Robert Lamphere joined the project as the FBI's liaison and controller of espionage information derived from the messages, giving Hoover knowledge denied to Washington policymakers.

Many names in the newspaper headlines of the 1940s— Elizabeth Bentley, Whittaker Chambers, Judith Coplon, Klaus Fuchs, Alger Hiss, Donald Maclean, and the atomic spy ring's Harry Gold, David Greenglass, Julius Rosenberg, and his wife, Ethel—are hidden in the messages. Lamphere, Hoover, and a few other intelligence officials gradually discovered that codenames in the messages fit the real names of these people, such as Arno for Harry Gold and Antenna for Julius Rosenberg. But the messages could not be used for prosecution because Venona's tightlipped stewards and the FBI would not reveal that U.S. codebreakers had penetrated major Soviet cryptographic systems.

Venona information was invaluable in many ways. From the messages investigators were able to identify atomic-bomb spies, explore the CPUSA's espionage underground, confirm code clerk Gouzenko's claims of widespread Soviet spying, and identify Soviet spies operating under diplomatic cover in Western embassies.

The Venona operation was formally ended in 1980; information about it was officially released in 1995. By 1997, about 3,000 messages had been declassified.

For a look at two Venona decrypts, see pages 290-91. When the decrypted messages were distributed to the small circle aware of the program, the format included notes explaining references in the message. In the Venona document on page 290, for example, the Soviet message refers to the founding conference of the United Nations and the NSA note says that ALBERT is an unidentified code name. Later, Venona analysts identified him as Iskhak Abdulovich Akhmerov, who, as "Bill" was Elizabeth Bentley's Soviet case officer. Akhmerov was married to Helen Lowry (cover name El'za), a spy and a niece of U.S. Communist Party leader Earl Browder (cover name Rulevoj), who also spied for the Soviets. Lt. Gen. P. M. Fitin was director of foreign intelligence for the Soviets. The code name BRIDE is one of several code words used for the program. VENONA was the final NSA code word. Venona and Bride were capitalized in NSA documents. The code words, randomly selected by the

J. Edgar Hoover, director of the FBI and of Venona operations in the 1940s.

United States and the United Kingdom, are neither acronyms nor abbreviations.

The document on page 291 provides a look at the espionage work of Antenna—Julius Rosenberg, who was convicted of espionage, as was his wife Ethel. They were both executed on June 19, 1953. Maj was the code name for Stepan Apresyan, Soviet intelligence "resident" in New York City, under cover as a diplomat in the Soviet Consulate. He signed hundreds of messages that Venona decrypted in the message traffic to and from New York and the Soviet intelligence headquarters called Moscow Center.

The Soviet penetration disclosed by the Venona decrypts extended throughout the government. One message from Moscow asked case officers to stop placing agents in the Treasury Department because too many were already there. Soviet agents were also in the White House, on Senate committee staffs, in the U.S. Army, the OSS, the State Department, the Justice Department, and the War Production Board.

Venona's cloak of secrecy had holes. Its existence was revealed to the Soviets by William Weisband, a Russian-language linguist who worked on the messages. To limit exposure of Venona, he was never charged with espionage. The Soviet master spy, Kim Philby, learned about Venona without having to spy. He was privy to Venona information as chief British intelligence liaison officer in the U.S.

Impact on History: For many years, Venona was the single most valuable source of U.S. counterintelligence, revealing the widespread and highly successful secret recruitment of Americans by Soviet intelligence agencies to serve as covert sources or penetrations in the White House, the State Department, the U.S. Treasury and other government agencies, as well as in the media, Hollywood, and other areas of U.S. society. The era was called by some the Golden Age of Soviet espionage in America. It revealed Soviet intelligence recruitment of nearly 350 such sources, about half of whom remain unidentified to this day. In the light of Venona and other evidence of Soviet intelligence activities, the FBI greatly expanded its counterintelligence program.

Memorandum

TO : MEMORANDUM FOR THE FILE

DATE: January 3, 1975

FROM : James A. Wilderotter
Associate Deputy Attorney General

SUBJECT: CIA Matters

CIA Director William Colby and CIA General Counsel John Warner met with LHS and JAW Tuesday, December 31 to discuss certain matters, including items apparently reported to the President by Colby in connection with the recent New York Times articles. Colby did not show us his report to the President, but paraphrased that portion of its contents which, in Colby and Warner's judgment, presented legal questions.

Colby began the meeting by describing the management style of former CIA Director Richard Helms. According to Colby, Helms utilized a very "compartmentalized" organizational structure, with each head of a constituent unit within the organization reporting directly to Helms. Colby described it as like "spokes from a hub," with Helms as the "hub" and the various compartmentalized units constituting the "spokes." It was possible to be in one "spoke" and have no knowledge of what the other "spokes" were doing.

Colby indicated that the various Watergate revelations touched the CIA in several ways, including: (a) Howard Hunt; (b) the matter of "psychological profiles;" and (c) the McCord letters to the CIA. Colby indicated that former CIA Director James Schlesinger sent a memorandum on May 9, 1973 to all CIA employees, directing them to report on all activities undertaken that may have fallen outside the CIA's charter. When the reports came in, Colby -- by then the CIA Director -- sent out "corrective" memoranda. According to Colby, the reports submitted in response to Schlesinger's May 9, 1973 memorandum constitute the "skeletons in the closet," and form the basis of Colby's recent report to the President. Colby and Warner are trying to track down more details about the various "skeletons."

The "skeletons" related to us by Colby are as follows:

(1) In 1964, a Russian defector was brought to the United States; apparently, CIA thought he was a "fake." The defector, a Russian citizen, was immediately confined in a house in

First page of the memo Wilderotter wrote after consulting with Colby and Warner, listing the CIA "Family Jewels."

The Family Jewels

CREATED: JANUARY 1975
SUBJECT: EXPOSURE OF
"QUESTIONABLE" CIA
ACTIVITIES

49 | President Nixon, engulfed in the growing Watergate burglary scandal, fired Richard Helms as Director of Central Intelligence in February 1973. Helms's successor, James R. Schlesinger, saying he did not want a Watergate on his watch, asked the CIA inspector general for a report on any activities that any employee thought were questionable and might come up at hearings of the Senate Select Committee to Study Governmental Operations with Respect to Intelligence Activities (also known as the Church Committee). The report went first to William E. Colby, Deputy Director for Operations, who remembered that Schlesinger said, "Goddam it, let's find out where these time bombs are." The preliminary summary was called "Potential Flap Activities." When the CIA's director of security made his contribution to the inspector general for inclusion in the report, he jokingly called them "the Family Jewels." The name was given to the entire report, and the name stuck.

Schlesinger's tenure was short. In July 1973 he was replaced by Colby, keeper of the Family Jewels. Colby, believing that the very existence of the CIA was at stake, decided to confidentially inform congressional oversight committees about the files. But secrets of the Family Jewels began to leak out. In December

William E. Colby, Director of the CIA in 1975, and the keeper of the "Family Jewels."

1974, The *New York Times* reported that "a check of the CIA's domestic files ordered last year . . . produced evidence of dozens of other illegal activities . . . beginning in the nineteen fifties, including break-ins, wiretapping, and the surreptitious inspection of mail."

Colby, looking back in 1988, explained his decision to cooperate with congressional investigators, saying, "In the context of the politics of the time, we had just had Watergate, you really weren't going to get away with stonewalling them."

In the furor that followed, Deputy Attorney General Laurence H. Silberman and Associate Deputy Attorney General James A. Wilderotter met with Colby and John S. Warner, the CIA's general counsel. Wilderotter wrote the memo (first page of which is shown on page 296) for his files. It describes 17 jewels:

- The confinement of a Russian defector for two years, which could have been regarded as a violation of kidnapping laws.
- Wiretapping of two syndicated columnists.
- Surveillance of columnist Jack Anderson and his associates, including Brit Hume, who became an anchorman for Fox News.
- Surveillance of *Washington Post* reporter Michael Getler.
- Break-in at the home of a former CIA employee.
- Break-in at the office of a former defector.
- Warrantless entry into the apartment of a former CIA employee.
- Opening of U.S. mail, 1953 to 1973—letters to and from the Soviet Union.
- Opening of U.S. mail, 1969 to 1972—letters to and from China.
- Behavior modification experiments on "unwitting" U.S. citizens.
- Assassination plots against Fidel Castro, president of Cuba; Patrice Lumumba, prime minister of the Republic of the Congo, and Rafael Trujillo, ruler of the Dominican Republic. Colby said the CIA had no role in the murder

of Lumumba, who was killed in a jungle execution in January 1961. Colby also said that the CIA had "no active part" but did have "a faint connection" to the assassination of Trujillo on May 30, 1961.

• Surveillance of dissident groups between 1967 and 1971.
• Surveillance of a particular Latin American female and U.S. citizens in Detroit.
• Surveillance of a CIA critic and former officer, Victor Marchetti, "to determine his contacts with CIA employees." Marchetti wrote *The CIA and the Cult of Intelligence* with John D. Marks, published in 1974.
• Amassing of files on 9,900-plus Americans related to the antiwar movement during Vietnam.
• Polygraph experiments with the San Mateo, California, sheriff.
• Fake CIA identification documents that might violate state laws.
• Testing of electronic equipment on U.S. telephone circuits.

Virtually all of the Family Jewels mentioned in the memo were disclosed in *Report to the President by the Commission on CIA Activities Within the United States*, issued in June 1975, and the *Final Report of the Select Committee to Study Governmental Operations with Respect to Intelligence Activities* (also known as the Church Committee), that was issued in April 1976.

In June 2007 the CIA released 702 pages on the Family Jewels. There were few revelations, but many new details, such as a note about E. Howard Hunt, Watergate burglar and former CIA operative, requesting a lock picker. Another note was written by the chief of the CIA Science and Technology Directorate, who said that Colby should keep himself uninformed about a program being run by an agency scientist. Although not mentioned by name, the program was undoubtedly MKULTRA, details of which had been aired in 1977 by the Church Committee, which made public a document in which the scientist mentions a project that "will include a continuation of a study of the biochemical, neurophysiological, sociological, and clinical psychiatric aspects of L.S.D," a psychoactive drug. As its absence from the memo indicates, Colby did indeed look the other way as this drug was being studied.

Impact on History: CIA Director Gen. Michael Hayden summed up the saga of the family jewels in 2007 when he released the hundreds of pages of notes about them. He called the notes "a glimpse of a very different time and a very different Agency." The changes in the Agency came especially after the end of the Cold War, when the CIA had to adapt to new ways in a new world of terror.

Bin Ladin Determined To Strike in US

Clandestine, foreign government, and media reports indicate Bin Ladin since 1997 has wanted to conduct terrorist attacks in the US. Bin Ladin implied in US television interviews in 1997 and 1998 that his followers would follow the example of World Trade Center bomber Ramzi Yousef and "bring the fighting to America."

After US missile strikes on his base in Afghanistan in 1998, Bin Ladin told followers he wanted to retaliate in Washington, according to a ▓▓▓▓▓▓▓▓▓▓ service.

An Egyptian Islamic Jihad (EIJ) operative told an ▓▓▓▓ service at the same time that Bin Ladin was planning to exploit the operative's access to the US to mount a terrorist strike.

The millennium plotting in Canada in 1999 may have been part of Bin Ladin's first serious attempt to implement a terrorist strike in the US. Convicted plotter Ahmed Ressam has told the FBI that he conceived the idea to attack Los Angeles International Airport himself, but that Bin Ladin lieutenant Abu Zubaydah encouraged him and helped facilitate the operation. Ressam also said that in 1998 Abu Zubaydah was planning his own US attack.

Ressam says Bin Ladin was aware of the Los Angeles operation.

Although Bin Ladin has not succeeded, his attacks against the US Embassies in Kenya and Tanzania in 1998 demonstrate that he prepares operations years in advance and is not deterred by setbacks. Bin Ladin associates surveilled our Embassies in Nairobi and Dar es Salaam as early as 1993, and some members of the Nairobi cell planning the bombings were arrested and deported in 1997.

Al-Qa'ida members—including some who are US citizens—have resided in or traveled to the US for years, and the group apparently maintains a support structure that could aid attacks. Two al-Qa'ida members found guilty in the conspiracy to bomb our Embassies in East Africa were US citizens, and a senior EIJ member lived in California in the mid-1990s.

A clandestine source said in 1998 that a Bin Ladin cell in New York was recruiting Muslim-American youth for attacks.

We have not been able to corroborate some of the more sensational threat reporting, such as that from a ▓▓▓▓▓▓▓▓▓▓▓▓ service in 1998 saying that Bin Ladin wanted to hijack a US aircraft to gain the release of "Blind Shaykh" 'Umar 'Abd al-Rahman and other US-held extremists.

continued

The August 2001 Presidential Daily Brief, declassified in 2004, which stated that Osama Bin Ladin was determined to strike the U.S.

For the President's Eyes Only

CREATED: AUGUST 2001
SUBJECT: PRE-9/11 WARNING
OF A TERRORIST ATTACK

50 | One of the most secret documents in Washington on any given day is the PDB—the President's Daily Brief—a document prepared by the Central Intelligence Agency for the CIA's most important customer. Accompanying the written brief, if the President prefers, is a briefer who is prepared to answer questions about that day's report.

The PDB is tailored for each President, providing timely information developed during the previous 24 hours. Little is known publicly about the circulation of the PDB, whose very existence was classified until the early 1990s. President Reagan got his PDB in a blue leather binder, which was shown (without any contents) at an exhibit in 2000 at the Ronald Reagan Presidential Library and Museum.

When George W. Bush made a PDB public in 2004, news reports said he was the first sitting President ever to reveal this for-his-eyes-only report. Not so, said the National Security Archive, a nongovernmental organization affiliated with George Washington University.

The Archive found 10 PDBs that had been officially declassified by the U.S. government. They were not particularly sensational. One of them, dated June 5, 1967, presented President Lyndon B. Johnson with information about the start of the Six-Day

War between Israel and its neighbors, Egypt, Jordan, and Syria. "Hostilities began early this morning," the PDB says. "Both sides report heavy fighting in the air and between armored forces along the Israeli border with Egypt. Israeli planes raided airfields in Cairo and other areas . . ." Another declassified PDB, commenting on the health of Indonesia's president, says: "Despite Sukarno's long-standing kidney ailment, for which he delays proper treatment, he has seemed quite chipper lately."

The CIA started producing PDBs under that name in 1964. Beginning in 1985, as part of the normal historical declassification program, PDBs from the Johnson administration were released, with redactions to keep sources secret. The CIA opposed the release of PDBs, which then essentially became exempt from declassification.

President George W. Bush backed the withholding of PDBs because he said the writers of the brief should "feel comfortable that the documents will never be politicized and/or unnecessarily exposed for public purview." He made this statement in October 2003. But a few months later, under pressure from the National Commission on Terrorist Attacks Upon the United States (also known as the 9/11 Commission), he declassified a two-page section of a PDB he received a month before the 2001 terrorist attacks. That section of the PDB appears on page 302.

The release of the "determined to strike" PDB touched off debates not only about the import of the warning but also about the worth of PDBs themselves. Future Secretary of State Condoleezza Rice, then Bush's national security adviser, testifying in a televised hearing of the 9/11 Commission, described the PDB as "historical information based on old reporting. There was no new threat information."

President Bush said that the "PDB said nothing about an attack on America. It talked about intentions, about somebody who hated America—well, we knew that . . . The question was, who was going to attack us, when and where, and with what." A *New York Times* analysis had a different interpretation: "In a single 17-sentence document, the intelligence briefing delivered to President Bush in August 2001 spells out the who, hints at the what and points towards the where of the terrorist attacks on New York and Washington that followed 36 days later."

The deep secrecy that surrounds the briefs is somewhat illusionary. The National Security Archive noted that the CIA's own history of presidential briefings says that about 40 percent of a PDB's content comes from newspapers and other open source material. And, said the Archive, President Reagan's first national security adviser, Richard Allen, wrote that the PDB "is, at best, a form of staccato information, a news digest for the very privileged. But it is rarely predictive. In fact, some would consider it pedestrian, even anodyne." President Clinton is said to have complained that "most days the PDB contained material he had already read elsewhere."

Impact on History: The creation of a Director of National Intelligence in 2004 raised questions about the future of the PDBs. What had once been a "flagship product" of the CIA's Directorate of Intelligence now is "coordinated" by the Office of the Director of National Intelligence (ODNI), drawing on contributions from the 16 agencies that form the U.S. Intelligence Community. Considering how many layers of secrecy that involves, it may be a long time before the public sees another PDB.

Acknowledgments

SPECIAL THANKS TO THE INTERNATIONAL SPY MUSEUM EDITORIAL TEAM: Peter Earnest, Executive Director; Anna Slafer, Director of Exhibitions and Programs; and Dr. Thomas Boghardt, Historian.

I also especially acknowledge my case officer, in the form of editor Olivia Garnett, who handled a frequently hectic operation with grace and skill. Thanks also to Roger MacBride Allen, Matthew T. Arnold, Raymond J. Batvinis, Bonnie Coles, Jeremy Felson, Jane Fitzgerald, Dr. John Fox and Mike Lilly of the FBI, Ron Olive, Hayden B. Peake, Norman Polmar, Christiana Simms, Joan Stanley, Michael Warner, Constance Allen Witte, Nigel West, and Jodi Zeppelin.

Bibliography

Allen, Thomas B. *George Washington, Spymaster.* Washington: National Geographic Society, 2007.

Allen, Thomas B. "Untold Stories of D-Day." *National Geographic* magazine, June 2000.

Allen, Thomas B. "Return to the Battle of Midway." *National Geographic* magazine, June 1999.

Allen, Thomas B., and Norman Polmar. *Merchants of Treason: America's Secrets for Sale.* New York: Delacorte, 1988.

Ambrose, Stephen E. *Undaunted Courage.* New York: Simon & Schuster Touchstone, 1996

Andrew, Christopher, and Vasili Mitrokhin. *The Mitrokhin Archive: The KGB in Europe and the West.* London: Allen Lane/Penguin Press, 1999.

Axelrod, Alan. *The War Between the Spies: A History of Espionage During the American Civil War.* New York: Atlantic Monthly Press, 1992.

Bakeless, John. *Turncoats Traitors and Heroes: Espionage in the American Revolution.* New York: J.B. Lippincott, 1959.

Bates, David H. *Lincoln in the Telegraph Office.* Lincoln, NE: University of Nebraska Press, 1995.

Bearse, Ray, and Anthony Read. *Conspirator: The Untold Story of Tyler Kent.* New York: Doubleday, 1991.

Benson, Robert and Michael Warner, *Venona: Soviet Espionage and the American Response, 1939-1957.* Washington: National Security Agecy, 1996.

Biddle, Francis. *In Brief Authority.* Garden City, NY: Doubleday, 1962.

Blackman, Ann. *Wild Rose: Civil War Spy.* New York: Random House, 2005.

Boghardt, Tomas. *Spies of the Kaiser: German Covert Operations in Great Britain during the First World War Era.* New York: Palgrave Macmillan, 2004

Brandt, Clare. *The Man in the Mirror: A Life of Benedict Arnold.* Random House, Inc., 1994.

Breitman, Richard, Norman J. Goda, Naftali Timothy, and Robert Wolfe. *U.S. Intelligence and the Nazis.* Washington: National Archives Trust Fund Board for the Nazi War Crimes and Japanese Imperial Government Records Interagency Working Group, 2004.

Breuer, William B. *Hoodwinking Hitler.* New York: Praeger, 1993.

Brown, Anthony Cave. *Bodyguard of Lies.* New York: Harper & Row, 1975.

Budiansky, Stephen. Her Majesty's Spymaster: Elizabeth I, Sir Francis Walsingham, and the Birth of Modern Espionage. New York: Viking Penguin, 2005.

Bullock, Alan. *Hitler, a Study in Tyranny.* New York, Harper & Row, 1966.

Burns, Michael. *France and the Dreyfus Affair.* New York: Bedford/St. Martin'S, 1999.

Carter, Miranda. *Anthony Blunt, His Lives.* New York: Farrar, Straus & Giroux, 2001.

Delmer, Sefton. *Black Boomerang.* New York: Viking Press, 1962.

Duane, Schultz. *The Dahlgren Affair.* New York: Norton, 1998.

Earley, Pete. *Family of Spies: Inside the John Walker Spy Ring.* New York: Bantam, 1989.

Eisner, Peter, and Knut Royce. *The Italian Letter.* New York: Rodale, 2007.

Fishel, Edwin C. *The Secret War for the Union: The Untold Story of Military Intelligence in the Civil War.* Boston: Houghton Mifflin Company, 1996.

Gates, Robert M. *From the Shadows*. New York: Simon & Schuster, 2007.

Goodwin, Doris Kearns. *No Ordinary Time*. Simon & Schuster, 1994.

Hamilton, Richard F., and Holger H. Herwig. *Decision for War, 1917*. New York: Cambridge University Press, 2004.

Haynes, John Earl, and Harvey Klehr, *Venona: Decoding Soviet Espionage in America*. New Haven: Yale University Press, 1999).

Hesketh, Roger. *Fortitude: the D-Day Deception Campaign*. Woodstock, NY: Overlook Press, 2000.

Ickes, Harold L. *The Lowering Clouds*, Vol. II *of the Secret Diary of Harold L. Ickes*. New York: Simon & Schuster, 1954.

Jones, J. William. "The Kilpatrick-Dahlgren Raid Against Richmond." *Southern Historical Society Papers*, Vol. 13 (1889).

Kahn, David. *Hitler's Spies: German Military Intelligence in World War II*. Cambridge, MA: Da Capo, 2000.

Kauffman, Michael W. *American Brutus: John Wilkes Booth and the Lincoln Conspiracies*. New York: Random House, 2004

Knightley, Phillip. *The Second Oldest Profession*. New York: Penguin Books, 1998.

Knox, Donald, ed. *The Korean War* Orlando, FL: Harcourt Brace, 1985.

Lamphere, Robert J., with Tom Schactman. *The FBI-KGB War: a Special Agent's Story*. New York: Random House, 1986.

Leahy, William D. *I Was There*. New York: McGraw-Hill, 1950.

Lochner, Louis P., trans. *The Goebbels Diaries: 1942-1943*. Garden City, NY: Doubleday, 1948.

Markle, Donald E. *Spies and Spy Masters of the Civil War*. New York: Hippocrene, 1994.

Martin, David C. *Wilderness of Mirrors*. New York: Harper & Row, 1980.

Masterman, J.C. *The Double-Cross System*. New Haven: Yale University Press, 1972.

Miller, Nathan. *Spying for America*. New York: Marlowe & Co., 1997

Modin, Yuri. *My Five Cambridge Friends*. London: Headline, 1994.

Montagu, Ewen. *The Man Who Never Was*. Annapolis, MD: Naval Institute Press, 2001.

Morison, Samuel Eliot. *Coral Sea, Midway and Submarine Actions May 1942-August 1942*. Boston: Little, Brown, 1961.

Murphy, David E., Sergei A. Kondrashev, and George Bailey. *Battleground Berlin*. New Haven: Yale University Press, 1997.

Niewyk, Donald L., and Francis Nicosia. *The Columbia Guide to the Holocaust*. New York: Columbia University Press, 2000.

O'Toole, G.J.A. *Honorable Treachery*. New York: Atlantic Monthly Press, 1991.

Olive, Ronald J. *Capturing Jonathan Pollard*. Annapolis, MD: Naval Institute Press, 2006.

Page, Smith. *A New Age Now Begins*. Vols. I and II. New York: McGraw-Hill, 1976

Parker, Geofrey. *The Grand Strategy of Phili*. New Haven: Yale University Press, 1998.

Persico, Joseph E. *Roosevelt's Secret War*. New York: Random House, 2001.

Philby, Rufina, Hayden Peake, and Mikail Lyubimov. *The Private Life of Kim Philby*. New York: Fromm International, 2000.

Pinkerton, Allan. *The Spy of the Rebellion*. New York: G.W. Carleton and Company, 1883.

Polmar, Norman, and Thomas B. Allen. *America At War: World War II 1941-1945*. New York: Random House, 1991.

Polmar, Norman, and Thomas B. Allen. *Spy Book, the Encyclopedia of Espionage*. New York: Random House, 2004.

Randall, Willard Sterne. *Benedict Arnold, Patriot and Traitor.* New York: Barnes & Noble, 1990.

Richelson, Jeffrey T. *Sword and Shield.* Cambridge, MA: Ballinger, 1986.

Ross, Ishbel. *Rebel Rose, Life of Rose O'Neal Greenhow, Confederate Spy.* Boerne, TX: Mckingbird Books. 1981.

Rowen, Robert. "Gray and Black Radio Propaganda against Nazi Germany." Presented to the New York Military Affairs Symposium, CUNY Graduate Center, April 18, 2003

Schultz, Duane. *The Dahlgren Affair* New York: Norton, 1998.

Sears, Stephen W. "The Last Word on the Lost Order," *Military History Quarterly,* Spring 1992.

Shogan, Robert. *Hard Bargain.* New York: Scribner, 1995.

Spence, Richard B. *Trust No One: The Secret World of Sidney Reilly.* Los Angeles: Feral House, 2002.

Steers, Edward, Jr., ed. *The Trial: the Assassination of President Lincoln and the Trial of the Conspirators.* Lexington, KY: Unversity Press of Kentucky, 2003.

Stern, Philip Van Doren. Secret Missions of the Civil War. Chicago: Rand MacNally. 1959.

Tidwell, William A., James O. Hall, David Winfred Gaddy. *Come Retribution: The Confederate Secret Service and the Assassination of Lincoln.* Jackson, MS: University Press of Mississippi, 1988.

Van Doren, Philip. *Secret Missions of the Civil War.* Skokie, IL: Rand McNally, 1959.

Vise, David A. *The Bureau and the Mole.* Atlantic Monthly P, 2002.

Weiser, Benjamin. *A Secret Life.* New York: Public Affairs, 2004.

West, Nigel. *The Illegals: The Double Lives of the Cold War's Most Secret Agents.* London: Hodder & Stoughton, 1993.

West, Nigel. *The Circus: MI5 Operations 1945-1972.*

Wilson, Jeremy. *Lawrence of Arabia, the Authorised Biography.* London: Heinemann, 1989

Wise, David. *Nightmover: How Aldrich Ames sold the CIA to the KGB for $4.6 Million.* New York: Harper Collins, 1995.

Wise, David. *Spy: the Inside Story of How the FBI's Robert Hanssen Betrayed America.* New York: Random House, 2002.

Selected Internet Sites

The Art of War by Sun Tzu: http://www.gutenberg.org/etext/132 or http://classics.
   mit.edu/Tzu/artwar.html
Aldrich Ames case: http://www.loyola.edu/dept/politics/intel.html
Berlin Tunnel: http://fas.org/irp/cia/product/tunnel.pdf
Anthony Blunt exposed: http://news.bbc.co.uk/onthisday/hi/dates/stories
   /november/16/newsid_3907000/3907233.stm
CIA "Family Jewels": www.gwu.edu/~nsarchiv/NSAEBB
   /NSAEBB222/index.htm
Civil War (Official records of the Union and Confederate armies): http://moa.cit.
   cornell.edu/moa/browse.monographs/waro.html
Codes and Ciphers: http://www.smithsrisca.demon.co.uk/crypto-ancient.html
Counterintelligence: http://www.fas.org/irp/ops/ci/docs/ci1/index.htm
Double-Cross System (Garbo): http://www.mi5.gov.uk/output/Page241.html
Drefus Case; http://www.dreyfuscase.com.
Daniel Ellsberg and Pentagon Papers: http://globetrotter.berkeley.edu/people/
   Ellsberg/ells.QA99.leak.html
Game against England: http://www.spymuseum.org/programs/educate/pdfs/back_
   game_england.pdf
Hanssen Case: http://www.fbi.gov/libref/historic/famcases/hanssen/hanssen
   .htm#anchor26782; more documents at: http://www.cicentre.com/Documents
   /DOC_Hanssen_1.htm
Holocaust: http://www.ushmm.org/wlc/article.php?lang=en&ModuleId=10005143
Intelligence Community: http://www.nsa.gov/notices/notic00005.cfm
Korean War documents: http://www.wilsoncenter.org/topics/pubs/ACF1A6.pdf
Mary, Queen of Scots: http://englishhistory.net/tudor/relative/maryqoschronology
   .html
National Security Council: http://www.state.gov/r/pa/ho/time/cwr/82209.htm
Alfred Naujocks (Nuremberg Trial Proceedings): http://www.yale.edu/lawweb/ava-
   lon/imt/proc/12-20-45.htm
Pentagon Papers: http://www.gwu.edu/~nsarchiv/NSAEBB
   /NSAEBB48/
Theodore Roosevelt: http://www.whitehouse.gov/history/presidents/tr26.html
Secrecy and History: http://www.historians.org/perspectives/issues/2000/0002
   /0002let1.cfm
Soviet Non-Invasion of Poland: http://www.wilsoncenter.org/topics/pubs/ACFB35
   .PDF
Spanish Armada http://www.britainexpress.com/History/tudor/armada.htm
   and http://www.rferl.org/featuresarticle/2005/08/8b89d311-5067-4c03-9aa6-
   72500d1f986d.html
Spy Letters of the Revolution: http://www.si.umich.edu/spies/index-about.html.
Wannsee Conference: http://www.yale.edu/lawweb/avalon/imt/wannsee.htm
Venona: https://www.cia.gov/library/center-for-the-study-of-intelligence/csi-
   publications/books-and-monographs/venona-soviet-espionage-and-the-
   american-response-1939-1957/venona.htm and http://www.nsa.gov/
   publications/publi00039.cfm
George Washington and Misinformation: http://www.founderspatriots.org/articles_
   wash_misinformation.htm

Illustrations Credits

16, British National Archives; 20, Library of Congress, Manuscript Division; 23, Library of Congress, Manuscript Division; 26, Clements Library, University of Michigan; 30, Library of Congress, Washington, D.C. #3a39917; 34, Courtesy of the North Carolina Office of Archives and History, Raleigh, North Carolina; 35, National Archives and Records Administration; 36, Library of Congress, Washington, D.C., #01246; 38, Pickett Papers, Manuscript Division, Library of Congress, Washington, D.C.; 42, Library of Congress, Washington, D.C., #3b49830; 44, George Dewey Papers, Manuscript Division, Library of Congress, Washington, D.C.; 46, National Archives and Records Administration; 48, National Archives and Records Administration; 52, National Archives and Records Administration; 54, National Archives and Records Administration; 56, National Archives and Records Administration; 59, National Archives and Records Administration; 62, Courtesy of the House of the Wannsee Conference Memorial and Educational Site, Germany; 66, Franklin Delano Roosevelt Presidential Library and Museum; 70, Library of Congress, Washington, D.C., #8e00858; 72-73, Courtesy of the Cold War International History Project, www.cwihp.org, at the Woodrow Wilson International Center for Scholars; 76, Three Lions/Getty Images; 78, The National Security Archive at The George Washington University; 82, The National Security Archive at The George Washington University; 84, The National Security Archive at The George Washington University; 94, James Madison Papers, Manuscript Division, Library of Congress, Washington, D.C.; 97, Library of Congress, Washington, D.C., #3c06865; 98, National Archives and Records Administration; 101, Library of Congress, Washington, D.C., #3a45443; 102, Library of Congress, Washington, D.C., #3a10370; 104, British National Archives; 108, Courtesy of the International Spy Museum and Graham Walker; 110, British National Archives; 114, National Archives and Records Administration; 116, Federal Bureau of Investigation; 119, Courtesy of The International Spy Museum; 122, National Archives and Records Administration; 130, Federal Bureau of Investigation; 134, Courtesy of Ronald Olive (originally appearing in his book, "Capturing Jonathan Pollard"); 138, Federal Bureau of Investigation; 142, Federal Bureau of Investigation; 146, Federal Bureau of Investigation; 150, Federal Bureau of Investigation; 160, George Washington Papers, Manuscript Division, Library of Congress, Washington, D.C.; 164, Library of Congress, Washington, D.C., #3b19847; 166, National Archives and Records Administration; 168, National Archives and Records Administration; 172, National Archives and Records Administration; 176, St. Ermin's Press, Little, Brown Book Group; 180, National Archives and Records Administration; 184, Hulton Archive/Getty Images; 192, Courtesy of The International Spy Museum; 198, Library of Congress, Washington, D.C., #04402; 200-201, Courtesy of the North Carolina Office of Archives and History, Raleigh, North Carolina; 204, Library of Congress, Washington, D.C., #03142; 206-207, National Archives and Records Administration; 212, Federal Bureau of Investigation; 214-215, Federal Bureau of Investigation; 222, British National Archives; 226, Parliamentary Archives, London, LG/F/205/1/1; 230, John F. Kennedy Presidential Library; 232-233, Franklin Delano Roosevelt Presidential Library and Museum; 234, Library of Congress, Washington, D.C., #3c09385; 236, The National Security Archive, "CNN.com / Cold War" online briefing book, Yalta Conference (http://www.gwu.edu/~nsarchiv/coldwar/documents/episode-2/05-02.htm; www.nsarchive.org); 238, Library of Congress, Washington, D.C., #3a10098; 240, Harvard Project on Cold War Studies, Davis Center For Russian and Eurasion Studies, Harvard

Index